C000177145

COMMUNISM, C
AND THE MASS MEDIA

The Media, Culture & Society Series

Editors: John Corner, Nicholas Garnham, Paddy Scannell,
Philip Schlesinger, Colin Sparks

COMMUNISM, CAPITALISM AND THE MASS MEDIA

Colin Sparks
with Anna Reading

SAGE Publications
London • Thousand Oaks • New Delhi

© Colin Sparks 1998

First published 1998

All rights reserved. No part of this publication may be reproduced, stored in a retrieval system, transmitted or utilised in any form or by any means, electronic, mechanical, photocopying, recording or otherwise, without permission in writing from the Publishers.

 SAGE Publications Ltd
6 Bonhill Street
London EC2A 4PU

SAGE Publications Inc
2455 Teller Road
Thousand Oaks, California 91320

SAGE Publications India Pvt Ltd
32, M-Block Market
Greater Kailash – I
New Delhi 110 048

British Library Cataloguing in Publication data

A catalogue record for this book is
available from the British Library

ISBN 0 7619 5074 5
ISBN 978-0-7619-5075-2 (pbk)

Library of Congress catalog card number   97-061828

Typeset by M Rules

Contents

Acknowledgements

We all know that, in theory, the author died a long time ago, but real books still obstinately demand someone's name on the spine. How else would we find them in the library catalogues? How else could British academics survive the Research Assessment Exercise? How else could US scholars get tenure? This book adopts a rather unusual formulation in naming the people who contributed immediately to its production, and it is only proper that it is explained very clearly right at the start. The writing of all of the text of this book, and thus the sole responsibility for the views and judgements expressed here, was the work of Colin Sparks. I, however, worked very closely with Anna Reading throughout the research phase of this investigation. Not only did her energy and linguistic talents mean that she was responsible for much of the actual field work, as a glance at the list of interviews will demonstrate, but we worked together on the development of the ideas embodied here. We published together a number of papers that were important to me in refining the intellectual framework of this book. So great is my debt to her, that her name appears with mine on the title page. There are some divisions of interpretation that have emerged between us. They are not great, being questions of emphasis rather than principle. Since they do not lead either of us to be unhappy about the formulations included in this book, nor to consider the omissions so severe as to be disabling, I have not, in the body of the text, specified exactly where our views diverge. I hope that Dr Reading's own analysis will soon also be publicly available, and those who are interested in the fine nuances of interpretation will be able to compare the two texts.

Work on this book would not have been possible without the support of the University of Westminster, since it proved predictably impossible to obtain substantial funding elsewhere. I am particularly thankful to Professor Nicholas Garnham, Director of the Centre for Communication and Information Studies, who took the decision to back this project. My colleagues in the Centre provided an argumentative audience at various stages in the development of my ideas. The Editorial Board of *Media, Culture and Society* were sufficiently flexible as to allow me to pursue my interests in their pages, and not too critical when I took up far too many of them.

Other organisations contributed, directly or indirectly, to helping me research this book. Among them are the British Association for Central and Eastern Europe, the British Council, the British Film Institute, the Polish Broadcasting Council, the Press Research Centre at the Jagiellonian University in Krakow, Budapesti Kommunikációs Rt., the Budapest

University of Economics, Eötvös Lorand University, the Faculty of Social Sciences, Charles University, the Faculty of Social Sciences, University of Ljubljana, the Department of Journalism and Mass Communication, University of Tampere, the Netcom Institute of Leipzig, and the Soros Foundation.

Of the many other people to whom I owe intellectual debts, I would identify first Slavko Splichal, of the University of Ljubljana, who provided the forum in which I first encountered many of the problems discussed here. The regular Euricom colloquia, of which he is the main inspiration, have been an invaluable source of contacts, ideas and excellent meals. In Ljubljana, I should also like to thank Marja Novak, Breda Luthar and Andrej Skreljep for insights into the transition in Slovenia. In Hungary, my main debts are to Ildiko Kováts and Mihály Gálik, both of the Budapest University of Economics, and Zoltan Jakab of Hungarian Television. In the Czech Republic, I must mention Milan Šmíd, of Charles University, and Helena Havlíková, of the Czech Broadcasting Council. No writer on broadcasting in Eastern Europe can escape the influence of Karol Jakubowicz, Chief Expert of the Polish Broadcasting Council, who also has many other important jobs. No matter who runs Poland, it seems Jakubowicz is indispensable to running Polish TV. Bolesław Sulik, of the Polish Broadcasting Council, combined in his own person the experience of both East and West, and was thus a source of invaluable insights. Neither is it possible to ignore the work of Wolfgang Kleinwächter, late of the University of Leipzig, and now of the Netcom Institute, who pioneered the study of the legal framework of post-communist media. There have been many other people, in both Europe and the USA, who have helped me either directly with information or indirectly through the chance to encounter their published work. Many are cited in the course of this book, but I would particularly like to identify Samuel Brečka, John Downing, Mary-Ellen Boyle, George Gerbner, Tomasz Goban-Klas, Svennik Høyer, Dina Iordanova, Owen Johnson, Frank Kaplan, Oleg Manaev, Valentina Marinescu and Kaarle Nordenstreng.

Stephen Barr, of Sage Publications, was as understanding a publisher as any author has a right to. When he moved on to higher things, Julia Hall took the final gamble of committing the company's money to getting this book into print. John Downing and Peter Goodwin read the first draft, and made penetrating criticisms to which I have tried to respond in reworking the material.

Naturally, none of the above would agree with all, or in many cases any, of the things I have written here. I hope those who have been so generous with their time and ideas are not too horrified when they find the uses to which I have put them.

Lastly, I have more than the conventional debts to Sue Sparks, and to Katie, whose habit of taking very long baths provided one of the spaces in which I could write.

Preface

This is a book about the changes that have taken place since 1989 in the media systems of what are sometimes known as the Visegrad countries: Poland, Hungary, the Czech Republic and Slovakia. It is primarily concerned with the restructuring of television, although it does have something to say about the newspaper press, and a very little about radio broadcasting. It supplements the literature attempting to review and understand the overall results of these processes of change and it builds upon a range of specialist studies of different countries. It is therefore a contribution to our knowledge of Central and Eastern Europe after communism.

To describe the book solely in those terms, however, risks misleading the reader. This work is emphatically not a detailed historical account of the different stages in the transition process as expressed in the mass media. It is, on the contrary, concerned with the general implications of these changes. As I argue in the opening chapter, the fall of communism presented a generalised challenge to what is here called 'the critical project'. It therefore involves consideration of quite wide-ranging issues not only in media theory but also in social philosophy, political theory and economics, at least as much as it involves a detailed study of the media.

It takes this form for two important reasons. In the first place, just as it is foolish to imagine that it is possible to consider the mass media in isolation from the society in which they operate, so it is impossible to discuss issues of media theory in isolation from broader considerations about our understanding of the nature of society. As John Downing, in a study closely related to this, has so elegantly shown, even those attempts to construct specific theories of the nature and functioning of the mass media considered in isolation from their broader social context in fact rest upon unstated assumptions about the nature of society and the relationship of the mass media to it (Downing, 1996: x–xvi). He demonstrates that what 'every social scientist knows' about the media and society is in fact a generalisation based upon the predominant relations in the USA, and perhaps Britain. Any attempt to discuss the mass media that is not explicit about the kind of society to which it refers runs the risk of inadvertently presenting its own unique case as intrinsically general. Given that, on almost everybody's account, something quite important has been happening in the last decade in Central and Eastern Europe, it is essential that any study of the media in that region confronts the main questions of social change.

If any attempt to isolate the mass media either theoretically or practically from the wider nexus of social relations is anywhere impossible to achieve, that is even more the case with critical theories of the media. Such work has invariably been self-consciously concerned with the ways in which its criticisms of the mass media were directly related to, and indeed dependent upon, far more general theories about society, both at the analytic and the normative levels. An obvious, if extreme, example is the notion of the media as 'ideological state apparatuses', derived from the work of Althusser. Even much more moderate figures, however, share a similar project. James Curran, for instance, built his general analysis of the shortcomings of the advertising-supported press and the remedies that might be taken to correct them on a theory as to the efficacy of the existing state in relation to modifications to the capitalist market. Since this study is, I hope, firmly located within the critical project, the general imperative to consider the broader social issues applies with double force here.

Second, I have located the changes in the media of former communist counties within a more general theoretical framework because it seems to me that this provides the opportunity for concretising and thus testing some of the more general propositions made in the overall discussion about communism and its aftermath. Such a procedure is in part the result of a particular conception of the nature of social investigation. Theory is, by its very nature, abstract and general. It has its own internal logics and its own procedures and it can be tested with reference to these. At this level, theories may be judged either coherent or incoherent, elegant or marked by redundancy. However, it seems entirely reasonable to argue that, in addition to this internal elaboration and critique, theories should also be required to illuminate, and be tested with reference to, the social realities they purport to discuss. Social theories that provide no purchase on the concrete cannot be true or false. They may be coherent and elegant, but they are certainly neither interesting nor useful. Theories that do engage with the concrete can be tested. They can be demonstrably false or probably true. They therefore have the potential to be both interesting and useful. The judgement upon truth and falsehood depends upon the evidence adduced in their discussion. We do not, I think, need to succumb to crudely positivist notions of experimental proof, or advance naïve empiricist views of the status of evidence, or hold the unsophisticatedly scientistic belief that it is possible to gain complete and certain knowledge of the world, in order to accept this modest view of the testability of theories.

The theoretical claims and counterclaims, some of them of quite fundamental import for our understanding of human society, made in the debate over the collapse of communism can therefore properly be tested only by means of their exposure to the actual evidence of the ways in which communism operated, the nature of its collapse, and the kinds of societies that are emerging in its aftermath. It is not simply because theories of the media depend upon more general social theories that the two must be brought together. On the contrary, the only ways in which those general social theories can properly make any claims to our attention is the extent to which they can be shown to be valuable in understanding the ways in which aspects of social reality, for example the media, have changed as a result of the end of European communism.

Critical studies of the mass media are a small part of what I have here termed the critical project, and I argue in Chapter 1 that this is in a serious crisis. By the term 'critical project' I am referring to the broad intellectual and social endeavour that has begun from a dissatisfaction with the nature of the contemporary world, attempted to mount a systematic and rational critique of the functioning of that world, tried to demonstrate how life might be lived differently and more humanly and, at least at its best, attempted to take steps to realise such a new world.

It is obvious from the stress on the comprehensibility and mutability of the world in my description of the critical project that it can trace its roots at least to the Enlightenment. It is also clear that the greater part of this project has, at least for the last 200 years, been socialist in inspiration, and that the many varieties of Marxism have been among its most developed forms. It is therefore tempting to drop the term 'critical project', and simply state that it is the Marxist, or at least the socialist, project that is in crisis as a result of the collapse of communism. Since, in the course of this study, I have some rather rude things to say about the use of obfuscating circumlocutions, it is incumbent upon me to give good reasons as to why my reluctance simply to discuss the crisis of Marxism is not just another example of that practice.

In the first place, I should make it quite clear that, by intellectual training and commitment, I am an adherent of one of the minor varieties of contemporary Marxism. To some minds, and not all of them the paid agents of capital, that is enough to render me at best the victim of an incurable nostalgia and at worst a sinister propagandist for evil incarnate. Since I do not believe that I am either of those things, nor a living, breathing dinosaur, and I wish to gain at least a hearing for my ideas, it is necessary for me to demonstrate why what I have to say is worth taking at all seriously outside of the very small circle of my immediate friends and fellow thinkers.

It is certainly true that, of all the forms of the critical project, the Marxist ones experience the current crisis most seriously. The official ideology of the communist regimes was Marxism, or rather Marxism–Leninism. In the name of Marxism, and of The Working Class, innumerable horrible crimes were committed, not least against the living embodiments of that very same working class. When the communist regimes collapsed, it became undeniably clear that the working class, in whose name these self-professed Marxists had ruled, had nothing but hatred and contempt for the system and its leading party. It is self-evidently the case that any contemporary Marxism that wishes to be taken at all seriously, either by intellectuals or by the putative agency of a socialist transformation, must do one of two things. One possibility is to accept that the communist regimes were Marxist in inspiration, but demonstrate beyond reasonable doubt that this outcome was not the inevitable result of the application of Marxism in practice. The alternative is to demonstrate that the communist regimes had nothing to do with Marxism and that, far from being compromised by the collapse of communism, Marxism is the system of ideas best able to account for the whole phenomenon. This book is written adopting the latter of these two positions.To the extent that it is possible to sustain that position, it is possible still to believe that Marxism remains not only the best way of understanding the world but also the only theory that can empower human liberation.

The crisis is, however, far wider than simply the bounds of the socialist or Marxist accounts of capitalism and its alternatives. Properly understood, the implications of some of the explanations of 1989 rule out the possibility of any systemic progress whatsoever, irrespective of its provenance. It is the extreme consequence of some accounts of the meaning of 1989 that it is no longer possible to hold to any theory of living differently and better, no matter what the nature of the critique or the shape of the alternative.

In this context, it is worth spelling out that the crisis that is here under review is broader than, although evidently inclusive of, the extremely well-known crisis of Enlightenment rationality, upon which by now every last undergraduate has a fixed and definite opinion. It is not, however, necessary to base a vision of a different future on Enlightenment values: More's Utopia, after all, was the product of a religious sensibility. To claim that it is not possible to think of living differently and better is to say something much broader than that reason is not a reliable guide to human practice.

Certainly, some of the explanations of the end of communism concatenate it directly with the end of modernity, and look to a specifically post-modern future in which the grand narratives of the Enlightenment are no longer credible. These are fundamental critiques of the Enlightenment and all its works. The ideas and values of the Enlightenment have been under severe attack ever since their first enunciation, but criticism has taken a new turn in the last decade or so. It is no longer the open reactionaries alone who decry reason and transformative purpose. The most severe critics of the critical project today claim to be much more radical than the heirs of the Enlightenment.

It must be admitted that, particularly in their critiques of the historically gendered nature of central categories like 'the public', and 'reason' itself, these writers have mounted an unchallengeable case. What I do not think follows from the demonstration of a contingently gendered category is the necessarily gendered nature of that category. That reason, and the rational understanding of the world, have been abused in the past to legitimise and naturalise a particular form of social domination does not imply that this must always be so. Deconstruction may be followed by careful reconstruction. The idea of rational enquiry, of understanding, of reasoned public debate, of a public sphere and thus of democracy itself can, I think, be rebuilt from their demolition, and in a form that is truer to their essence than was their actual historical manifestation.

There are, however, very influential explanations of what happened with a rather different focus than the above. According to many accounts, the failure of communism is not the failure of grand narratives in general but of one particular class of grand narrative in particular. Others remain viable. The fundamental distinction between these criticisms and those that reject the Enlightenment in its entirety is that the shape of the future envisaged by these explanations here reviewed is recognisably a child of the Enlightenment: liberal capitalism. For many commentators on the fall of communism, it is only those grand narratives of human liberation and social progress that have been thrown into crisis. The grand narratives of the global market and the capitalist state remain entirely, indeed robustly, healthy. It is true that in these presentations, the scope of enlightened reason has been stripped of its critical edge: if it is not possible to conceive of a better society, then the sole function of reason is to make the one we have run a little smoother.

In an honest intellectual accounting, it seems to me, any debate over the end of communism and the nature of its successor societies raises unavoidably these central questions of social theory. Unless the critical project, in whatever manifestation, can give a convincing account as to why the end of communism did not mean the end of the hope of a better world, then it certainly cannot expect to command general interest, let alone determined and confident adherents. To the extent that the Marxist version of the critical project confronts this crisis most acutely, if it can be shown that it is able at least to answer the charges against it, then other versions of the critical project may also be assumed to retain viability. The choice between the various versions remains one between living alternative ways of thinking about the same aims, rather than a purely antiquarian interest.

The intellectual project of this book, then, is first to try to show that the events of 1989 do not constitute a disproof of the Marxist account of society. Second, I hope to show that, in point of fact, the ideas of Marxism actually provide the best available account of what the nature of the communist regimes really was, the manner of their decline and fall, and the reasons for the peculiar features of the successor societies. To the extent that I succeed in these two tasks, I will have achieved an essentially negative goal: I will have shown that it is not possible simply to dismiss Marxism as an outmoded way of thinking that has been disconfirmed by history. Positively, I will have put forward an argument about an important social phenomenon that at least has some purchase on reality and over which debate can take place.

What I will not have done is to furnish a positive demonstration of how Marxism provides a guide to the positive transformation of society. As we shall see, the reasons for this lie in the nature of the transformation itself, and in particular in the very limited extent to which the fall of communism was accomplished by the active self-mobilization of the mass of the population. Since such actions are central to the Marxist project of human liberation, the events under study prevent me from making a positive claim along the lines that 'I have been over into the future and it works'.

Another aspect of this book that requires some explanation here is the claims made to the generality of the results. The theories that are reviewed are ones that apply to the whole problem of post-communism, but the evidence adduced here relates overwhelmingly to four countries. Some additional material is presented from the former East Germany, Bulgaria, Romania and Slovenia, but there are wide areas even of European communism that are barely considered. The former USSR and the bulk of the former Yugoslavia are the two most important omissions within Europe, and the Asian and American versions of communism are also neglected.

The obvious reason for this is that this book is already longer than was originally envisaged, and any attempt to analyse in detail more examples would only have worsened that problem. Such a drastic reduction in scope, however, carries with it the danger that the views presented here may be rejected on the grounds that there is inadequate evidence for such generalised conclusions.

To such a charge it is possible to make three replies. The first is simply to claim that the only validity of this exercise is with respect to the countries reviewed. In that case, the main issue would be whether the evidence adduced here actually does sustain the conclusions drawn about these countries alone. No claims would be made about other countries and no generalisability of the results would be suggested. Second, although it might be conceded that the current evidence applies only to a small part of the problem, it could be argued that it indicates trends which, in the absence of more detailed studies, it is reasonable to believe hold good more generally. It may well be the case that detailed studies of other countries would reveal that what appears to be the case here is contradicted elsewhere. If that were to be shown to be so, then we would have either to modify our assessment of the theories or, at the very least, to recognise the limits to their scope.

The third argument, which is the one advanced here, is that the conclusions to be drawn from the study of these particular countries are ones that can indeed be generalised. They may need to be modified by the results of more detailed work, both on the countries themselves and on other national experiences, but there is a high probability that at least the general contours revealed by this study will be replicated elsewhere.

The reason for this claim is that I believe that we may consider these countries to be 'typical' of the end of communism and the transition to a market economy. In claiming this, I am not claiming that they represent an average case, between the extremes, but that we find in them the working out of the general problem in its most complete form. The features that make East Germany very different from the Visegrad countries are not central to the nature of the transformation as a general social phenomenon. Rapid and complete union with the largest and most successful capitalist economy on the continent is not an option for any other former communist state, at least in Europe. At the other extreme, the fragmentation of single economic unit between different competing nations, which is a leading characteristic of the post-Soviet experience, is not a uniquely post-communist phenomenon.

The transition in the Visegrad countries has been far from uniform, and far from unidirectional. On the other hand, in every case the transition has been worked out by purely internal forces. There have been no direct external interventions. There have been no powerful internal blocks to change. The national question has so far been resolved without recourse to civil war. The achievements and failures of the transition from communism in these four countries has been what I want to call a 'typical' transition, which reveals the general features of such a process without the obscuring features that are to be observed elsewhere.

That is not to say that these unique features are unimportant to the transition, nor that the process as a whole has many aspects that might be better illuminated by examining other cases. My claim here concerns the central two events of the transition: the end of communist political rule and the collapse of the command economy. We may illustrate what I mean by typicality by contrasting the examples I discuss here with what appears, at least at first sight, to be the directly contrary case: that of China. In the Visegrad countries, there was a sequential logic to the order of transformation. Despite the important changes that took place in the economic sphere before the collapse of communist political rule, it was the latter event that was decisive for the subsequent economic changes. In the case of China, there appears to be strong evidence that, particularly in the case of the mass media, the process of economic change is preceding the end of communist political control. This difference is obviously real and important, and its implications deserve fuller analysis. My claim in this book, however, is that despite this difference in sequential logic, there is an underlying social logic that is the same in both cases, and that in this respect the Visegrad countries can be regarded as exemplifying typical features of the transformation. That social logic I identify as the transformation of the collective ruling class of the communist epoch into the individualised rulers of a private capitalist economy. Whether my argument is correct, and whether I have here presented sufficient convincing evidence to support it, is, of course, another matter.

Any book of this kind poses considerable difficulties of vocabulary. The terminology of political discussion is itself politicised, and always carries with it a heavy burden of its own history and contemporary usage. A clear example is the term 'social democrat'. In the last years of the nineteenth and early years of the twentieth centuries, 'social democrat' meant someone who was implacably opposed to capitalism and its state, to the nation, the army and the family. The official title of the party that led the Russian Revolution was the Russian Social-Democratic and Labour Party (RSDLP). Already, however, there were changes going on. The official title of the party that supported the German war effort in 1914 was the German Social Democratic Party. These changes have continued apace in the years since then. By the 1980s, the rightist split from the British Labour Party chose as its title that of Social Democratic Party. In Britain today, a 'social democrat' is someone who is to be distinguished from the much more left-wing 'democratic socialist', whom the original social democrats would undoubtedly have, in their turn, denounced as a lackey of capitalism.

The main difficulty in this particular study concerns the term 'communism' and its cognates. This is an even more difficult word, since so many of the great hopes of our century have borne this name, as have so many of the great crimes. Any usage of this term comes dripping with good faith misplaced and bad faith triumphant. It was to the title 'Communist Party' that the RSDLP turned because it believed the traditional party name was now hopelessly compromised. Later, 'communist' came to be the commonly applied label to a range of societies with very different formal titles: Communist China, for example, is officially the Peoples' Republic of China. The term is hopelessly mired in historical controversy, in the noblest dreams, the worst nightmares, and the most systematic hypocrisies of the twentieth century. It is very difficult to say what it actually meant at each turn.

In order to clarify this confusion, I have adopted a crude and simple method in this book. I simply use the term 'communist', except where there is an important distinction to be made by using a more specific term. So the Hungarian Socialist Workers' Party, the East German Socialist Unity Party and the Polish United Workers' Party all appear as the 'Communist Parties' of their respective countries. Countries are called 'communist', and by extension 'post-communist', irrespective of the legal names they enjoyed prior to 1989.

I think that this simplification will not cause the reader any serious problems, particularly if it is accepted that this sort of usage cannot possibly sustain any normative or analytic dimension. When I call countries or parties 'communist', I am not claiming that they are good or bad. Neither am I claiming that this term means the same here as it did for Marx, or even Lenin. I am simply using a term that is easy and convenient, and which everybody understands, to specify a certain group of historical phenomena whose internal workings need to be analysed and whose ethical status was once hotly debated. Part of the work of this book is to ask exactly what was meant by the term 'communist' as applied to the mass media, rather than to assume that because they were 'communist' everyone understands what was at stake.

That is not to say that I do not use normative terms. In this book, 'communist' is often linked with 'regime', and 'post-communist' with 'government'. There is no reason for this other than prejudice, since it does not pretend to have any scientific status: it does not correspond directly with the distinction between democratic and undemocratic, for example. Strictly speaking, I ought to submit this manuscript to a global 'search and replace' operation. The fact is, however, that the term came naturally to me in the course of writing, and the reason for that is that it carries with it strongly disapproving connotations. This is a prejudice I am happy to acknowledge and see no need to remove.

Some other contentious terms concern geography. The focus of this book is on European communism and its aftermath, and in particular the four countries that are often termed the Visegrad group. Taken together, these occupy a large part of the European continent, and it is convenient to find some geographical label for them collectively. Various terms suggest themselves: middle Europe, East-Central Europe, Central Europe, Central and Eastern Europe. Almost all of these carry with them geopolitical implications, and choice between them is a difficult matter. I have mostly used some combination of 'east' and 'central', coupled with Europe, to name the region. By this, I intend no commentary upon any of the political issues involved, since they play no major part in my analysis. To put it frankly, the supposed cultural boundaries of 'Europe', and whether certain kinds of social behaviour are properly 'European', are not subjects that interest me, and the question is not one that I believe to be either open to serious analysis or useful to illuminate reality. To the extent that the fact that people believe that 'Europe' is anything other than a category of geography, and to the extent that this belief influences social action, then it is worth analysing just as much as are other ludicrous ideological constructions like 'British'. I use terms like 'Eastern and Central Europe' because, on a map read from a small island off the western fringe of the European continent, which is where I happen to be writing, that is the easiest way to describe the location of these countries.

In general, I hope that no one will try to read too deep a significance into the use of words like the ones discussed above, or any other terms that I use. I try to use words in their simple, indeed common, sense as far as is possible. When I employ an important term whose meanings are the subject of debate, like 'totalitarianism' for example, I try to provide a discussion that illuminates the sense in which I understand it. If there is something important at stake in a particular terminology, I try to spell out what it is. No doubt I have failed in numerous cases, and for the obscurities that ensue I apologise.

Because of the aims of this book, it is obliged to consider material not directly related to questions of communication. To the extent that the view of communication, and in particular of the mass media, advanced here, is one that holds that it is impossible to understand these phenomena in isolation, no justification for these digressions is necessary. It might, however, be useful to the reader if I briefly state here why the book is structured the way that it is.

I begin, in Chapter 1, with a discussion of the dominant discourses that have surrounded the end of communism. These are various, but they all seem to point to it as a fundamental turning point in human history. In particular, whether they find the outcome desirable or disastrous, they are all agreed that the collapse of the communist states represented the end of the dream of an alternative and better society that has inspired the critical project for more than a century. Turning to the views of the erstwhile proponents of alternative views, I argue that, whether particular strands within the critical tradition realise it or not, the collapse of communism does constitute a crisis and that, if the project is to continue as anything other than a residual structure of feeling, there are charges that must be answered. The most important of these is to understand what happened and why, and to reanalyse some of the central categories of contemporary social theory in the light of such an understanding. Within the field of media research, the direct consequences have been less obvious, but that does not mean that they are not equally far reaching. This book attempts to undertake part of this essential reanalysis through the lens of the changes to the media system.

In the second chapter, I explain what was particular, and particularly interesting, about the mass media in communist countries. I argue that the fusion
of political and economic power that was so characteristic of these societies
presented the problems of the mass media in a rather different light to that
common in the West. I argue that the concept of totalitarianism, despite
having been put to scoundrelly uses, remains an essential one for understanding the position of the mass media in communist societies.

The third chapter considers the dominant Western theories of the mass
media and society, and in particular that associated with Wilbur Schramm.
This theory, the communist societies's own conceptions of their media systems, and a major alternative approach sketched by Raymond Williams, are
examined in the light of their utility in understanding the declining years of
the communist system. It is argued that a theory of the mass media that pro-
ceeds from what are claimed to be the core beliefs of a social system, and still
less one that claims to be derived from a few fragmented texts by a political
activist, are quite unable to provide any purchase on the real historical development. An approach that begins from an analysis of the real relations in
society, and in particular the differential distribution of different kinds of
power, is much better able to understand what actually happened.

The discussion then moves, in the fourth chapter, to a consideration of different kinds of theoretical explanations for the collapse of communism. Four
main positions are identified, ranging from those who believe that the end of
communism was the end of history through to those who believe that it
marked no change at all in the most basic social relations. These are then
examined in the light of the evidence of the actual changes to broadcasting.
The evidence shows that the changes are much less than predicted by theories
of radical transformation, but that there has been sufficient change as to
render pure continuity theories inadequate. It is argued that the fall of communism was indeed a revolution, but that this was primarily constituted at the
level of political relations, and that institutions like broadcasting display
marked degrees of continuity.

In the fifth chapter, the idea of civil society, much used by the opposition
during the last stages of communism, is critically examined. Three main variants of this position are identified. These again are examined with regard to
the evidence of the restructuring of the media. In particular, the broadcasting
legislation of the region is scrutinised as to how far the ideas of civil society
are embodied in the governance of television. It is concluded that the more
enthusiastic proponents of the idea of civil society were mistaken both as to
its nature and effectivity. The only version of civil society that offers any serious purchase on the actual course of events was that version of the classical
theory that more or less equated it with the capitalist economy.

In the sixth chapter, an attempt is made to show how the ideas about
broadcasting embodied in the legal instruments of the region have fared in
practice. In particular, it is demonstrated how the idea of public-service
broadcasting, which was important in many of the debates around the new
laws and is embodied in many of their founding clauses, was negated by the

realities of constant government intervention that effectively rendered state broadcasting a partisan political instrument. It is concluded that an over-stress upon legal arrangements, as embedded in the importance given to 'a state of laws', is quite inadequate to understand real developments. In the case of broadcasting in particular, the pressures of the political culture are at least as important as the letter of the law.

Finally, in Chapter 7, an attempt is made to categorise the emerging media systems of the region. It is argued that the evolution of both the commercial and public broadcasters has been inevitably politicised, and that the emerging media systems are deeply marked throughout by this reality.

The main conclusions of the book are then summarised and it is concluded that, on the basis of the evidence presented, the critical project is well able to account for the demise of communism, and that it is possible, provided it is clearly distanced from the statism and nationalism that so deeply marked both the Stalinist and social democratic versions of the project, to reconstruct it as a viable programme for human liberation. The implications for these conclusions for the study of the mass media are considered. It is argued that, while materialist theories of the media are clearly superior to the alternatives, the evidence suggests that a purely economistic model of media–society relations is inadequate to grasp the nuances of change.

Books take time and money to write, to produce and to read. Scarce human resources should not be squandered lightly on worthless projects. There really ought to be justifications for producing books that are of a different order than the simple desire for promotion, tenure or esteem.

In this case, it is quite easy to provide such a justification. Irrespective of the quality of the work that I have produced, the fact remains that the subject is important. No one can imagine that the end of communism was not an important event. No serious student of society can imagine that the collapse of a social order is not worth investigating. No engaged intellectual can pretend that the collapse of one of the main claimants to embodying the human future is an irrelevance. In the course of writing this book, I have been continually struck by how little attention the community of communication scholars has been prepared to pay to these questions. There have recently emerged a number of excellent books on aspects of the collapse, and I am deeply in their debt, but the field is far from saturated. I am certain that the topic justifies the book. I can only hope that the book does justice to the topic.

1

Introduction:
A Crisis of the Critical Project

The events of the autumn and winter of 1989 were greeted with enthusiasm around the world. The sense of joy at liberation from an ancient tyranny was as real and as great as that felt in other great revolutionary moments. There was the same sense that, with the collapse of the old order, it would now be possible to build the world anew, and build it better. The suffocating paralysis that had gripped half a continent for half a century, and which had provoked an equal paralysis in the other half, would now be replaced by a new energy and dynamism. Everything, or at least everything good, was now possible.

The comparison that was most often drawn was with 1848, the 'Springtime of the Nations', in which the old multi-national states of Central and Eastern Europe were shaken by national risings, and when the political stasis imposed upon the European continent at the end of the Wars of the French Revolution was finally shattered. The hopes of democratic life that had been crushed at the Congress of Vienna blossomed once again in the capitals of Europe. This time round, it was decisions of Yalta and Potsdam that were overthrown. The legacy that was ended was that of Churchill, Roosevelt and Stalin, in place of Metternich, Talleyrand and Canning. There was, however, the same sense that an attempt to freeze the continent into a pattern acceptable to the victors had been shattered.

The comparison was given an added dimension because, along with the fresh winds of freedom and democracy, 1989 also saw the collapse of another despotic empire that had denied the national aspirations of its subject peoples. In one important respect at least, the prognosis for 1989 was even better than that for 1848. The hopes of the earlier revolutionary moment were eventually drowned in the blood shed by the intervention of reactionary forces, most notably those of the Tsar. Recent European history, particularly events in Hungary in 1956 and Czechoslovakia in 1968, demonstrated that the possibility of Russian counter-revolutionary violence choking off the shoots of democratic development was no distant historical memory. This time around, though, the Russian regime itself was in crisis. The weakening of the communist system, the faltering attempts at reform associated with *Glasnost* and *Perestroika*, and the public repudiation by Mikhail Gorbachev of any intention of intervening to stop the tide of democratisation, both strengthened the confidence of the oppositions in Russia's European empire and signalled to the local defenders of the existing order that they would have to fight for their own survival unaided by outside forces. In the event, in most countries, they decided against the military option and negotiated their own loss of power without violence.

Within two years, communist political rule had collapsed even in Russia. Gorbachev had been toppled, the Communist Party declared illegal, and the *soi-disant* democrat Boris Yeltsin had taken power with promises to extend and speed up economic and social transformation. The old USSR was no more. In its place stood a range of newly independent and semi-independent states, and many groups and nations that aspired to independence. In the place of a monolithic ruling party there was now a multitude of competing factions based on ethnic, geographical or industrial interests. In the place of a centralised command economy there was now a firm commitment to an unbridled free market of the wildest kind.

Echoes of 1989

These great historical changes have produced a profound intellectual crisis around the world. In this, events again followed the pattern of earlier upheavals. The shots fired at Lexington allegedly were heard around the world, and stimulated to new thinking and new action people far distant from Colonial America. The images of the fall of the Berlin Wall certainly were seen around the world, and their impact was unquestionably global. They aroused hopes and fears in the hearts of people facing other tyrannous systems. On the one hand, the strongest of strong states, the most totalitarian of political systems, the most ruthlessly repressive of dictatorships, had been shown to be vulnerable. The tanks and the guns and the legions of secret policemen had proved in the end as powerless to defend the Kremlin from its own people as had the Cossacks and the Okhrana before them. On the other hand, whatever its internal horrors, the communist regime had been a source of aid, of arms and, indeed, of inspiration to many of the bravest opponents of other brutal oppressors. Joe Slovo and Chris Hani are only two of the best-known names out of thousands whose heroism in the fight for political freedom in South Africa was matched by their devotion to the belief that the Soviet Union embodied the highest aspirations of humanity. Those who rejoiced at the practical demonstration of the fragile rule of tyrants were partly balanced by those who saw the end of a source of aid and the extinction of a beacon of hope.

People in situations like these embodied in acute form a crisis that was felt much more widely. The most influential of the traditional poles of the left–right spectrum in political life had been exposed as a hollow and worthless sham, whose rhetoric was not believed even by its own ideologists. Whether Evil Empire or Socialist Motherland, something essential had disappeared from the familiar political terrain. It had collapsed so conclusively and in such ignominy as to demonstrate its rotten foundations. Such a collapse was bound to create the most profound crisis in the minds of all those who had believed what the system said about itself, whether they loved it or hated it.

It is tempting to think of this crisis as affecting only the traditional left. Certainly, it is a crisis for the left. The world impact of 1917 had left powerful organisational echoes in the shape of the communist parties that commanded substantial followings around the world. To a greater or lesser extent, most of the parties that stood in that lineage still, in 1989, despite decades of evidence to the contrary, looked to the 'socialist camp' as a proletarian Utopia of the kind they wished to construct in their home countries. The collapse of this Utopia, however it was explained, removed the living embodiment of an alternative to the capitalist West. Whatever the outcome, the adherents of the orthodox Moscow-line communist tradition needed to engage in some very fundamental rethinking of their past, present and future.

It would be wrong, however, to consider the crisis as only one for the left. In a number of important ways, the intellectual problem reproduced itself in every serious current of thought. This is at its most obvious in political life. For decades, anti-communism had provided the ideology of the dominant right-wing political forces. In the name of anti-communism, any alliance could be justified, no ally was too vile, and no compromise too base. If communism was often presented as a form of religion, anti-communism has been plausibly presented as the US national religion. The collapse of this common enemy meant that much of the social cement that had held together the right began to weaken. When children stop believing in the threat of the bogeyman, there is bound to be a crisis for the kind of parental authority that is based entirely on that fear. The intellectual certainties of anti-communism needed new consideration every bit as much as did those of the erstwhile communists. The triumphalism of much of the right masks a deeper crisis.

Italy provides the clearest example of the extent of the problem. We can see there the extent to which this crisis was not only one of the left, but of the whole political spectrum. Indeed, we can see that in some ways the crisis was a deeper one for the right than for the left. The direct inheritor of the mantle of communism, the Italian Communist Party (PCI), was already in 1989 far removed from its revolutionary past. Compared to many other communist parties, it had put a great distance between itself and the regimes of the Warsaw Pact. The catastrophe of communism provoked a further revision of the party's aims and structure. It split into a more moderate 'Party of the Democratic Left' (PDS) and a more traditionally leftist 'Party of Communist Refoundation' (RC). Despite the crisis, both of these parties retained substantial memberships and considerable voting support.

But the crisis not only shattered the old left. It destroyed its traditional enemies too, and perhaps even more thoroughly. The Christian Democrats (DC) had governed Italy ever since they, the Vatican and the United States Navy had worked together to ensure the defeat of the PCI in the March 1948 elections. As the bulwark against communism, the DC had been excused any fraud or corruption. In the 1980s, it had been joined in government, and in corruption, by a reconstructed Italian Socialist Party (PSI), whose sole claim to support was that it was reliably anti-communist. So long as the Cold War continued, the DC and the PSI could count on the backing of the bulk of business and the state machine. Once the Cold War ended, this entire structure collapsed. It was no longer necessary to pay the price of personal and political corruption the DC and the PSI demanded. No longer able to mobilise the terror of communism, the political élite were unable any more to control the lower echelons of the state machine. The result is that, while the successors of the PCI, the PDS and the RC continue and modestly thrive, many of the most prominent figures of the old governing parties are in jail or in exile. Bettino Craxi, sometime leader of the PSI, cowers in his villa in Tunis to avoid spending five and a half years in the jails of the country of which he was once prime minister. It was necessary completely to rebuild the parties of the right, and to allow the fascists into the government for the first time since the fall of Mussolini, in order to stave off the electoral challenge of the left. Even this, eventually, proved unsuccessful and, for the first time since the Liberation, the left actually entered the government.

It is therefore evidently the case that, far from being of interest only to specialist students of communist countries, or to the political left alone, the echoes of 1989 have been of much wider significance. They have provoked intellectual, moral and spiritual crises around the world, and across the political spectrum. Their impact is far from exhausted. In all of those countries that experienced communist rule, political debate is still fundamentally oriented around the consequences of its collapse. In China, in North Korea and in Cuba, communist parties still cling to power, although each is finding its own ways of adapting to the new world. Elsewhere, too, the impact of 1989 is working its way through the intellectual and political structures. Although the nature of the collapse, and the shape of emerging societies, is much clearer now that it was in the immediate aftermath of the events themselves, the process is far from complete in the former communist countries. Elsewhere, outside the immediate impact zone, the effects are perhaps more subtle and slow working, but they remain powerful. The year 1989 was one of those turning points in world history, like 1917 and 1933, which demand serious consideration from everyone who makes any claim to think about the nature of human society as a whole, or about its major constituents.

A sense of an ending

Although 1989 provoked joy and enthusiasm from all but a hard core of committed Stalinists, that mood of euphoria has not lasted. Not only have there been different conclusions drawn from the events of the period by people thinking and writing from different perspectives, but people have also sometimes changed their minds over the years, and to a dramatic extent.

These shifts have been particularly marked amongst those who have the most direct experience of communist rule and its aftermath. In many countries, the first free elections resulted in victories for parties who were determined opponents of the old communists and everything they stood for. That electoral mood has certainly changed. As the Hungarian joke of the early 1990s had it: 'The democrats succeeded in one year in doing what the communists failed to do in 40 years: they made us love communism.' The same Poles whose persistent oppositional heroism played such a central role in the collapse of communism have, today, more or less freely elected a president and a government who are both politically direct descendants from the hated party of the past. In Hungary, the Prime Minister and leader of the largest party in Parliament is a man who, in the aftermath 1956, was so convinced of the rightness of the Moscow line that he joined the special party militia fighting its opponents. These politicians, of course, have changed their minds from the days when they were pillars of the Stalinist system, but so too have the voters who elected them. While the big votes for ex-communist parties should not be interpreted as a desire to return to the old days, they certainly signify a shift in popular views of the costs of changing the system. No doubt the situations in Poland and Hungary do not represent stable settlements, and there will be future, equally dramatic, changes in political fortune. What is certainly the case, however, is that assessments of the nature of the changes amongst those most directly and immediately involved have varied widely over time.

These shifts in mood have been closely allied to the differing emphases that have been given to the interpretation of the events and process of the period. In the following pages, I want to review some of the assessments of communism and its aftermath. I first consider those assessments that come from outside the critical project. Each of these, in different ways, poses a general challenge to the critical project. I then consider the leftist responses to these events, and consider what implications flow from them.

If one reviews the different accounts of the impact of 1989, it is impossible to avoid confronting the widespread belief that it marked the end of something. This was the first, and perhaps the most widespread, of reactions. Partly, at least, it is obvious why this should be the case. The world order established in 1945 came definitively to an end. The old Europe, frozen into hostile camps in the late 1940s, thawed overnight. The fundamental political, economic and military polarity between West and East vanished. The geopolitical universe in which almost everyone in the continent had spent the bulk of their lives no longer existed.

While the new world was not without problems, they were new and apparently novel ones, and they appeared fluid and transitory compared with the fixed certainties of the former order. The old Europe, with its iron boundaries and its rigid ideologies, had not seemed susceptible to change. The new Europe, in which state boundaries were revised overnight, at worst on the battlefield and at best at the conference table, has a much more transitory air about it. Change, even to the most apparently fundamental markers of social existence, now seems not only possible but normal.

This sense of a historic punctuation mark was powerfully aided by the proximity of the millennium. The old century of revolution, class war and communism had come to an end, 11 years before its appointed time. However arbitrary we may know the measure of historical time we use to be, the great dates it marks out nevertheless exert an immense psychological pull on our imaginations. We want to believe that the end of a century, and still more the end of a millennium, amounts to something more than a simple passage of time no different to any other moment in the history of the universe. In the fall of communism was found what was obviously an event of historical significance to give the end of a millennium the sense of also being the end of a distinct passage in human history. It seemed necessary to say something more than that politics were henceforth different, or that economic life had changed fundamentally, or even that it was necessary to find new ways of thinking about the world. It was rather that all of these things had to be taken together and seen as parts of some fundamental change in human life. There are various vocabularies in which this sense of total change could be expressed. One might say that a new structure of feeling had emerged; that a new century had begun a little early; even that a new epoch of world history had come into being.

One could almost construct a succession of such epochs, starting in 1789 and punctuated by great revolutions, and call literary witnesses to their birth. Goethe had witnessed the death of absolutist Europe in the mud at Valmy, and with it the birth of the new epoch of bourgeois liberty. Serge had witnessed the birth of the epoch of proletarian revolution in the aftermath of a failed insurrection in Barcelona. He marked the nature of the change through his new relations with the Russian consul, formerly a bitter enemy and now a cautious ally. In 1989, Havel stood in Wenceslas Square at the centre of the Velvet Revolution that ushered in the new, and as yet unknown, age. The historical actor and the literary witness were fused in the one personality.

But if there was unanimity as to the fact of an ending, opinions as to what it was that had ended, and just what was replacing the old order, were much more varied. The first to win wide recognition, and the most grandiose in its claims, was that of Francis Fukuyama. According to him, 1989 marked nothing less than the end of history. I shall return to his views in more detail in a subsequent chapter. Here, let us note only that by this claim Fukuyama meant not that events and struggles would now pass from the world, but that the course of human development was finally and decisively set in the pattern of life appropriate to US capitalist democracy. There was no longer the possibility even of thinking that there might be a different and better way of organising human life. There was no longer any believable alternative ideology to that enshrined in the Constitution, and embodied in the daily practice, of the United State of America:

> We who live in stable, long-standing liberal democracies face an unusual situation. In our grandparents' time, many reasonable people could foresee a radiant socialist future in which private property and capitalism had been abolished, and in which politics itself was somehow overcome. Today, by contrast, we have trouble imagining a world that is radically better than our own, or a future that is not essentially democratic and capitalist. Within that framework, of course, many

things could be improved: we could house the homeless, guarantee opportunity for minorities and women, improve competitiveness, and create new jobs. We can also imagine future worlds that are significantly worse than what we know now, in which national, racial, or religious intolerance makes a comeback, or in which we are overwhelmed by war or environmental collapse. Be we cannot picture to ourselves a world that is *essentially* different from the present one, and at the same time better. Other, less reflective ages also thought of themselves as the best, but we arrive at this conclusion exhausted, as it were, from the pursuit of alternatives which we felt *had* to be better than liberal democracy. (Fukuyama, 1992: 46)

In this view, Fukuyama joined a chorus of official voices celebrating the final triumph of the system from which they so conspicuously benefit. The old nightmare that, somehow, all might not be for the best in the best of all possible worlds could be shown to be false. The other in its various horrible guises might still be there, stalking the ghetto streets or beating against the closed doors of the immigration departments, but its political expressions are no longer to be feared. They can no longer pretend they are motivated by the dreams of a better, freer, world. They are simply envious. The US Department of State put the final official seal of approval on the total defeat of the opposition: it closed down the journal *Problems of Communism*.

From another direction, and standing at a much greater distance from the world of officialdom than does Fukuyama, less influential in the corridors of power but taken more seriously by intellectuals, Zygmunt Bauman argued that 1989 constituted the final end of modernity. According to him, the project of modernity had been the attempt to subordinate all aspects of human life to the dictates of reason. Modernity was ultimately inspired by a terror of contingency and chance, and thus sought to eliminate them from the determination of human experience. Its most grandiose attempt at the rational ordering of human life was the socialist system, in which the contingencies of economic life were to be overcome by means of The Plan:

Throughout its history, communism was modernity's most devout, vigorous and gallant champion – pious to the point of simplicity. It also claimed to be its only true champion. Indeed, it was under communist, not capitalist, auspices that the audacious dream of modernity, freed from obstacles by the merciless and seemingly omnipotent state, was pushed to its radical limits: grand designs, unlimited social engineering, huge and bulky technology, total transformation of nature. (Bauman, 1992a: 179)

But this great project proved illusory. The project did not deliver the intended social and personal benefits: 'Life did not seem to become more comfortable or happy, needs . . . did not seem to be better satisfied than before, and the kingdom of reason and harmony seemed to be more distant than ever' (*ibid.*).

The failure of the socialist project thus marked the termination of the overall aim of modernity as well. It is now necessary to construct a new, post-modern, account of life and of the human condition. This account starts from the fact that there is no longer any possible alternative to the capitalist system, but recognises that this is not the simple and unproblematic system of unalloyed benefits its unthinking adherents proclaim it to be. The post-modern account recognises the limits, the uncertainty, the contingency that is a central feature of human life and proposes only limited, local and partial resolutions to the problems that this contingency entails. Unlike the drive towards unity and completeness of modernity: 'The most conspicuous features of the postmodern condition [are] institutionalised pluralism, variety, contingency and ambivalence' (Bauman, 1992a: 187). It is in the recognition and celebration of these elements that the distinctive features of the postmodern project are to be found.

On a more modest scale, Ralph Dahrendorf claimed that the end of communism also meant the end of any kind of socialist project (Dahrendorf, 1990). According to him, the attempt to construct a different way of organising society was logically independent of the particular communist means for realising it. What collapsed with communism was not the particular means, but the common end of both socialism and communism. In this, he undoubtedly has a point. Whatever differences and disagreements about the methods of achieving a socialist society there may have been between the main currents of communism and socialism, there was indeed a unity of conception about the kind of society they were trying to build. In both of their accounts, the direction of human labour and energy from above was a common and central theme. The Plan as the product of the reflection of the expert, to be imposed upon the mass of humanity, constituted as much the core of the Fabian project as it did of Stalinism. It was not for nothing that George Bernard Shaw got on well with Stalin and the Webbs wrote a massive tome hailing the USSR as a new civilisation. To the extent, then, that even the mildest of social democrats shares this version of socialism with the least repentant of Stalinists, the lesson of 1989 is that this dream is unrealisable. A rational social order cannot be imposed on the mass of the population by the far-sighted technical intellectual acting in everyone's long-term interests. The price of attempting to force the unruly drives of humanity into the logic of the centralised plan is brutal repression and social stagnation.

It is clear, then, that despite the different positions each of these writers takes upon precisely what it is that has ended, they have a basic agreement that the attempt to construct a different, and better, society has proved futile. They may regard this as a great triumph for capitalism, in the manner of Fukuyama and Dahrendorf. They may, like Bauman, regard it as a challenging and threatening, but ultimately liberating, release from the false certainty of progress embodied by the modern project.

If these writers are correct, then the scope for the human imagination, for the social theory that embodies it, and for our ideas about the mass media, have been dramatically reduced. It is simply no longer meaningful to consider how the affairs of society, or of the media, might be organised differently. They are not perfect, and we are free to point to their many flaws and shortcomings, but the way things are is, at root, the best way that things can be. Attempts to modify the basic features of our world will inevitably lead to worse outcomes. Perhaps we may tinker with the structures in which we live in order to overcome the most glaring shortcomings. As Fukuyama admits, many of these tinkerings would materially improve the lives of great swathes of the world's population. But one thing is certainly off the agenda: whether in its communist or social democratic form, the idea of a systematically different and better society has to be abandoned.

Critical responses

It was this belief, that it was indeed possible to construct a better society, that was the unifying core of all the bewildering varieties of the critical project. It was, of course, at its clearest in classical Marxism, but exactly the same ambition glimmered somewhere inside the withered souls even of Beatrice and Sydney Webb. If that core idea is now false, then the critical project in all its variants is now at an end. It follows that, unless we can show that the apocalyptic accounts of the meaning of 1989 are wrong, and that it is possible still to imagine and to theorise alternatives to capitalism and the capitalist media, then there is no future for the critical project as a route to positive human development. If we can no longer even see an alternative to capitalism, then it is certainly impossible to mobilise against it. While it might still be possible to point to the failings and shortcomings of actually existing capitalism, unless it is also possible to point to how the world might be made different, then critical thought will become a truly residual category. It will express the anger and rage against the present of those who look back to an imaginary glorious past as their inspiration. Some of us, who came to political and intellectual maturity before 1989, will no doubt persist in the errors of our youth: John Bunyans railing against the defeat of our cause. Many others will be more sensible and adapt to the new order. But we residual critics will be unable to recruit fresh forces to our project. As new generations, who were never misled into imagining that there could be alternatives to capitalism, come to maturity, so the critical project will wither and die with its current proponents. The furthest extent of the new critical thought will be proposals for tinkering with the workings of an established system.

The adherents of the critical project have made a number of responses to this challenge. The most surprising one has been public silence. Outside of the realms of the specialists, the impact of the fall of communism has been little registered, at least in the scholarly literature. Despite the fact that it would be fair to claim that the critical project has, or had, many adherents amongst those professionally engaged in the study of the mass media, the number of studies has been tiny. There was, it is true, an initial flurry of interest, but that has died down. There have been no major international conferences dedicated to the subject. The number of books is small, the number of articles in scholarly journals scarcely larger. Like the sages of Greece and Rome, the majority of critical academics 'turned aside from the awful spectacle, and pursuing the ordinary occupations of life and study, appeared unconscious of any alterations in the moral or physical government of the world'. This supine inattention is all the more surprising in that there can be no ironical intention in the description of the evidence as overwhelming and irrefutable.

Apart from the sound reason that the questions raised are very difficult to answer, and the more questionable motives of self-deception, there is one easily understood reason for the lack of attention to the crisis of the critical project: academic specialisation. The links between the collapse of communism and the study, say, of the relations between journalists and their sources, is far from immediate. It lies rather at the level of the most general theoretical questions. It is quite possible, and quite proper, to continue with narrowly focused social scientific enquiries and leave the more general questions to the engaged, or general, intellectuals. The consequences of this professional blindness are, however, in the long run severe. Even the most narrowly focused studies are in the end informed by general theoretical considerations. If the critical project collapses as a general theoretical statement of possibility, then ultimately that will affect the kinds of questions that can be posed in even the most specialised areas. The self-distanciation from the implications of 1989 may be understandable, but it is surely mistaken.

Not everybody on the left has followed the route of silence. For some, the nature of their professional activity itself, as much as their public obligations, has forced them to confront the problem. The best-known example is Eric Hobsbawm, who argued that the collapse of communism was the end of the 'short twentieth century'. The dates of this spiritual century were from the outbreak of the First World War, which marked the end of the 'long nineteenth century' inaugurated in 1789 by the great French Revolution, up to the collapse of the Communist Party of the Soviet Union in 1991. This short century had been marked by the attempt to build socialism. However dreadful in its practices, the project itself was a noble one of human emancipation. Now that project had finally failed and the future seemed grim and almost hopeless. For Hobsbawm, as much as for Fukuyama, there is now no visible alternative to the rule of capital, but in Hobsbawm's account that victory is seen as carrying with it the looming threat of barbarism and human extinction. The imperative to change the world remains, but the belief that the author once held, that at least the main lines of the path to that change were clearly visible, is no longer credible. The closing passage of the magnum opus of one of the most prominent of a great school of Marxist historians runs thus:

> The future cannot be a continuation of the past, and there are signs, both externally and, as it were, internally, that we have reached the point of historic crisis. The forces generated by the techno-scientific economy are now great enough to destroy the environment, that is to say, the material foundations of human life. The structures of human societies themselves, including even some of the social foundations of the capitalist economy, are on the point of being destroyed by the erosion of what we have inherited from the human past. Our world risks both explosion and implosion. It must change.
>
>   We do not know where we are going. We only know that history has brought us to this point and – if the readers share the argument of this book – why. However, one thing is plain. If humanity is to have a recognizable future, it cannot be by prolonging the past or the present. If we try to build the third millennium on that basis, we shall fail. And the price of failure, that is to say, the alternative to a changed society, is darkness. (Hobsbawm, 1994: 584–5)

Before 1989, it was possible to think that the Soviet Union represented some sort of alternative, however limited and distorted. It was possible to believe that the traditional labour movement, however limited and distorted, represented a starting point for any plan to change the world. It was possible to see traditional political action as the special means by which society could be changed. That whole set of beliefs has now been shown to be a sham. Hobsbawm sees no basis for the transformation of capitalism, and therefore has no hope for the future. In this gloomy and pessimistic conclusion, Hobsbawm speaks almost as much as the official voice of the bulk of the reflective left as Fukuyama did for the right.

For others on the left, particularly those writing about the political life of societies in which the pressures of hunger, poverty and war remain the central existential realities of the mass of the population, the collapse of the critical project, Marxism–Leninism in this version, was due to the treachery of the leaders of the USSR. In the days of good old Joe, things were fine in the Soviet camp. Then, after his death, decline set in:

> The rot, the downhill process along the road leading to the restoration of capitalism, started with the triumph of Krushchevite revisionism at the 20th Congress of the CPSU [Communist Party of the Soviet Union] in 1956, and the distortions of Marxism–Leninism in its aftermath and under its direct stimulus in the fields of philosophy, political economy and the class struggle. (Brar, 1992: vii)

It therefore follows that the way to reconstruct the critical project is to return to the old verities. In this, historical development will prove a powerful ally. Socialism raised the living standards of the Soviet masses, gave them a range of free material and cultural benefits, and secured for them their jobs and the futures of their children, 'but very soon the Soviet workers will be able to have a first-hand taste of the "freedoms" of a market economy' (Brar, 1992: xi). They will have the same access to unemployment, poverty, homelessness and general miserable insecurity as the workers of established capitalist economies.

The views advanced by Brar might perhaps be dismissed as extreme, but they are merely one end of a spectrum that stretches through to those whose attitude towards the old regime is more one of nostalgia (Ahmad, 1992: 24–7). What unites this version of the critical project is the belief that the Soviet Union was indeed the living embodiment of a society that was, at the least, an imperfect embodiment of a better way of life. The reasons for the collapse were either internal treachery, the predations of imperialism, or some combination of both. The remedy is to try again, without making the same mistakes as last time.

These views have in common with Hobsbawm the claim that the Soviet Union and its satellites were fundamentally different to the West. In this, the resurrection men are at one with the voices of the Western right. Both saw the world as one polarised between fundamentally different systems, although they evaluated the two poles quite differently. Located in the context of the real immediate needs that remain the lot of the majority of the world's population, such a view is at least understandable. For all its shortcomings, it can

be argued, the Soviet Union achieved impressive levels of national development, transforming the country from one dominated by backward peasant
agriculture to an urban and industrial society. That achievement still seems to
many worth emulating. For others, it is a matter of regret that the project
failed, and that circumstances prevent its repetition. But starting from the
premise that the communist societies were radically different forms of economic life that were, in some way or another, at the very least the precursors
of socialism leads one inevitably either to Hobsbawm's pessimism or Brar's
resurgent Stalinism.

The reasons for thinking that this approach does not provide a route to the
reconstruction of the critical project are relatively straightforward. The historical evidence as to the undemocratic nature of the society that spawned
The Plan is irrefutable. The achievement of economic growth, measured in
tons of coal and steel, was directly coincident with the abolition of the last
rights of the urban workers and with the bloody civil war against the peas-
antry in the countryside. Let us dismiss as unworthy of serious discussion the
idea that these horrible events did not occur. They did, as historians of almost
all persuasions agree. The collapse of communism has finally negated the
claim that these deeds were justified in the long-run triumph of socialism.
Unless it can be shown conclusively that these immense historical atrocities
were independent of the rapid economic growth, then while the Stalinist
model may or may not continue to represent a viable strategy for economic
growth, it cannot possibly be considered a strategy for human liberation. In
the absence of any such demonstration, convincing or otherwise, it is impossible not to accept the argument that forced labour was the literal lifeblood of
forced economic growth. The critical project cannot be rehabilitated by
bathing it in the blood of Stalin's victims.

Debates about the nature of communism

There is, however, another possibility. It might be the case that, whatever
was proclaimed about them, Stalinist societies were not the living embodiment of the critical project. They might, indeed, have been its negation. This
view has much more to commend it. The view that Stalinist societies had
nothing to do with attempts at human liberation are not all constructed with
the benefit of hindsight. There has never been unanimity about the nature of
communist societies. That has been an issue of strong contention ever since
the Bolshevik seizure of power. The majority view internationally, held by all
communists and many social democrats, was that these countries constituted
new and essentially democratic societies that marked out the road to a better
future for humanity in general. The alternative view, held by most of the
right and some on the left, stressed the undemocratic nature of these regimes
and saw them as engines of oppression.

It is important to recognise that this division of opinion was not a simple
split between left and right. To be critical of Western capitalism did not

automatically mean that one became uncritical of Stalin and all his works. Conversely, to be critical of communism did not mean that one was automatically an enthusiastic agent for the British Empire, or the CIA, or Christian Democracy. There have always been left critics of the USSR, and not all of them were people who had made their peace with capitalism. One of the earliest and most notable critics of the Soviet regime was Luxemburg, whose revolutionary socialist credentials could hardly be doubted, and who would have repudiated the charge that she was some kind of 'anti-communist' with contempt. She was followed in the 1920s and 1930s by a line of more or less distinguished left critics, including Pannekoek, Serge, Rosmer and, of course, Trotsky. The tradition continued after the Second World War in the work of writers like Mandel and Cliff.

Despite their many differences, these thinkers were united in the fact that they laid heavy stress upon the fact that communist societies were not evolving naturally towards peace and democracy. They tended to stress the extent to which the Soviet Union, and later other similar societies, were dominated in every respect by a pervasive, dictatorial bureaucracy that effectively controlled all the levers of social power. The differences lay in their conception of the nature and probably longevity of this bureaucracy. These disputes, although apparently arcane, are important to the prospects of reconstructing the critical project, and therefore require a little examination. The fundamental division was between those, like Trotsky, who saw the Soviet Union as at least partially the embodiment of social principles different from those of the capitalist world, which rendered it something of an approximation to socialism, and those others who claimed that it was the negation of socialist principles.

The school of thought associated with Trotsky, and later Mandel, famously believed that the Soviet bureaucracy was a 'sphere balancing on a pyramid', and predicted the imminent collapse of such an unstable formation. In this, they were among the few theorist of communism who saw it as a transitory phenomenon (Lipset and Bence, 1994: 199). The problem with accepting this view as the best predictor of real events is what may be called the 'stopped clock' effect: the same prediction of imminent collapse was made from the middle of the 1930s right up to the end of the 1980s. Sooner or later, it was right. The theory said it would be sooner. It turned out to be later.

One of the major reasons for Trotsky's reluctance to accord any degree of historic stability to Stalinism was that he believed that the USSR was, at the bottom, some kind of workers' state, radically different from the West. In this, despite his early and unsparing criticisms of the undemocratic features of Stalinism, he was at one with his bitter enemies in both the West and the East. An alternative view, equally critical of the internal terror, but more prepared to concede the relative stability of communist societies, is provided by those that consider them to be new forms of class rule. These constitute the basis for a quite different approach to the problem of the future of the critical project.

This difference of estimation as to the internal structure of the communist societies in fact constitutes the fundamental divide between different versions of the critical project. We might sum up the overall differences by saying that there are, or were, two kinds of theories about the nature of communist societies. The major group of theories, advanced by the vast majority of commentators both hostile to and supportive of communist societies, from Cold War warriors through to Trotsky, held that they were what they claimed to be: socialist societies. They were no longer characterised by an exploiting class. Power was held by the working class, or at least by their representatives, and the societies were at least capable of being reformed in the image of that class. The intention was to build a new world without class divisions, and The Plan and its ancillary apparatus was designed to achieve that end. The horrors arose from the failings and imperfections of the attempt to achieve a laudable goal.

The alternative group of theories, held by some opponents of the regimes, and some who in the course of their careers were equally fervently both supporters and opponents of the regimes, albeit at different times, was that societies of this type represented different forms of class rule. There continued to be an exploiting class, and The Plan and its ancillary apparatus was designed to continue the rule of that class. The horrors of the *Gulag* were a necessary part of those fundamental social relations, since they were part of a process of industrial development analogous to the primitive accumulation of capital that left such a deep scar on the Atlantic economies.

Within this latter group, there was a further important division between those who believed that communism represented some new form of class society, and those who held that it was a special and distorted version of capitalism. According to 'new class' theories, of whom the best-known contemporary representatives are the group around the journal *Critique*, the bureaucracy constituted a special form of collective exploiter of the other classes in society. This kind of society was more analogous to slavery or feudalism than to capitalism, since the exploited classes neither enjoyed the freedom of movement normal in capitalism, nor were they able to bargain collectively over the reward for their labour in the manner of an industrial proletariat. The all-embracing Plan meant both that there was no labour market in a communist society and that the rewards of labour were determined in advance by the planners. To the extent that money remained an element in these societies, it was a fiction concealing relations constituted essentially through the direct use of a monopoly of political power.

The alternative position argued that the ruling group in communist societies constituted a special form of the capitalist class. This view is best represented today by the journal *International Socialism*. Like their identical opposites in the West, the bureaucracy were obliged to accumulate as a condition for competitive survival. Because the unit of competition in this special case was the state rather than the firm, the object of accumulation was weapons rather than capital per se. But in order to produce modern weapons, it was essential to have modern industry, so the accumulation of capital in the narrow sense was indeed the ultimate motor of the economy. The Plan was designed to produce the heavy industry that could produce weapons. In order to accumulate, they were obliged to extract a surplus from a working class in exactly the same way as do their Western competitors: by buying labour at a lower value than that of its product. Consequently, they were confronted in industry by a classical proletariat.

Any attempt to reconstruct the critical project in the aftermath of the collapse of European communism has to orient itself towards these debates. The supporters of the existing order say that the critical project was embodied in communism, which was in turn embodied the societies of Eastern Europe. These were not only manifestly tyrannous – they also ultimately collapsed under the weight of their own shortcomings. There are, as we have seen, among the adherents, or erstwhile adherents, a variety of possible responses. One accepts that the argument of the right is correct, and despairs of ever changing the existing order. Another argues that the communist states did indeed embody the critical project, and their barbarous features, probably much exaggerated, were a necessary price to pay for future rewards. The critical project can be reconstructed by a return to the pure form of the system, when it was robustly aggressive. A third position argues that the communist states embodied at least some elements of the critical project, but that the barbarous features were avoidable excrescences upon a healthy principle. The task is to rescue the healthy principle and to avoid repeating the mistakes. The final position argues that there was no connection between communist societies and the critical project, and that these societies were simply another form of exploitive rule. The future of the critical project begins by demonstrating clearly how great the distance was between actually existing socialism and the aspirations of humanity.

The preferences, or prejudices, of the current author are probably already sufficiently clear, but they do not even begin to settle the questions at stake. They can only be resolved by considering the actual evidence. It is in principle possible to discriminate between the above positions on the basis of the extent to which they explain reality. It might be possible to show that the communist societies were in fact radically different from Western capitalism; that they were the true embodiment of the critical project; that their barbarous features were an integral part of that project; that their collapse was the inevitable consequence of their organising principles. On the other hand, it might be possible to show that one or all of these propositions cannot be supported by the evidence. The choice between different positions is one that can convincingly be made only on the basis of systematic investigation.

The media and the transition

The issues raised by the such an investigation are immense. They range across the full range of the human sciences. They can only be resolved through extensive theoretical discussions and empirical research. Practical considerations aside, the current author is eminently ill-equipped to give definitive answers to questions that must involve enormous specialist knowledge.

Probably, the task of a conclusive study is beyond the range of any single individual. Partial studies, however, can take us some way towards understanding the real historical processes and provide us with indicators as to the likely outcome of the overall question.

I want to argue that a study of the transition in the mass media of the communist societies is a particularly valuable place to conduct such a local investigation. The first reason for this is that social crises, and no crisis could be more serious than a final crisis, illuminate the fundamental structures of societies more clearly than do normal periods. What is essential can be more clearly distinguished from what is contingent when a system dies. To use a biological metaphor, an autopsy can reveal the inner decay of an individual through methods that were not available during the life of the patient. The end of communism showed quite clearly what sort of things the system could tolerate and what sort of things it was bound to reject as alien to its very nature. From this, we can start to understand what the system actually was.

Second, I want to argue that the mass media, and in particular television, form a privileged point of entry into the understanding of any society. In saying this, I do not wish to claim that the kinds of experiences focused by the mass media were more important than the social realities of labour in the socialist factory, or the mechanisms for conflict resolution in single-party states, or the problem of economic calculation in a command economy, or whatever. Rather, I want to claim that certain features of the structures of society are more clearly illuminated through this optic than through others. This is partly because of the fact, regarded as a banality by most of us who study communication, but regarded as a revelation by other social theorists when they intermittently stumble across it, that the mass media are 'constitutive of the experience of modernity'. Social life, in the sense of a knowledge of and interaction with aspects of the world outside the circle of proximates, exists overwhelmingly through the mechanisms of the mass media.

More importantly for this study, however, there are certain features of the modern mass media that render them particularly valuable as the site of evidence about communist societies. As we shall see, these depended upon a particular kind of articulation between politics and economics that was different from that prevailing in the West. These differences were immediately apparent in the case of the mass media. The character of the changes to the mass media consequent upon the fall of communism could therefore be expected to be particularly revealing about the differences between the different kinds of social systems.

One can illustrate this point by considering the question of democracy. This, by common consent, is one of the key points at issue in terms of the relationship between communist societies and the critical project. Democracy, in the modern senses of the word, is literally impossible without the media. It is a characteristic claim of Western societies that they are democratic precisely because they have both regular elections and a free media. One of the charges brought against the countries of Eastern and Central Europe was that, whatever they claimed about themselves, they were not democracies because these two conditions were absent. If the shift from communism to the new order in the region is really one of a shift between fundamentally different systems, then one would expect that to be registered particularly clearly in the mass media. If one of the faults of the mass media in the old system was that they were closely controlled by politicians, and therefore were not able to act as the forum for the kinds of public debate essential to a democracy, then we would expect to find that the changes to the mass media are fundamental and far reaching if the societies in question have in fact become democracies. If, on the other hand, the nature of the transition is more nuanced than that, then we would expect to find a greater degree of continuity in the media. The close relation between different kinds of media performance and the structure of political life in a given society means that the former will act as an important indicator of changes in the latter.

Previous studies of the problems

Most of the existing scholarly studies of the mass media have addressed these questions at best obliquely. It is probably true to say that almost everyone who writes on the post-communist societies is, either openly or covertly, concerned with the fate of the critical project. Having said that, however, the engagement is very often indirect or implicit. Relatively few studies confront directly the more general questions that we have here broached.

Probably the majority of the writers accept that the changes are best interpreted as a one-way process of change, for good or ill, from command media to market media. Tomasz Goban-Klas's study of Poland, for example, demonstrates conclusively that, seen through the perspective of media policy:

> The collapse of the Communist system was not a phenomenon of a deus ex machina type but was the result of a long, painstaking, and gradual process of transformations of the system through internal political and economic struggles leading to social compromises and mutual adaptations. (Goban-Klas, 1994: 4)

Goban-Klas shows how the newly emerging media system in Poland owes a considerable debt to its communist predecessor, and details the ways in which the politicians of the new system retain many of the attitudes of the old days (Goban-Klas, 1994: 257–8). He does not, however, extend his analysis to consider the systemic implications of these developments and indeed seems sometimes to regard them as teething problems in a system that is bound to evolve towards norms of complete freedom, independence and democratic vitality.

A similar view can be found in the scattered, but extremely influential, writings of Karol Jakubowicz, cited throughout this work, who records in considerable detail the vicissitudes of the media in post-communist societies, while at the same time apparently holding to the view that there is a teleology operating that will lead them ever more closely to resemble an idealised version of the kind of media imagined to exist in the West.

Peter Gross's study of Romania is rather gloomier about the prospects of a

Western model taking root in Romania in the short term, but he is an open and convinced believer in the fact that 'journalism [will] progress from a purely commercial or political endeavour to one that is societal in scope' (Gross, 1996: 168). I think that it is fair to say that the latter study, directly, and the other two at least by implication, answer the central problems posed by this book in favour of drawing a radical distinction between communist and capitalist media. I do not know what the personal attitude of any of these writers is towards what I have called the critical project, but it would not be unreasonable to conclude, on the basis of their books, that they would fall within that segment of opinion that holds that it has definitively ended.

Two more general studies address my central concern more directly, but have rather different emphases. Slavko Splichal's early study of changes in the region is concerned to show how the development of a market orientation for the mass media has not resolved the problems of political intervention. He is very far from imagining that there exists some holy grail of a Western media system towards which the benighted East will surely progress. He distinguishes usefully between different kinds of Western media system, and places the emerging post-communist systems as variants of the 'Italian' type (Splichal, 1994: 143–8). Again, the issue of the critical project is not directly addressed, but it would be reasonable to assume, on the basis both of the general tenor of his analysis and in particular his remarks about 'the most excessive case of transplanting a Western model of deregulation to a former socialist country', that while accepting the idea of the fundamental difference between socialist and capitalist societies, he wishes to recast the critical project in terms of a radical democratisation that transcends debates over forms of property (Splichal, 1994: 34).

John Downing's study of the transition, besides having a much greater focus on the former USSR than this work, is certainly in part addressed to what is recognisably a version of the critical project. At one level, the analysis presented in Downing's book is concerned to establish the similarities between the systems prevailing during the communist period and other, capitalist, examples. The main differentiation is not between communist and capitalist but between a small number of Western states and the rest of the world:

> I have argued that despite the specificities that characterize sovietized and post-Soviet nations, and despite the specificities that always distinguished Soviet bloc nations from each other, their fierce conflictual brew of state power, communication, social movements, cultural change, economic dislocation and all the rest, is far more characteristic of planetary society than is the relative stability of Britain or the United States (the predominant sources of empirical illustration in media theory). (Downing, 1996: 229)

Downing's main focus is much more upon the consequences of this fact for media theory, which he impressively argues has been too ready to universalise the narrow experience of the USA and Britain. It is, however, clearly the case that he believes that a corollary of this position is that the critical project is distinguishable from the fate of the communist societies.

The argument of this book, then, is not without precedents. The earlier major studies of the media after communism have clearly at least touched upon the issues raised here. They have not, however, taken them as central to their concerns. I am here making quite large claims for a study of a particular set of media in a small number of countries over a relatively brief period of time. It is my contention that the issues at stake are very important ones indeed, not simply for the ways in which we can understand the mass media, but also for our general understanding of our social world and our prospects for bettering it.

Conclusion

It may well be that some readers will wish to bracket out those more general concerns and concentrate their attention on the mass media. For those who decide upon that route, it is only polite to offer a more immediate guide to what is at stake. In terms of the media, a great deal of critical effort has gone into ways of exploring the relationship between the mass media and other centres of political and economic power. One of the aims of this has always been to effect changes in the mass media so that they act to empower the mass of the population in their lives as members of democratic societies. This is the critical project, or at least one version of it, specified in terms of the mass media.

If the critical project is over, then that effort will have been wasted. We might make some minor adjustments to this or that aspect of broadcasting regulation in order to ensure that the cultural needs of small or poor sections of the audience receive at least some parity of treatment with those of larger and richer groups. We might introduce this or that measure to modify press competition in order to cater for that section of the population that would like to read serious popular journalism in order to understand its world better. We might argue that there should be provisions for equality of access to the services provided by any new information infrastructure in order that all citizens might have an equal chance of participating in democratic political life. But even as we argue for all of this, we must make it clear that we accept as given the framework of a market-driven, profit-motivated media system. We can quarrel over the relative importance of advertising funding and subscription in the future of broadcasting, but we must accept that outcomes in the real world will be determined by the operations of the market. That, history has demonstrated, is the best and most durable system that human beings have been able to devise. All others are worse.

If, on the other hand, it can be shown that the critical project remains viable, then we can be rather more ambitious than this. We would, of course, want to question whether some assumptions that were taken to be central to critical analysis were still valid. We might, for example, now think that the idea of a television service responsive to the plurality of its audience flourished despite its historic relation to the state, rather than because of it. But we would also still be able to try to find ways in which the huge variety and great richness of human self-expression could find its place in the mass media independently of the mere consideration of what might be profitable. We could still try to think of ways in which the stranglehold over access to public communication exercised by the owners of the media and their loyal servants could be broken down and replaced by a system in which communicative entitlements were more equally distributed. We could, in short, continue to think radical thoughts about the mass media. And if we can still think radical thoughts, we might perhaps also dream of doing radical deeds.

2

Totalitarianism and the Media

In this chapter, I discuss the background to the position of the mass media, and particularly television, in communist regimes. In order to illuminate that question, I first make some general remarks about the overall nature of the communist system, and its distinguishing features. I suggest that, with care and precision, it is possible to apply the term 'totalitarian' to regimes of this type. Despite the obvious difficulties with this term, arising from its Cold War usage, I argue it nevertheless comes closer to pointing up the unique features of the political regimes in communist societies than other alternatives. In particular, from the point of view of our main concern with the mass media, it illuminates very productively the differences between communist societies and the Western, mostly democratic capitalist, societies in which theories of the media have been most intensively developed. Like Downing, I suggest that some of the basic ways in which we think about the mass media require revision if they are to account for the specificity of communist, and by extension post-communist, societies. The area that requires most extensive revisions is in the way we think about the relations between the mass media and other centres of power in society.

Varieties of political system

Both the supporters and the opponents of communism claimed that the regimes set up in Central and Eastern Europe after the Second World War were radically distinct from those of Western Europe. For most commentators, the new societies were, more or less, imitations of that existing in the Soviet Union, to which they were obviously closely tied, economically, politically and militarily. There were, of course, differences of emphasis in descriptions of the systems, and most certainly a cleavage as to the assessments of the worth and viability of these ways of organising human affairs. For the supporters of communism, these new societies were the embodiment of the highest human aspirations. For its opponents, communism represented a new and uniquely savage form of repression and exploitation calculated to crush the independent human spirit. Despite these differences, however, there was something of an overlap of opinion about the main features of the societies. In particular, both sides could agree that communist societies, whatever their various individual characteristics, all displayed structural differences with their major post-Second World War antagonists: the societies of Western

Europe and North America. One of the easiest ways to appreciate the unique features of communist societies is to consider just these structural differences.

While I would certainly want to reject any claim that there is some necessary link between capitalism and democracy, the major Western societies were, during this period and up to the present, both capitalist and, more or less, democracies. As capitalist democracies or, in the classic terminology, 'bourgeois democracies', they display a characteristic and clear distinction between political and economic life. While it can readily be admitted that in practice the two influence each other to a considerable degree, they are in theory different and separate spheres of activity. Political life is concerned with the common interest and the public good. Political power follows upon successes in free and competitive elections. Economic life is concerned with the pursuit of private interest and only takes notice of the common interest to the extent that this is a condition for, or restriction upon, its own pursuits. Economic power follows on from the ownership of productive property.

This separation is further embodied in the distinction between the state machine, with its various permanent military and civil bureaucracies, and the elected, and therefore transitory, political apparatus of government, both national and local. Politicians and business leaders are very often different people, and when the two sets do overlap there are elaborate precautions designed to prevent advantage accrued within one sphere being used to further the interests of the individuals involved in the other sphere. Both government bureaucracies and business are, in principle at least, permanent structures that endure beyond their individual inhabitants. Governments, at least in principle, are subject to the possibility of regular change.

Within the economic sphere, too, power and control are dispersed amongst different groups. While there may in practice be marked tendencies towards the concentration of ownership within areas of business, and between different areas of business, there remain in all known cases distinct and different centres of power. Thus ownership of the major mass media, for example, is often independent of ownership of other kinds of productive capital, and is usually divided between at least two competing firms. To the extent that media institutions are owned not as private economic enterprises but as public property, as in the case of the public-broadcasting systems that have historically been so important a feature of Western European democracies, there are usually elaborate rules designed to ensure the independence of these media from government control. To the extent that the unchecked workings of economic laws are thought to lead to an undue concentration of economic power, there are often provisions for political intervention in the market designed to thwart these tendencies towards monopoly. One of the main functions of the elaborate structures of laws and regulations that surround media ownership and operation in even the most de-regulated of capitalist societies is to ensure that there is both a relative dispersion of media ownership and a relative degree of media independence from political power.

Commentators have drawn different conclusions from these characteristics. It is possible to argue that the fact that there are many different and distinct centres of power means that it is distributed, and that there is no single ruling group. In terms of a politico-academic slogan, we would say that there is a plurality of élites: minimally, as in Pareto's seminal formulation, a 'governing élite' and a 'non-governing élite'. These élites may be made up of different functional groups, like the military élite, the educational élite, the media élite, and so on. They may be divided along ethnic, linguistic, religious or political lines, or some combination of these, as for example in contemporary Belgium. They are, however, sufficiently differentiated as to have distinct and different interests and policies. This is the dominant view of the nature of bourgeois democracies. Political conflict, it is argued, takes the form of struggles between different élites.

On the other hand, we might wish to follow Ralph Miliband's classic argument that these different élite groups have important features in common. They are radically distinct from those outside the élite sphere. They depend on a common set of structures and have a common set of interests. They can therefore be shown to constitute a distinct and homogenous grouping that we may term the ruling class (Miliband, 1973). While there may indeed be conflicts between different sections of the ruling class, they will tend to be united in the face of challenges from other classes. Politics may thus take the form both of struggles between élite groups within the ruling class, as with Republicans and Democrats in the USA, and between the representatives of different classes, as in much of Europe.

For our purposes here, it is not necessary to resolve that lengthy debate. It is my personal view that the description of the ruling group in society as constituting a class is the more useful way of thinking, at least with regard to the historical dynamics of capitalist societies. Within bourgeois democracies, however, this ruling class has observable internal differences. In normal circumstances, it is advisable to modify the simplistic description of it simply as a class and to think of it as a porous and loosely articulated ruling class. The conflicts within the ruling class, the clash of élites if one chooses to adopt that terminology, are real, and the political struggles organised around those élites are substantive. They may indeed all take place within a framework of the domination of one class over others, but in circumstances in which that class struggle is not at the centre of social life, élite struggles can and do occupy the political terrain. It is very difficult to understand the functioning of the mass media in bourgeois democracies without a theoretical conception that recognises the extent to which there can be genuine conflicts between the mass media and the government, not to mention between different political forces. I would add that it is equally difficult to understand these problems without a conception of class rule, and that the two theoretical positions can be seen as differences of perspective from the point of view of class theory.

Whichever position we take upon this long-running debate, however, it is certain that we would wish to distinguish bourgeois democracies from many other kinds of twentieth-century rule. Historically, such democracies are relatively rare, even in Europe. The communist societies form one extreme version of that much larger group of societies in which the internal dis-articulation of the ruling class is much less marked than it is in bourgeois democracies operating under normal circumstances. This grouping is not defined by its economic characteristics. Alongside communist societies, it certainly includes classical fascism, military dictatorships of the most free-market stripe like that of Pinochet in Chile, bourgeois democracies facing internal and external crises, and numerous other different kinds of economic relations. What is distinctive is that in all cases within this diverse group of political forms, the distance between the economic and the political is greatly reduced. At the same time, differentiations within the different spheres of economics and politics are often also attenuated.

At one end of this spectrum of what one might almost term 'co-ordinated' societies, lie bourgeois democracies operating in exceptional circumstances, of which major wars are the clearest examples. In Britain during the Second World War, for instance, the political apparatus extended its direct control over large areas of society, including industry and the mass media, which usually enjoy a degree of independence. Labour and raw materials were allocated to industries not according to a price mechanism but according to the political priority of the war effort. One eminent historian wrote that after 1940 Britain had: 'in the interests of survival . . . the most state-planned and state-managed economy ever introduced outside a frankly socialist country' (Hobsbawm, 1968: 208). A similar high level of intervention marked the production and dissemination of information.

In the middle of this spectrum lie the 'ordinary' military dictatorships which, for example, ruled most of Latin America in the recent past. In Argentina, for instance, the military élite directly intervened, not simply by murdering its opponents, but also by directing many areas of social and economic life, most notably the mass media. Journalists were arrested and murdered, and 'military "intervenors" were put in the command of all civil and social organizations in Argentina: from radio and TV stations, to the Ballet company, the Housewife's organization or the animal rights groups' (Cerutti, 1994: 64).

The concept of totalitarianism

It is in the context of these kinds of measures that the concept of 'totalitarian' societies begins to be useful. This is such a difficult and contentious term when used as anything other than an abusive epithet that, in order to make it quite clear what is at stake here, an extensive discussion is necessary. The term appears to have originated in discussion of the nature of the Mussolini regime in Italy, but it was subsequently extended to Nazi Germany and, particularly after the Second World War, to the Soviet Union and similar societies (Schapiro, 1972). By their use of the term, its proponents mean to signify that totalitarian societies have special features that mark them out from other forms of coercive rule. As one of the leading contemporary theorists of this idea wrote:

> Totalitarianism is a system in which technologically advanced instruments of political power are wielded without restraint by the centralized leadership of an élite movement, for the purposes of effecting a total social revolution, including the conditioning of man, on the basis of certain arbitrary ideological assumptions proclaimed by the leadership, in an atmosphere of coerced unanimity of the entire population. (Brzezinski, 1967: 46–7)

On this definition, there would be room for debate as to whether the Argentinian military dictatorship, which, according to Timmerman, saw itself as waging war on Marx, Freud and Albert Einstein in the name of Christianity, constituted a totalitarian regime or a mere military dictatorship (Cerutti, 1994: 64)

It is important to note that while this term bears with it distinctly negative connotations, and has been used to extremely demagogic ends, it was not solely designed as a term of political abuse. It is not a claim about the particularly brutal nature of some regimes. It is not properly part of the theory of totalitarianism that in such societies the ruling group is more horrible or murderous than that of, say, an 'ordinary' military dictatorship. It should be recalled that it was Italian fascism that provided the occasion for the first discussions of the idea. The proportional butchery of the domestic population carried out by a military dictator like Pinochet in Chile was far greater than that perpetrated by the undoubtedly fascist and arguably totalitarian regime of Mussolini. Some later writers, understandably overwhelmed by the horrors of the *Gulag* and the Holocaust, have tended, mistakenly in my view, to identify totalitarianism with systematic mass murder (Arendt, 1958). The history of humanity demonstrates, regrettably but incontrovertibly, that the systematic slaughter of whole peoples is not a unique characteristic of totalitarian regimes.

The view that a society is 'totalitarian' rests upon claims that have little to do with the degree of violence they exercise against their internal opponents, or their propensity to launch wars of aggression outside their borders. In classic formulations, there were six distinguishing features of totalitarian societies:

> The basic features or traits which we suggest as generally recognized to be common to totalitarian dictatorships are six in number. The 'syndrome' or pattern of interrelated traits of the totalitarian dictatorship consists of an ideology, a single party typically led by one man, a terroristic police, a communications monopoly, a weapons monopoly, and a centrally directed economy. (Friedrich and Brzezinski, 1956: 9)

Friedrich and Brzezinski insisted that it was the co-presence of these factors that constituted a regime as totalitarian. As a general theory, this will not do. Some of the factors were not, in fact, even true of many of the societies that these writers wanted to place in the category. For example there were, formally at least, a number of different political parties in some Eastern European countries throughout the post-war period (Berglund and Dellenbrant, 1994: 14–35; Berglund et al., 1988). Again, a 'weapons monopoly' hardly seems a distinctive features of totalitarian states, and a stress upon this element might simply be an optical illusion produced by residence in the USA. Max Weber's well-known theory of the state argues that this is

precisely what characterises all states, and it is empirically the case that contemporary bourgeois democratic Britain exercises a 'weapons monopoly'
over firearms of a particularly restrictive kind.

For our purposes, two underlying ideas are important. The first of these
has to do with the way in which the different sections of the ruling class, or
different élites, are articulated together. In totalitarian societies, there is a
direct subordination of all of the élite groups to the political élite. Brzezinski,
for example, argued that the purge was a necessary part of totalitarian societies because it achieved precisely this unification, and attributed the internal
decay of communism partly at least to its failure to sustain such a coherent
élite group (Brzezinski, 1956, 1989). In the case of these kinds of regimes, the
fusion of the different élites makes the concept of a ruling class irresistibly
powerful: there simply are not the divergences between different groups that
give other interpretations their persuasive edge. In this, communist societies
appear as sharply differentiated from bourgeois democracies: 'The fundamental difference between a society of the Soviet type and one of the Western
type is that the former has a unified élite and the latter has a divided élite'
(Aron, 1950: 10). It seems to me that only ideology can prevent such a unified
élite being described as a class.

The ruling class is organised in the ruling party, which in principle attempts
to encompass all of the leading positions in society, and which persecutes
those who do not meet its criteria of loyalty. The mass media are the particular objects of the attention of the totalitarian party, which seeks to ensure
that all of them are directly subordinated to its own the political goals. There
is, in principle, direct and close supervision by the political élite over the
daily workings of all of the mass media.

The second important distinguishing feature of totalitarian systems concerns the relationship between the ruling class and the various subordinate
classes. Totalitarian parties tend to have developed programmes for the radical destruction of the existing order and the positive reconstruction of society
in their own mould. This factor is not wholly absent from some other forms
of dictatorship, but it is particularly well developed in totalitarian regimes. As
Brzezinski put it:

> Totalitarianism, being a dictatorship, characteristically includes the coercive qual-
> ities noted in [such] varied dictatorial systems. But unlike most dictatorships, of the
> past and present, the totalitarian movements wielding power do not aim to freeze
> society in the status quo; on the contrary, their aim is to institutionalize a revolu-
> tion that mounts in scope, and frequently in intensity, as the regime stabilizes itself
> in power. The purpose of this revolution is to pulverise all existing social units in
> order to replace the old pluralism with a homogenous unanimity patterned on the
> blueprints of the totalitarian ideology. (Brzezinski, 1967: 42)

To this end, the party strives to control and to organise as much of the life of
the general population as is at all possible. In particular, it is extremely hostile to independent organisations, particularly mass organisations. It seeks to
destroy not only independent political and economic organisations like other
parties and trade unions, but also ones like the Boy Scouts to whom it might

be thought to have little direct political objection. In the eyes of the totalitarian regime, these constitute possible sources of independent thought, values and opposition that need to be removed. In their place, the regimes place their own, closely controlled, mass organisations. In developed totalitarian regimes, these directly politicised mass organisations seek to encompass every area of social life from extreme youth to old age and to direct activities towards the building of the new world. To anticipate a later argument, what totalitarian societies manage to do is to destroy those informal social organisations that are sometimes called 'civil society' and replace them with institutions that are more or less direct manifestations of the party state.

Once again, the media have a particularly important role to play in this form of social organisation. All of the plethora of specialised publications that are used by different organisations of civil society are replaced by politically directed material produced in conformity with the ideological needs of the totalitarian party. According to Friedrich and Brzezinski:

> All in all, the system of propaganda and mass communication developed in the totalitarian systems is of crucial importance for the maintenance of the regime. . . . In a very real sense, it dehumanizes the subjects of the regime by depriving them of a chance for independent thought and judgement. (Friedrich and Brzezinski, 1956: 117)

Thus, in the theory of totalitarianism, the mass media have an important and special role. They are the mechanism through which the primary organisation of the symbolic universe of the ruling group is disseminated and generalised. To the extent that they are successful, they are the central instrument of the totalitarian project.

The value of the concept of totalitarianism for our purposes lies in the degree to which these two central features of the theory provide a way of illuminating the differences between fascist and communist societies on the one hand and bourgeois democracies on the other. These latter are commonly marked by the existence of democratic rights that are absent in totalitarian regimes. Freedom of association and of assembly, and freedom of publication, although to a greater or lesser degree circumscribed in all bourgeois societies, are nevertheless constitutive of the essence of bourgeois democracy. Unless opposition can form opinion, publicise that opinion, and coalesce its supporters into political parties, then it is difficult to see how even a minimal definition of democracy can be sustained (Dahl, 1991: 10). The direct and extremely close supervision of the mass media, and the extent to which the whole range of the mass media is part of a single socio-political project, are two factors that mark totalitarian societies out sharply from bourgeois democracies.

Objections to totalitarianism as a theory

There are several major objections to the usage of the term totalitarian that I have proposed here. The first minor one is that we have ignored the role of the single leader that is characteristic of totalitarianism. This does not seem today to be such an important part of the social form. It may well have some importance from the point of view of a study of the social psychology of such societies, but from our point of view, nothing is lost from the discussion presented here by excluding that category, and nothing is gained by including it. It is, simply, not important one way or the other. At best, it is one of the mechanism by means of which the resolution of social and political conflicts within the ruling group may be achieved.

The second minor objection is that there is nothing in the theory of totalitarianism that suggests its historical frailty. On the contrary, the classical formulations tended to stress the 'hopelessness' of all opposition to such regimes. No doubt influenced by the examples of fascist Italy and Nazi Germany, both of which were destroyed by outside military intervention, the authors most associated with this school of thought believed that communism could only be overthrown from outside: 'One possibility should be excluded, except in the satellites: that is the likelihood of an overthrow of these regimes by revolutionary action from within' (Friedrich and Brzezinski, 1956: 300). Since communism did collapse as the result of internal pressures, history has certainly proved this theory wrong. One may reply, first, that outside pressure in the form of Western miliary competition was indeed a vital ingredient of the collapse (Brzezinski, 1993). Second, and more substantially, we may agree that these theories did tend to marginalise the internal opposition that eventually proved decisive in the overthrow of communism, but that this was part of a more general problem they had with accounting for the economic trajectory of such societies. Their crucial limit is that, while they describe a political form rather well, they have no adequate account of its relation to economic life. 'Totalitarianism', despite the intentions of its original theorists, is only useful in illuminating an aspect of communist societies: it does not explain them. It is only in that limited political sense that we are using the term here.

The first major objection is that the boundaries between actually existing societies are a great deal less clear than the theory presented here. It is obviously the case that the boundaries between some kinds of military rule and totalitarianism are extremely blurred. It is also true that bourgeois democracies, even the most advanced like Weimar Germany, which tolerated death squads and ordered its police to fire on demonstrators, are capable of undertaking very high levels of repression against internal dissent and attempting to exercise considerable control over the symbolic universe of their subjects, as Brecht's famous encounter with the Prussian censor demonstrated. It is further the case that, in actual practice, many regimes that fall under the definition of totalitarianism advocated here are or were a great deal less complete than the theory suggests. Both Mussolini's Italy and Jaruzelski's Poland, for example, were unable to subordinate the church to their direct control, although both were able to come to quite comfortable agreements with its hierarchy. Nevertheless, particularly in Poland, it is clear that the church as an institution was an important source of oppositional values to the communist

regime. More generally, as evidence presented in the next chapter demonstrates, the actual practice of communist societies in their last years often
differed very widely indeed from the prescriptions of theories of totalitarianism. Particularly with regard to the mass media, the societies of Central and
Eastern Europe were a great deal less monolithic than the theory I have outlined here suggests they should have been.

In answer to that objection, I can only make a methodological defence.
This takes the form of a brief restatement of more general propositions about
the nature of social theory, which, as I argued more extensively in the Preface,
underlies the other central arguments in this book every bit as much as it does
this discussion of totalitarianism. Social theory is an abstraction from social
reality. It is not here, never can be, nor should be expected to be, a complete
mapping of actual social life. Its function is to illuminate the structure and
dynamics of social life. One of the tests of its validity is the extent to which it
helps us to understand the world. (The other is its internal logic, consistency
and completeness.) Boundaries in actual social life are inevitably messy and
blurred. Actual social formations always display a greater richness and com-
plexity than the theoretical abstractions we use to understand them. We are
forced to use those abstractions because we cannot hope to understand reality simply by observing its surface features. We need social theory, but we
should not expect it to provide complete, total and final answers to the problems we examine.

From this point of view, we may therefore readily accept that the boundaries between bourgeois democracy, military rule and totalitarianism are less
clear in reality than they are in theory. The idea of totalitarianism, however,
helps us to understand what is special and distinct about societies like Nazi
Germany and Soviet Russia. It is therefore a useful concept in social theory.
We can usefully see the different kinds of political organisation as arranged
on a scale (see Table 2.1), with those in which the ruling group is least fused,
bourgeois democracies, standing at the far end from those in which the ruling
class is most fused, communist countries, at the other end.

Table 2.1   *The degree of fusion of ruling groups in different societies*

Least fusion				Greatest fusion
Bourgeois democracy	'Besieged' democracy	Military dictatorship	Fascism	Communism
		$\to \to \to \to \to \to \to \to$ More totalitarian		

The second major objection is that I have here capitulated to one of the
crudest ideological ploys of the Cold War, and accepted what was essentially
an instrument designed to demonise the USSR and to argue for its identity
with the thoroughly discredited Nazi regime. In answer to this charge, one
must begin with the admission that it is certainly true that the idea of totalitarianism was used to fight the Cold War. One of its leading contemporary

proponents is the right-wing US academic-cum-politician Zbigniew Brzezinski, whose views are quoted extensively above. The worst example of this trend is another right-wing US academic-cum-politician, Jean Kirkpatrick. She credits herself with providing the intellectual ammunition for the second Cold War, and certainly waged it with some vigour as Reagan's ambassador to the United Nations. She made a crucial distinction between 'traditional' and 'revolutionary' autocracies (Kirkpatrick, 1982: 49): the latter were much worse, so it was entirely legitimate to provide military aid to the former while waging covert war on the latter. It might be argued that this abuse of the idea has rendered it useless, or worse, from the point of view of serious enquiry. There are three reasons why this is not the case.

The first is that good and true ideas are sometimes used to justify foul activities. The ideas of Karl Marx, for example, have been used to justify a range of horrible crimes. The Social Democrats who were responsible for the murder of Luxemburg and thousands of other German militants called themselves Marxists. Stalin and Pol Pot called themselves Marxists. It does not follow that because the ideas have been used in such ways they are no longer of any value whatsoever. There is, fortunately, no guilt by association in the world of ideas. It is certainly true that ideas that been used in such a way have to be examined very closely to see whether they have some intrinsic relationship with the deeds they have been used to justify, but that requires rather more precise intellectual work than simply pointing to the record of the people who have used them to describe themselves. After all, on such a logic, Christians would be in real trouble. In the case of 'totalitarianism', as we have seen above, there were undoubtedly strongly ideological elements in its stress upon the role of the single leader, upon the hopelessness of internal resistance and the lack of a serious economic dynamic, that rendered it of dubious value. The denial of the possibility of successful internal resistance, for example, served directly to justify preparations for military aggression in order to achieve 'roll back'. In criticising these elements of the classical theory, we are certainly using the term in a different and much weaker sense than did its classical, cold warrior, advocates.

Second, it is not true that the idea of totalitarianism is a product of the Cold War, nor that it has always been used by the right. As has been stated, the origins of the term lie in discussions of fascist Italy, and it was only later that it came to be used to discuss communist regimes as well. The idea that there was in some sense an identity between Stalinism and fascism, if not always the exact term 'totalitarianism', has been widely used by leftist critics of Stalinism. Trotsky, for example, argued on more than one occasion that, in terms of their political methods, the major difference between the Hitler and Stalin regimes was that the latter was worse. Trotsky, of course, was murdered before witnessing the Holocaust. It can be argued that might have led him to revise his judgement. As it was, he could only compare the undoubted brutalities and murders the Nazis had inflicted upon their political opponents and the Jews with the wholesale extermination of elements of the rural population, the construction of a vast system of labour camps, and the systematic torture and murder of the Left Opposition. In that light, his judgement looks relatively accurate. Stalin did seem worse.

The final response to this kind of criticism is that it is correct. Stalinism and fascism were not identical phenomena. Trotsky was quick to qualify his own statements about the identity of political methods between the two political systems with a stress upon their different forms of economic organisation. One does not need to accept Trotsky's own analysis of the nature of the Soviet economy in order to see the real differences. Although the state machine in Nazi Germany intervened very heavily in the capitalist economy, it did not attempt to abolish private capitalism. The Nazi state was prepared to breach the laws of property insofar as they interfered with military preparations and war, provided support for political opposition, impeded the achievement of their anti-Semitic ideological programme and obstructed efforts at personal enrichment. It did not, however, even faced with defeat in total war, make any attempt to expropriate the private capitalists wholesale. Even in the press, the methods used by the Nazis to gain ownership of the newspapers held by 'Aryan' private capitalists were in the main business dealings rather than simple political seizure (Hale, 1973).

Stalinism, of course, was radically different. Even before the apparatus of totalitarian control was established, private property in the means of production played a subordinate role in the economic life of the Soviet Union. The establishment and consolidation of the totalitarian state coincided precisely with the radical marginalisation of private productive property in both the city and the country. Totalitarianism in the Soviet Union was built upon the graves of the last remnants of private capitalism.

This difference, however, does not negate the concept of 'totalitarianism' as a description of political forms. On the contrary, it simply highlights the extent to which Stalinism represented the purest form of this phenomenon. The fact that fascist totalitarianism tolerated and coexisted with private economic power represented an important limitation upon its programme of total control. Economic power, in any developed economy, is one of the most pervasive and influential forms of social power. To the extent that they coexisted with other sources of power, the fascist regimes fell a good way short of the totalitarian ideal. It is this element that constitutes a small particle of truth to the infamous distinction between totalitarian and authoritarian regimes that has been used to justify various examples of Cold War aggression (Garfinkle and Pipes, 1991; Kirkpatrick, 1982, 1990). While there is no ground for considering the latter morally or politically superior, they are forms of social organisation in which there are, at least potentially, other sources of social power than the party-state.

The third major objection to this position is that the theory of totalitarianism does not describe the reality of communist societies. As a matter of demonstrable fact, Poland in the 1980s did not resemble a society in which whole classes were exterminated, in which the entire population was mobilised to achieve political goals, where the only permitted forms of social organisation were tightly controlled by the party-state, and in which the individual whims of the ruler overrode the established norms of political life.

This criticism is true, and as will be demonstrated in a later chapter, the mass media of Central and Eastern Europe in the 1980s often departed rather far from the role prescribed for them by the totalitarian model. In reply, it is necessary to make a distinction between two historical forms of totalitarianism. In its classic form, in Stalin's Russia for example, there was indeed one leader, one party, one goal. There was indeed systematic mass mobilisation. There certainly were chronic, unpredictable and bloody purges that reached far even into the political élite.

These factors were not present in Central and Eastern Europe in the last years of communism. Traces of them, often very substantial, remained and operated with varying intensity in different countries. What was identical between the classic form and the late form was that there was more or less systematic integration of economics and politics and a formally integrated ruling class. This constitutes, we might say, the rational kernel of totalitarianism.

It might perhaps be wise to try to find some new term that carries with it less dangerous baggage, but short of that there is a good case for retaining at least this weaker version of the notion of totalitarianism. We should also accept that, in theory, it applies more fully to the Stalinist type of regime than to the original fascist models. In particular, because of the genuinely integrated aspect of the ruling class, transitions away from dictatorial regimes based on the communist model pose different problems than they do in the case of other forms of totalitarian societies, like classical fascism, in which there is a distinction between the holders of political and economic power. The nature of the ruling group in communist societies, the extent of its internal cohesion and the degree of its control over the rest of society are thus key points in our analysis.

The *nomenklatura*

The integrated and organised ruling group in communist societies took the form of a bureaucracy, which is generally termed the *nomenklatura*. It is important to distinguish this from the party as a whole, since under the organisation of the communist parties, which they called 'democratic centralism', power over the membership as a whole resided with a hierarchy of committees at the apex of which was the Central Committee. The party itself was everywhere a relatively small and élite group, entry to which was quite difficult. But party membership was not the same thing as membership of the ruling group in a communist society. In order to run something important, to actually become a member of the *nomenklatura*, it was necessary both to be a party member in good standing and to be nominated by the appropriate party committee.

A study of the phenomenon by a Russian dissident quoted a Communist Party source defining the term thus:

The nomenklatura is a list of the highest positions; the candidates for these positions are examined by the various party committees, recommended and confirmed. These nomenklatura party committee members can be relieved of their positions only by authorization of their committees. Persons elevated to the nomenklatura are those in key positions. (cited in Voslensky, 1984: 2)

As this quotation makes clear, the *nomenklatura* was in practice both a list of the leading posts in society and a list of the people held fit to discharge such duties. It was out of this list of persons, approved by the party apparatus and responsible only to that apparatus, that the senior managers of industry, the rectors of universities, the directors of collective farms, the ambassadors to the USA and to every other country however small, the editors of newspapers and the directors of television stations, were appointed.

The power to appoint key individuals to key posts extended throughout the whole of society. The most prominent national and international posts in both the party and the state were nominated by the Central Committee. Less exalted posts, right down to the locality, were appointed by the corresponding lower party committees. For every position of any influence whatsoever, there was a formalised hierarchy of appointments that specified in great detail exactly who was entitled to make the appointment. Since this applied to party positions as much as state posts, its effect was to concentrate power not simply in the hands of the *nomenklatura*, but of the élite group within it. In these very peculiar workers' democracies, final control over every aspect of social life was concentrated in the hands of a tiny élite at the top of a vast pyramid of power in which the lines of power ran from apex to base and the lines of accountability ran from the base to the apex.

The formal arrangements in the case of Poland gave the Central Committee of the Polish United Workers' Party (the Communist Party) responsibility for the appointment of the 'chief and deputy editors of Trybuna Ludu' and three other papers produced by the Central Committee, the 'chairman, deputies and director-general of the Radio and Television Board', the 'chief editors of national circulation dailies, weeklies and monthlies', the 'directors-general of Polish Radio and Television', the 'president and secretary-general of the Society of Polish Journalists', and a host of other appointments relating to culture and the media nationally. The regional committees had responsibility for appointing the editors of regional party publications, the 'chief and deputy directors of Polish Radio broadcasting stations and of Polish Television centres' and the 'chief and deputy editors of the main local dailies and cultural and social magazines', not to mention the 'rectors and vice-rectors of higher education establishments' (Walker, 1993: 257–62). I have cited here mostly positions that granted control of the mass media, but it is important to realise that this system of appointment extended to every area of social life: youth clubs, hospitals, railways, factories, trade unions, the Polish–Soviet Friendship Association – all were subject to a similar regime.

It is also important to note that, alongside its pervasive and hierarchical nature, the *nomenklatura* was organised with no distinction between party functions and those of the rest of society. One might quite accept that the

Central Committee has a perfect right to appoint the editor of a magazine that it owned and which it set up with the express purpose of propagating its views in some field. That, after all, is exactly the right that the most rigorous forms of bourgeois legality grant without question to other media owners like Rupert Murdoch. One might also accept that, in practice, even bourgeois democracies have a *nomenklatura* of their own that gets appointed to posts in the state gift, like governors of public broadcasting institutions. In Britain, this group even has a name: it is known as 'the great and the good'. In communist societies, however, the right to make appointments to even nominally independent publications lay with the leadership of an élite minority party. Party, state and social organisation were intentionally fused under the control of the Central Committee.

In addition to these posts of responsibility, the party also maintained a network of branches in all major organisations, including the mass media. The secretaries of these party cells were, of course, themselves appointed from above. In the Polish case, it was the responsibility of the district party committees to appoint the '(full-time) secretaries of Party base committees and organisations in enterprises coming under the district *nomenklatura*' (Walker, 1993: 263). Since to be a member in good standing of the Communist Party was a more important qualification for high office in a communist country than a private education is in Britain, the local enterprise committees were a vital part of the promotion ladder by means of which individuals could seek advancement. For the ambitious, the route out of the working class lay through enthusiastic support for the 'party of the working class'.

In addition to these social structures, the party leadership also controlled a massive network of police terror, professional internal spies, amateur informers and, of course, various mechanisms of formal censorship. However, as one observer argues, these external constraints were far from being the main mechanisms used to control the media. According to Downing, the ability to control membership of élite groups and of the means of access to them, together with the positive appeal of aspects of the regime's official ideology, most notably nationalism but also its claims to be pursuing social justice, meant that direct censorship was not the main mechanism of control even in the USSR. On the contrary, 'the chief way in which control was exerted was for journalists to censor themselves' (Downing, 1995: 194). Just as in any hierarchical society in which the élite guards access to very considerable rewards, the pressure on the ambitious is to conform to values of the hierarchy, whatever their private beliefs (Karch, 1983: 119). It is one of the clearest marks of the difference between the communist societies of the recent past, which I have termed late totalitarian, and those of the period of classic totalitarianism, that it was these dull routines of accepted practice, rather than the spectacular purges complete with show trials and executions, that constituted the main mechanisms whereby control of the mass media was maintained.

This kind of process is not a unique characteristic of totalitarian societies. It also flourishes in other hierarchical societies, including bourgeois democracies. A 1995 survey of British news journalists found that 6 per cent of them intended to vote for the governing Conservative Party at the next election (Delano and Hennigham, 1995: 13). Thirty per cent of these journalists were employed by the then 11 national daily newspapers, eight of which supported that party at the last election. Clearly, journalists in the UK keep their political views to themselves, and write what they know will please their bosses. In a society in which there was only one boss, the pressure to conform was commensurately greater. The shift that the journalists of Central and Eastern Europe were to experience was not one from total terror to total freedom, but from one master to many.

It is a matter of some dispute as to exactly what kind of social phenomenon the *nomenklatura* constituted. According to the official ideology of the system, they were the representatives of the working class, exercising power on behalf of the toiling masses (see for example, Pospelov, 1971). According to many critics, they were a bureaucratic caste that had usurped the role of the working class and who ruled in the interests of their own material gratification (see for example, Westoby, 1981: 343–4). According to other commentators, they constituted a ruling class every bit as much as do the dominant groups in other kinds of societies (see for example, Cliff, 1974).

As I shall show below, these different views of the *nomenklatura* had important consequences for one's understanding of the end of communism and the prospects for the media in the outcome. Irrespective of these differences, however, it is generally agreed that the *nomenklatura* had certain special features that set them apart from other twentieth-century ruling groups. The ruling classes of communist societies were not divided into a political élite, entrepreneurs, civil and military bureaucracy, and so on. In private capitalist societies, even highly repressive ones, there are structural differences between different capitalists: they genuinely compete with one another both economically and politically, and they may enter into struggles against the state itself. The *nomenklatura* formed a single, bureaucratic, ruling group. The condition for the continued rule of each member of the *nomenklatura* was the continued rule of the bureaucracy as a whole. They exercised power collectively and they exercised power over the whole of society uniformly, including the mass media.

Conclusion

The concept of totalitarianism is thus both a valid and a useful one to describe distinctive features of the structures of power in communist societies. It most certainly has its limitations, particularly with regard to the economic dynamics of societies with this kind of political formation. In spite of this, it is particularly valuable from the point of view of understanding the structural relations of the mass media to other centres of power, which forms the central point of our investigation.

The utility of the concept is evident if we contrast the ideal type of communist totalitarian rule with the ideal type of bourgeois democratic rule. These differences are schematically represented in Table 2.2. In this much simplified representation, I have ignored those grey areas between the two, like classical fascism, military dictatorships and 'besieged' bourgeois democracies. It is also of course the case that we could probably never find actual societies that operated in such a neatly delimited fashion. Nevertheless, the significance for the study of the media clearly emerges.

Table 2.2   *Power, media and audience in communist totalitarian and bourgeois democratic societies*

	Communist totalitarian	Bourgeois democracy
Political and economic élites	Fused into one	Separate and independent
Mass media	Politically subordinated	Economically subordinated
Social position of audience	Politically and economically subordinated	Politically free, economically subordinated
Social organisations	Politically controlled	Politically independent

At the level of the media themselves, the form of control of the mass media in totalitarian societies is direct political intervention. To the extent that economic factors play a role in these systems, it is a marginal and subordinate one. In bourgeois democracies, on the other hand, the primary form of control of the mass media is through economic power, and it is political intervention that forms the marginal and the exceptional circumstance.

The audience, too, is in a different position with regard to the mass media and to other forms of social power. In bourgeois democracies, the majority of the citizens who make up the mass audiences of the media are formally free and able to exercise, admittedly only very occasionally, a vote that helps to determine the composition of the government. Their subordination in society is primarily economic in form. In totalitarian societies, on the other hand, the main form of subordination is both political and economic: the political freedoms existing in the constitutions of those countries are recognised by the vast majority to be entirely illusory. The media thus confront their audience as part of a unified and oppressive power structure from which the population is comprehensively excluded.

Neither does the audience have access to independent forms of social organisation that might allow it to develop alternative critical responses to the media themselves. What the populist tradition in cultural studies likes to call 'popular productivity' surely depends upon the existence of alternative value systems embodied in forms of social organisation not wholly subordinated to the ruling class. These conditions for independent and alternative readings of media artefacts are commonplace in bourgeois democracies: they are often elevated to the status of 'civil society'. They were, at least in principle, absent in communist societies.

The overall consequence of these differences is that we need to think very carefully about the fundamentals of media theory. As John Downing has pointed out, these have been most fully developed in bourgeois democracies. One might go rather further and say that the bulk of media theory has been developed in the USA. This is not only the model bourgeois democracy, but also very large, very rich and very stable. The result is that the underlying ground rules, the unconscious definition of normality, have been derived from that historical experience. Particular kinds of relationships between the mass media and social power have been assumed as natural and self-evident, and the communist system has appeared as a wholly different and aberrant case. This was entirely understandable and unavoidable, and affected critical theory as much as it did conservative writings. It arose from the nature of the reality with which the analysts were confronted. For example, critical writers have devoted very considerable effort to trying to explore how far, and to what extent, the mass media were dependent upon the views of the holders of political and economic power. This was legitimate and important. It was, however, not a problem that appeared in the same light in communist societies. To the question 'Do the mass media reflect the views of the government?' the logical and obvious answer was: 'Yes, and they are intended so to do.' A much more interesting research question in a communist society would be: 'Under what circumstances is this proposition not true?'

Another strand of critical thinking, represented most famously by Adorno and Horkheimer in their essay on 'The culture industry: Enlightenment as mass deception', expended considerable intellectual effort in a vain attempt to demonstrate how, despite the apparent differences, the mass media in Nazi Germany and the USA displayed the same repressive features. Their argument slides from examples of Göbbels to examples from *Life*, without pausing to consider the gap between the different societies. They move from Germany to the USA without differentiation:

> In bringing cultural products wholly into the sphere of commodities, radio does not try to dispose of its culture goods themselves as commodities straight to the consumer. In America it collects no fees from the public, and so has acquired the illusory form of disinterested, unbiased authority which suits Fascism admirably. The radio becomes the universal mouthpiece of the Führer. (Horkheimer and Adorno, 1973: 159)

This, and passages displaying an identical lack of discrimination, were written and published before the defeat of the Nazis, by authors who were the direct victims of Nazi persecution and the direct beneficiaries of US bourgeois democracy. A similar, if less obviously grotesque, elision of these differences can be traced in Althusser's very different but equally famous discussion of the ideological state apparatuses. Questions of political morality and judgement aside, the failure to make an elementary distinction between these two kinds of societies, and the structure and function of the mass media in each of them, seriously incapacitates the critical project. Not only does its magnificent disregard of evidence open it to serious criticism from the uncritical, but it fails to illuminate either of the systems it purports to describe.

The mass media in totalitarian societies operated under different rules than those in bourgeois democracies. That is not to say that the popular image of the constantly ringing telephone on the desk of the news editor was necessarily a correct picture of the mundane reality of subordination. The issue is rather that the real relations of power, formal and informal, between the media and the élite were different. Their articulation with the powerful was different and their social functions were different. It is to those functions, and to various attempts to theorise them, that we must now turn.

3

Media Theory and the Decline of the Communist System

In this chapter, I look first at some of the distinctive features of the mass media in communist societies. The characteristics of totalitarian societies that were analysed in Chapter 2 are here used to explain important aspects both of the functioning of the communist media and the distinctive ways in which they decayed. Second, I explore three major theoretical accounts of the nature and function of the communist media, one internal to the systems themselves and two originating in the West. These theoretical accounts yield different predictions as to the possibilities for changes to the media systems. The final decade of the communist media is then explored. The validity of the different theories of the communist media are considered with reference to this empirical evidence.

Media as indicators of social change

In order to undertake this investigation, we need first to explore a number of features of the communist media that made them uncertain indicators as to the nature and progress of change in communist societies. In most versions of the history of Western societies, evidence derived from the mass media is one of the key elements in any account of social change. While specialist studies of the mass media have cast doubt on the value of such evidence, historians continue to cite newspaper reports as one of their primary sources. It is also true that much media theory has been concerned with the relationship between the media and social change. In one current of investigation, there is concern with the ways in which the mass media cause changes to their audience's knowledge, attitudes and behaviour. In another tradition, the stress is upon the ways in which the mass media serve to preserve existing social relations. Despite the wide differences of methodology and perspective, the formative assumption of both is that the mass media have a special and privileged place with regard to social changes.

We cannot automatically assume that the same will be the case in communist countries. It is an assumption that requires substantiation that the media will either be centrally involved in, or even reflect very accurately, more general social changes, let alone play any initiating role. There are factors in the constitution of the media in bourgeois democracies that might be argued to lead it to play such a role, but these do not necessarily apply to the communist

countries. On the contrary, there were powerful factors that made it unlikely
that the mass media would be direct indicators of change, much less in its van-
guard.

As we saw in the last chapter, there is a considerable difference in the degree
to which the ruling groups in communist societies are fused into one bloc,
compared even with other versions of totalitarian political systems. This difference has two important consequences for our analysis of the mass media in
communist societies. In bourgeois democracies, of course, a degree of distance
between the owners of commercial newspapers and the leaders of political
parties is commonplace, although of recent date. The very dis-articulation of
the ruling groups means that their differences are often reflected and debated,
and perhaps even exaggerated, in the mass media. The existence of different
political currents, with their own organisations, means that any representation
of political debate necessarily involves public dissent. While these debates
may be presented in accordance with the views of this or that press owner, it
is only in the cases where that owner is also a political party that there is a
direct and unmediated link between the media and political power. Since, generally, there tend to be divisions between different political and economic
groups, the normal situation of the media in a bourgeois democracy is that it
contains differing views about at least those issues that divide powerful
groups.

In totalitarian societies, there is much less space for this. The fusion of the
ruling group means that there is much less likelihood of its internal debates
becoming public. Communist societies represent an extreme form of this,
since the fusion of the ruling group is much greater than in other cases. Even
in totalitarian regimes resting on private capitalism, it is possible for the mass
media to be owned and controlled by people not directly answerable to the
regime. Thus, in Nazi Germany, Alfred Hugenberg continued to own the
Scherl Verlag, and thus important newspapers, right up until he was bought
out by the Nazis, for cash and shares worth RM64,106,500, in September
1944 (Hale, 1973: 308–12). Admittedly, Hugenberg was a right-wing nationalist politician, and his media outlets had given the Nazi Party aid and
comfort on the road to power, but he was not a Nazi. When he was finally
separated from his newspaper empire, he was still an independent economic
figure. Very far from being expropriated, he was able to bargain hard over the
amount and kind of compensation he would get for his press interests. Even
in the depths of total war, and confronted by the certainty of defeat, Nazi
totalitarianism was very far from having achieved the kind of fusion between
different kinds of social power that was routine in communist societies.

In communist societies, on the other hand, there was no obvious independent source of social and political power, and the extent to which the media
could act independently of the regime was thus structurally limited. That is
not to say that the mass media were always and necessarily univocal in their
interpretation of the world. Different media could and did, in periods of
internal conflict amongst the *nomenklatura*, reflect the views of different currents in the struggle, but they were incapable of doing more than acting in a

supporting role. A great deal of 'Kremlinology' in the Cold War was devoted precisely to teasing out exactly what minor differences in media treatment of events and politicians might tell us about the internal strains of the *nomenklatura*. The terrain of the media, which in many capitalist countries provides an opening for all sorts of critical voices, albeit usually not very radical ones, was particularly unreceptive to such figures in communism.

This structural incorporation at the level of ownership was reinforced by the fact that the media did not operate with a commercial dynamic. On the contrary, the prime determinant of the media was the political interest of the *nomenklatura*. This was not entirely a unique feature of communism: political media, particularly newspapers, have a long tradition in private capitalism. There is no automatic identity between private capitalist societies and commercial media. One prominent historian of the British press argues that the primarily political form of the newspaper only finally collapsed after 1945 (Koss, 1990: 1095–7). Most commentators would place the shift to a commercial model rather earlier than this, but it is certain that the form is no longer dominant, at least in Britain and the USA. The fact that newspapers are run as commercial enterprises means that they have, up to a point at least, to take some account of the expectations of their readers and their advertisers, and are thus forced to operate, if not against the wishes of, at least in tension with, the views of their owners. It may make good commercial sense for the owners of particular newspapers to give editorial space to opinions radically different from their own. The presentation of dissenting opinion can, for example, help a newspaper to attract and retain a particular kind of reader who may be valuable either in terms of their direct purchase of the paper or as a target for advertisers.

As we shall see, in common with most features of communist societies, the mass media were run according to the logic of a central command economy, embodied in The Plan. This meant that there was in principle little to be gained by commercial success. Cover prices were set by political criteria rather than economic calculation, and advertising was limited or non-existent. The basic costs of the newspaper were agreed in advance and any predicted shortfall was covered by some form of subsidy from the state. There were thus no countervailing pressures to the demands of the party leadership for political subservience. To publish dissenting voices brought no apparent economic benefit and certainly incurred considerable political risks.

The mass media were thus directly incorporated into the ruling group in a manner not common in a capitalist democracy. This has an immediate consequence for our study. Because of this dependence, the mass media were unlikely to be the most important arena in which social developments were debated and thus in which social crisis was evident. Neither, since they answered directly to the *nomenklatura* rather than their readers or advertisers, were they particularly concerned with sensitivity to the popular mood: to the extent that they attempted to achieve certain kinds of effects, these were decided from above and their characteristic rhetoric was that of the *nomenklatura*. We might therefore expect to find traces of the decay of the system in the media, but they are not likely to be anywhere near as evident as in agriculture or the trade balance.

Totalitarian media practice

At the most general level the mass media held a central and relatively unproblematic place in the totalitarian system. Just as commentators supportive of, and hostile to, communism shared a great deal in their accounts of the nature of those societies, so there is general agreement about some of the distinctive features of the mass media. Once again, the nature and importance of these is best illustrated by a contrast with the situation existing in bourgeois democracies. As we shall see, although these differences are not quite as fundamental as is sometimes alleged, they were nevertheless sufficiently deep and general as to make the different media distinct social forms.

The mature Soviet system that emerged after 1929 insisted that all newspapers had to function as organisers of the masses and that all writers had to follow the party line as determined by the General Secretary. By extension, the same principles were applied to film and radio, and later to television. In theory, the whole of the symbolic life of the state came to be subordinated to the directives of the leading committee of the sole legal party. In later extensions of the system to the 'people's democracies' of Central and Eastern Europe, there was sometimes more than one legal party, often with its own press, but in reality the main features of the symbolic universe were still determined by the Central Committee of the Communist Party.

The mass media were supposed to have a militant, organising function quite different from that of the media in the West. These differences were allegedly systemic, although they were often rather overstated by commentators from both camps. Nevertheless, they were present at the level of the political direction, of the intended function, of the character of the material presented, of their relationship to their audiences and of the economic basis for media activity. The differences were part of the official view of the media even in the later days of relatively liberal communist countries (Szecskö and Fodor, 1974: 30).

The media in communist regimes were politically supervised and their output co-ordinated to an extent not usual in Western capitalism. All politicians are concerned as to whether the media report their speeches and activities, and communist politicians were no exceptions. However, perhaps to the envy of their ostensible enemies, leading politicians in communist countries could expect to be reported completely, and to have their priorities determine the news agenda of the day. If they were disappointed, they could and did intervene directly to rectify the mistake. It would, of course, be extremely naïve to imagine that there is not political intervention in the mass media of the more democratic capitalist states, even in conditions of relative peace and stability. In wars, in national emergencies and in other extreme situations, this kind of intervention is clear and open. A recent, relatively small-scale, example, was the British government's ban on the broadcasting of the voices of members of Sinn Fein, a legal Irish political party, which at one point during the ban counted a member of the British House of Commons amongst its representatives. Political intervention in the running of the mass media in communist societies was of a quite different order. It was a regular, systemic and acknowledged dependence of the media upon the political authorities. The major difference between the communist system and that prevailing in countries such as the UK was thus that the principle of political intervention and co-ordination was accepted and proclaimed as a normal and central part of the day-to-day running of the mass media rather than as an exception to a more general rule of independence that would often be hotly contested and was usually justified by appeals to exceptional circumstances.

In theory, the communist media were supposed to present news and opinion in such a way as to organise and mobilise the masses. Their task was to deliver enthusiastic support for the construction of socialism and the defence of the motherland. Again, this was not a uniquely distinguishing feature of the communist press. Quite apart from the more general question as to whether any interpretation of the world necessarily carries within it some latent injunction to social action, the popular press in capitalist countries also intermittently attempts such manifest and direct mobilisations. The British newspaper the *Sun* has made a number of attempts to carry out precisely such narrowly political mobilisations, most famously against the then EC President Jacques Delors. Again, the difference is not that such things happen in the capitalist press, but that they are incidental, rather than central, to its functioning. The communist press, in theory at least, had as its main structural purpose this organising and mobilising function.

In addition, the nature of the material the media carried was supposed to be quite different. Journalism did not make the same claims to objectivity and fairness which, it is said, characterise the Western media, and in particular those of the USA. On the contrary, the function of journalists was to explain and to educate and to help by their writing to win support for the construction of the new socialist world. Once again, we may note that the actual practice of the Western media departs very often from this idea of objectivity and fairness. It is evident, for example, that British press coverage of general elections is heavily and consciously politically biased. The point, however, is that this coverage is presented as being an abnormal activity appropriate to those occasions when citizens choose their rulers. Normally, it is argued, a different set of rules apply in which the duty of the journalist is to record events rather than select and interpret them. Conscious bias, by which is meant the knowing selection and construction of material in order to demonstrate a particular view of the world, was, on the contrary, the organising principle of the communist press.

The balance of the content in both the press and broadcasting was not determined by considerations of audience maximisation. In the case of the Western media, getting and retaining the right audience, defined either in terms of sheer numbers or demographic composition, is a central part of their activity. Although much of the communist media did indeed have very large audiences, and some publications reached the key decision makers in society with a precision and completion that the *Financial Times* could only envy, the output of television, radio or the press was not designed to ensure that audience's loyalty to a particular medium.

For one thing, there was no real competition between the mass media. In theory, at least, the mass media were as subject to central direction, usually called 'planning', as any other aspect of society. As with the rest of the economy, the volume and nature of the mass media as business enterprises was determined according to the dictates of The Plan. The supply of newsprint, which determined the maximum possible circulation of the press, was settled by prior negotiation with each print enterprise. The number of television receivers produced, and thus the possible audience for the limited number of television channels, was likewise a matter of prior planning.

It goes without saying that the mass media that were supposed to fulfil these ends were financed by political subsidy rather than the advertising subsidy common in capitalist countries. Even when, as with the printed press, there was a direct price for the consumer to pay, this was reduced as the result of heavy subsidies to production. Individual and party subsidy of the press is not unknown today, even in the developed capitalist world, but it is clearly a passing form: even *L'Unità* is attempting to float itself as an independent commercial entity. In the press, state subsidies are more widespread than is usually credited, particularly in Western Europe, but it is really only in Scandinavia that the concern to maintain a diversity of press opinion has led to specific and differential schemes. In broadcasting, of course, state subsidy, either direct or mediated through a licence fee, is much more common and up until the recent past was actually the norm in Western Europe. Even these subsidies, however, exist within an environment where cultural activities are primarily commercial, or at least have a commercial element. In the case of the communist media, this was emphatically not the case. For example, the sale of rights to cover major sporting events in the Warsaw Pact was negotiated by the media's own broadcasting organisation, which set prices far below those dictated today by the market. One of the reasons for the very high levels of newspaper readership in some of these societies, and the frequency of multiple purchases, was that the price of each copy was kept very low by political rather than advertising subsidy.

Perhaps most importantly, the basic aim of the media was didactic enlightenment rather than diversion. The triad of 'information, education and entertainment' has always sat a little uneasily even on those organisation, like the BBC, that are constitutionally enjoined to pursue such goals. In the more directly commercial media, and in particular the printed press, it is more than arguable that diversion, consisting mostly of entertainment material pure and simple but also of some information and education presented in as entertaining a manner as possible, has long been the real aim of editorial policy. In theory, if not in practice, in the communist media, the objective of media production was to improve the morale and the consciousness of the population and to make them more able to carry out the tasks of socialist construction. To the extent that involved entertainment, it was as a means to the end of greater enlightenment, not as a distraction from the sober business of life.

It was the combination of all of the above factors, their systemic character, and their self-conscious acknowledgement, rather than the unique presence of this or that element, that constituted the differential specificity of the communist media. While we can find traces of this or that aspect in various of the media in Western capitalist countries, there they tend to constitute the exceptions. Particularly in the case of the press, the commercial model is more or less completely dominant. In broadcasting, it is more contested, but the general direction of policy in most countries is clearly towards a commercial model. The communist media were different: they did not fit the standard categories that we use to understand the media in the West, and their analysis requires a distinctive theoretical framework, to which we must now turn.

Theories of communist media

The most influential of Western theories of the mass media in communist countries accepted the self-descriptions offered by the communist parties more or less at face value. Of course, the value signs were reversed. What the communist system praised as the loyalty and political acuteness of its noble proletarian media workers, the Western commentators regarded as the servility and craven self-censorship of downtrodden party hacks. What the communist system praised as brilliantly dialectical analysis, the Western commentators dismissed as distorted propaganda. Both, however, agreed that the media in communist regimes were fundamentally different to those in capitalist democracies. Where there was much more disagreement was in the theoretical accounts they gave of why the mass media had such characteristics.

The ruling groups in communist societies claimed that the distinctive characteristics of their media could be traced to what they termed the 'Leninist theory of the press'. This theory was normative, in that it prescribed what the press, and by extension the mass media as a whole, should be like, how they should function and what their political role should be.

Lenin wrote many texts about the mass media, and in particular about the press, in response to the widely different conditions in which he found himself politically active. The most elaborate and consistent examples of his thinking on this subject come from the period in the first few years of this century when he was part of a small, illegal and persecuted party riddled with factional disputes. Of these, one minor and two major texts deeply influenced communist thinking about the mass media. In many ways, the relatively minor text *Where to Begin?* was the seminal work with regard to the press. In that work, as part of an argument for patient and protracted political work, Lenin first advanced the view that:

> The role of a newspaper . . . is not limited solely to the dissemination of ideas, to political education, and to the enlistment of political allies. A newspaper is not

only a collective propagandist and a collective agitator, it is also a collective organiser. In this last respect it may be likened to the scaffolding round a building under construction, which marks the contours of the structure and facilitates communication between the builders, enabling them to distribute the work and to view the common results achieved by their organised labour. With the aid of the newspaper, and through it, a permanent organisation will naturally take shape. . . . (Lenin, 1961, V: 22)

This is clearly a theory of the social function of the press in particular circumstances, which Lenin elaborated in the first major text, *What is to be Done?* He stressed the isolation of the small groups of revolutionaries throughout the vast Russian Empire, their lack of contact with each other, and their complete political inexperience. In this account, while the content of the paper is important, it is only one part of its major function, in which the collective production and distribution of the journal is at least as important:

> The mere function of distributing a newspaper would help to establish *actual* contacts (if it is a newspaper worthy of the name, i.e. it is issued regularly, not once a month like a magazine, but at least four times a month). At the present time, communication between towns on revolutionary business is the exception rather than the rule. If we had a newspaper, however, such communication would become the rule and would secure, not only the distribution of the newspaper, of course, but (what is more important) an exchange of experience , of material, of forces, and of resources. (Lenin, 1961, V: 507)

This idea of the organising and partisan nature of the working-class press was neither original nor unique to Lenin. On the contrary, like much of the argument underlying *What is to be Done?*, including the famous line about political consciousness coming to the working class from outside, it was derived from a study of what was then the dominant model of a revolutionary party, the German Social Democratic Party (SPD). This had a very large press apparatus whose prime task was to articulate and organise the discontents of the proletarian masses. According to its main historian, it had 60 daily local papers in 1890, and around 100 newspapers and periodicals by 1910 (Hall, 1977: 30–1). Karl Liebknecht, editor of the central party paper *Vorwärts*, demonstrated the way in which the SPD press was an integral part of the party apparatus and closely linked with its organisational and agitational role, when he wrote of his job:

> I can hardly ever spend a complete working day in the editorial offices as I should do, let alone be there every day. I have to be responsible for the work of political agitation in general, hold meetings and be present in the Reichstag. (cited in Hall, 1977: 32)

The SPD, during this period, was a mass party that existed in conditions of legality – albeit under considerable pressure from the state machine. Its press had less of a 'scaffolding' function than that envisaged by Lenin for the RSDLP, but it was nevertheless clearly the model for the Russian plan. The key political figures in the SPD had roles as journalists and editors; the party press not only argued the party line but also organised the work of the party and its associated unions. The preparation for a large demonstration, for the franchise for example, would be the result of the co-ordinated efforts of the whole party apparatus, including the press.

It should also be stressed that this model of press–party integration was not the only successful version of socialist newspaper and magazine production available at the time. There was also a tradition of commercially successful publications, particularly in the USA. These tended to be much more independent of the political movement than were the German examples, and to depend more on the efforts of talented leftist entrepreneurs to produce the sort of publication that could raise its own funds, through circulation and advertising, to make them successful businesses (Shore, 1988). In theory, then, Lenin had a choice even within the international socialist movement, and may be said to have selected his views of the press from competing models. In practice, it is difficult to see how the commercial model could have been applied to the Russian situation, given that the level of political repression was much higher than in the USA, and the country was much less developed, particularly as regards its advertising industry.

The origins of Lenin's theory of the press therefore have to be seen as lying in one of the more general traditions of the socialist movement. While the tradition that Lenin followed was by far the dominant one in Europe and internationally, there were alternatives. The choice that Lenin therefore made was, in this as in much else in his political thought, an attempt to adapt the central ideas of European, and particularly German, social democracy to Russian conditions. It is important to stress this point very firmly, since there is a strong tendency to imagine that everything that Lenin produced was both totally original and either demonic in intent or the expression of the highest human wisdom, depending upon one's political persuasion. Apart from its inherently objectionable methodology, this quasi-religious attitude presents some difficulties when we come to consider the overall validity of his theory as an explanation of the media in communist states.

The second major text was *Party Organisation and Party Literature*. It is this work that is usually cited to demonstrate that Lenin was in favour of the complete subordination of all cultural practice, from the press to poetry, to the line of the Central Committee. In this short article, Lenin argued that: 'Literature must become *part* of the common cause of the proletariat. . . . Literature must become a component of organised, planned and integrated Social Democratic work' (Lenin, 1961, X: 45). The first thing to note about this statement is that it was written in radically different conditions than *What is to be Done?*. In November 1905, Russia was in the midst of revolution. Socialist organisations were effectively legal, as was their press, and commanded a mass audience. The world of the tiny clandestine group of conspirators was past: 'we are now becoming a mass party all at once, changing abruptly to an open organisation' (Lenin, 1961, X: 47–8). It is sometimes argued that in taking this line Lenin was simply following the Russian tradition in which literature is much more deeply politicised than is the case in most other Western societies (Vaughan James, 1973: 1–22). In fact, while this

Russian tradition may have been part of the background, the explicit aims of the article were much narrower and less philosophical. Essentially, Lenin was concerned to argue that writers who were also members of the RSDLP were under a duty to use their special skills to help the party. They could not claim some special licence to write as they pleased and expect to remain members. Just as a political party demanded of its proletarian members that they participated in the process of deciding policies and then carried out the decisions they had reached together, so it demanded that writers who chose to join the party took the same responsible attitude to their political actions. These political actions included writing for newspapers and other public literary acts. Those who disagreed, Lenin argued, were quite at liberty to write as they pleased: 'First of all, we are discussing party literature, and its subordination to party control. Everyone is free to write and say whatever he likes, without any restrictions' (Lenin, 1961, X: 47). The only restriction that Lenin was seeking to place on writers was that upon those who chose to become members of the RSDLP. Those who wished to write other things or in other ways were entirely free to join other parties or to remain outside organised politics.

Much later, after the Bolshevik Revolution in 1917, Lenin faced a quite new set of problems. Not only was a small and isolated oppositional party now a mass organisation that wielded state power, but it had also achieved this in conditions of invasion and civil war. It was never possible in Lenin's active lifetime for him to attempt to develop a theory appropriate to a stable and democratic Soviet state. Such theoretical contributions as he attempted towards defining the press during this period were limited and fragmentary. In general, they tended to concentrate upon three things. First, he stressed the rationale for banning hostile publications in circumstances when the state found itself in acute danger from within or without, for example his draft 'Closure of the Menshevik newspaper undermining the country's defence' of 22 February 1919 (Lenin, 1961, XXVIII: 447–8). Here, he made much the same sort of arguments as the British government used to justify banning the *Daily Worker* in the early years of the Second World War. Second was the defence of what Lenin saw as a new kind of press freedom, in which the ability to express an opinion was not dependent upon the whims of the wealthy and powerful but was open to every worker and peasant. This line of thinking was embodied in, for example, his 'Draft resolution on freedom of the press' of 4/17 November 1917 (Lenin, 1961, XXVI: 283–4). Third, he stressed the duty of the press to expose the shortcomings and limitations of the new Soviet state, to publicise the best working methods in industry and to educate the mass of the population (Lenin, 1961, XXVII: 203–9). To these latter two ends, there tended to be a stress upon the involvement of non-journalists in the writing of reports for newspapers.

According to the protagonists of the communist system, these texts constituted a 'theory of the press' that was valid everywhere and that guided their own, highly repressive, practices in later years. As late as 1987, one could encounter arguments taken more or less directly from the classic model and only slightly modernised to take account of technological change:

The mass media and the propaganda system belong to the most powerful tools for the formation and expression of public opinion. As a tribune of public opinion Soviet mass media contribute to improving the administration of social phenomena and the activation of the masses. The mass media and the propaganda system are included in the administration scheme because they can help the party shape people's outlook and values. . . . Television renders reliable assistance to the party in solving important social and economic problems. It initiates and puts forward socially loaded problems, stimulates the search for their solution, shapes the economic thinking of the people and thus directly promotes the perfection of socialist production and the vital functions of society as a whole. (Gagarkin and Kushnereva, 1988: 51)

The conclusion that this line of thinking constitutes a fully formed theory of the media derived from Lenin's scattered writings seems highly suspect, for two basic reasons. In the first place, it is doubtful whether the scattered writings we have reviewed actually constitute a 'theory of the press' at all. They certainly make a sharp distinction between the official, bourgeois, press and that of the working-class movement, and propose that the two have different purposes and methods of organisation. They do not, however, elaborate how this might be related to other general features of social life, nor do they have any systematic character. The sum of these writings is better described as a series of penetrating insights, or perhaps the elements upon which a theory of the working-class press in opposition might be built, rather than as a general theory of the press as such. Second, as we have seen, the actual content of these writings is highly situational: in different phases of the struggle in Russia, Lenin made radically different pronouncements about the nature of the working-class press. We could easily add others, like the period of extreme openness involving the legal *Pravda*, immediately before the First World War, in which something else again is argued (Cliff, 1975: 338–52). This situated character of Lenin's writing not only reinforces the difficulty with considering his work on the press as constituting a recognisable theory, it also raises the question of what elements should properly be generalised. Lenin's successors were happy to generalise the organising role of the press taken from the writings of the earlier period, but they ignored the strong stress upon press freedom from that period. Instead, they took the much more restrictive pronouncements of the civil war as mainly constitutive of their systematising efforts.

The elevation of these scattered ideas into a fixed and definite theory of the press and the selection of elements from a contradictory corpus of writings tell us more about the successors to Lenin and the conditions in which they found themselves than they do about the man himself. Taken together, it is hardly possible to speak of anything more than a series of scattered insights and ad hoc pronouncements:

It is inaccurate to refer to Lenin's 'theory of the press', as if it were an academic treatise. His collected writings on the press are more in the realm of operating principles. He worked them out during his career as a revolutionary, often to justify or to plead for certain actions. Thus, Lenin's press theory is actually a conglomeration of essays or a few paragraphs of editorials written in the heat of battle. (Hopkins, 1970: 54)

As the state hardened towards Stalinism, so the practices born out of the exigencies of civil war became weapons in the struggle to establish the complete power of the new ruling group. The independent cultural and political life that had survived the civil war, and the cultural and press organisations that sustained it, were either crushed or transformed (Hopkins, 1970: 72–4, 92–8). What had been conceived as appropriate to the press of an opposition became a theory of the press as a whole. What had been adopted as the desperate solution to desperate circumstance became codified as the basis for normal life. The 'Leninist theory of the press' was, in fact, very little more than a crude justification of totalitarian practice decorated with selective quotations adopted in a hagiographical, rather than critical, manner.

By far the best known and most widely diffused of the Western theorists of the communist media was Wilbur Schramm. He contributed the chapter on 'The Soviet Communist Theory' to a collective work contrasting different media systems called *Four Theories of the Press* (Siebert et al., 1963). In many respects, Schramm's work represents the clearest and most systematic attempt to theorise the actual practice of the communist regimes and, as such, it is perhaps the best available account of the 'Leninist theory of the press'. Despite having been originally published over 40 years ago in 1956, the intellectual framework sketched in this book retains a strong currency in ways of thinking about the media up to this day, and is apparently still placed upon undergraduate reading lists. The main European textbook on communication theory, by Dennis McQuail, continues to have a heavy debt to this work. The 1987 edition of his standard work reproduced Schramm's categories exactly (McQuail, 1987: 111–18). The major modification was to add two new ones. The 1994 edition, recognising historical developments, changed the structure somewhat, but is still explicitly and recognisably indebted to *Four Theories of the Press* (McQuail, 1994: 127–33). There are certainly a number of projects designed to replace or supplement this and the other theories underway today. For the reason of its historic position, its continuing intellectual influence and, indeed, its status as the clearest exposition of the system it opposed, Schramm's account still needs to be taken very seriously.

The provenance of the text was in the depths of the Cold War, in which Schramm was to be an engaged participant, working directly for US government agencies on problems of the media, particularly with regard to the question of national development (Keever, 1991; Tankard, 1988). There can be no doubt that this political atmosphere influences the intellectual structure of the press theory book. The 'four theories' turn out in actual practice to be two – the 'libertarian' and the 'Soviet communist'. The 'authoritarian' model was one located firmly in the past, and identified as residual in its presentation. It was closely allied in some of its main features with the Soviet communist theory, which was 'a new and dramatic development' of the authoritarian theory (Siebert et al., 1963: 5). The 'social responsibility' theory, on the other hand, was 'an emerging theory', which was designed to supplement the libertarian theory dominant in the USA and to cover some of its more obvious lacunae (Siebert et al., 1963: 103). These two great theories stood in direct and explicit opposition:

> Thus the two systems line up almost diametrically opposite in their basic tenets, although both use words like freedom and responsibility to describe what they are doing. Our press tries to contribute to the search for truth; the Soviet press tries to convey pre-established Marxist–Leninist–Stalinist truth. We think of the audiences of our press as 'rational men', able to choose between truth and falsehood; the Soviets think of theirs as needing careful guidance from caretakers, and to this end the Soviet state sets up the most complete possible safeguards against competing information. We bend over backward to make sure that information and ideas will compete. They bend over backward to make sure that only the line decided upon will flow through the Soviet channels. We say that their press is not free; they say that our press is not responsible. (Siebert et al., 1963: 5–6)

This theme also closed the book. It ends with a highly tendentious contrast between the communist and US media, which Schramm clearly saw as being engaged in a desperate struggle for global leadership, in which 'the next few decades will tell' which is the best kind of media (Siebert et al., 1963: 145–6).

Despite its clear Cold War origins, it would be wrong to dismiss this account solely on the grounds of its ideological motivation. Just as with the theory of totalitarianism, to which it is closely allied, it is quite possible that the worst of motives might nevertheless lead to interesting and valuable conclusions. A similar view of the nature of the media in communist regimes was often advanced by writers of a radically different political persuasion. Thus, one writer well known for his opposition to both capitalism and communism wrote of the Hungarian press treatment of a show trial in the late 1940s that: 'Up to the day on which Rajk was arrested, all the papers in Hungary competed in singing his praises. . . . When on 15 June 1949 it was announced that Rajk had been arrested as a "Tito-fascist", all the press, without exception, attacked him in a most vicious manner' (Gluckstein, 1952: 225). The same writer later wrote of China that: 'Total control over the means of communication facilitates the dissemination of any propaganda lie the authorities might wish to put over' (Gluckstein, 1957: 334).

In pursuing the opposition between the US and Soviet press systems, Schramm, who wrote the chapter on the Soviet communist theory of the press, ascribed a number of major features to the communist media:

> Mass communications are used instrumentally – that is, as an instrument of the state and the Party.
> They are closely integrated with other instruments of state power and Party influence.
> They are used as instruments of unity within the state and the Party.
> They are used as instruments of state and Party 'revelation'.
> They are used almost exclusively as instruments of propaganda and agitation.
> They are characterised by a strictly enforced responsibility. (Siebert et al., 1963: 121)

As we have seen, this not only corresponded to the supposed features of the media in the communist countries, but is also based upon, and very closely parallels, the official version on the nature of that press.

One of the key charges here is that the mass media are 'instrumental', in that they are used as a means of conscious social engineering. In this, they are contrasted sharply with the US press, which is portrayed as pursuing truth as an end in itself. It is certainly possible to dispute this opposition and to argue, for example, that a commercial press is essentially instrumental in the production of profit, but in the central point Schramm had clearly identified an important distinctive dimension of the communist press. According to him, it is of the essence of this model that everything is subordinated to these instrumental ends:

> In other words, here is deadly serious broadcasting, missionary broadcasting. It carries good music. But chiefly it is a teacher and a lecturer. It tells millions what the agitators would tell them face to face, if it were possible to reach them. (Siebert et al., 1963: 157)

The theory thus leads to the definite conclusion that the kinds of material in the media must be primarily determined by political considerations, since this is the central characteristic of the system.

The central problem with the view advanced by Schramm is that it is based on the belief that the social order, and thus the mass media, are more or less direct reflections of the ideas and beliefs that people hold. Thus, with his co-authors, he wrote at the start of the book in question that:

> To see the differences between press systems in full perspective, then, one must look at the social systems in which the press function. To see the social systems in their true relationship to the press, one has to look at certain basic beliefs and assumptions which the society holds: the nature of man, the nature of society and the state, the relation of man to the state, and the nature of knowledge and truth. Thus, in the last analysis the difference between press systems is one of philosophy, and this book is about the philosophical and political rationales or theories which lie behind the different kinds of press we have in the world today. (Siebert et al., 1963: 2)

This view of the nature of society is what philosophers call 'idealism'. This sociological version is derived ultimately from Max Weber. The view that it is the ideas and beliefs that people hold that are determinate of social relations is one that obviously gives great importance to the mass media. It is also one that seems to have operated in other areas of Schramm's work, most notably his engagement with the role of the mass media in national development. Along with Daniel Lerner, Schramm was a major proponent of the notion that it was the task of the mass media to disseminate the ideas and attitudes appropriate to 'modern' men and women to the rural populations of developing countries as a prerequisite for changing the social structures of those countries and permitting them to launch themselves on a pattern of economic development and modernisation. At that level, the idea expressed in abstract theoretical form about theories of the press has indeed had an enormous practical effect, although of course Schramm's own prescriptions for the media in developing countries were highly 'instrumental' towards the end of national economic development.

There are major methodological questions at stake in deciding the intellectual validity of this position. Fortunately, we do not need to explore them in detail here. I would merely suggest that this kind of approach tends to lead to a concentration upon what people say about themselves and their beliefs, rather than the concrete realities of their lives and actions. It is a commonplace of social science precisely to explore the gap between actors' accounts of a situation or process and the features that present themselves to outside observers. Second, it is quite possible to hypothesise that in any given society there might be conflicting 'basic beliefs and assumptions' and we would need to find some reason outside the mere holding of such beliefs to explain why a society was dominated by one set of beliefs and not the other. In Poland, for example, there were clearly two rather different systems of belief, communism and Roman Catholicism, that commanded considerable support in the country. The reason why communism, probably the minority in terms of numbers of adherents, was the socially dominant one, requires us to go beyond the simple statement of 'basic beliefs'. Third, this kind of theory explains changes in the material world as being consequent upon changes of beliefs and ideas. Thus, in this instance, we would expect the communist media system to persist intact so long as, and only for as long as, the central ideas governing the societies remained intact. We would not, therefore, expect to find that there were any major departures from the picture outlined by Schramm while the communist regimes remained intact. The media would be 'deadly serious' and entirely instrumental throughout their life. Once the ideas of communism collapsed and were replaced by new value systems, we would expect to find a complete and total transformation in the media system as well.

Paradoxically, exactly the same predictions would be applied to the 'Leninist theory of the press', insofar as, despite the self-proclaimed 'materialism' of its proponents, it in fact constitutes a view of the media that derives their main practical features directly from the ideas held about them by the leading figures in society. There is a very striking parallel in the nature of the views about the media held by the theorists of the two major contenders in the Cold War. Not only did they share many points of textual reference, detail and interpretation in their accounts of communist media, differing only in their evaluation of its desirability, but they had in common a methodological approach that began from the values of the dominant group and attempted to demonstrate how these determined the actual practice of the mass media. Both, as consequence, present very rigid views of the nature and functioning of the communist media, and have no apparent room for any contingent evolution or change independent of the central value system of the dominant social group.

There was, during exactly the same period as Schramm was writing, a much less well-known attempt to construct another 'four theories of the press', which would seem to have been conceived as a more or less conscious alternative. It is remarkable that this version has received so little attention since its author was Raymond Williams, whose reputation today is probably as high and as widespread as that of Schramm himself. Since Williams was both a socialist and a critic of communism, his version of media theory is less marked by ideological warfare than Schramm's. Also, since Williams frequently wrote with what we may charitably term a certain detachment from the immediate and the concrete, it is a great deal less specific. It does, nevertheless, represent a serious attempt to address the same problem from a quite different perspective and therefore deserves equally serious attention.

Williams shared with Schramm and his fellows the starting point of the 'authoritarian' media system, in which 'the first purpose of communication is to transmit the instructions, ideas and attitudes of the ruling group' (Williams, 1962: 89). His second category was the paternal, which was 'an authoritarian system with a conscience: that is to say, with values and purposes beyond the maintenance of its own power' (Williams, 1962: 90). In both of these systems, control of the content and nature of communication was in the hands of the minority who run society. The Soviet system would fall into one of these two groups, depending upon how one interpreted the ends of the *nomenklatura*: the language of Williams's account suggests that it is into the former that he would personally have placed the Soviet Union.

Against these two systems, he opposed the commercial system. Whilst this contained a certain liberatory potential in that it freed expression from the control of state power, it contained within it its own problems, due to the difficulty of making money out of some kinds of expression:

> Thus the control claimed as a matter of power by authoritarians, and as a matter of principle by paternalists, is often achieved as a matter of practice in the operation of the commercial system. Anything can be said, provided that you can afford to say it and that you can say it profitably. (Williams, 1962: 92)

Overall, the US media system would probably have fallen into this category. That in the UK was a mixture of the paternal (broadcasting) and commercial (press), with some elements of surviving authoritarianism and small experimental examples of Williams's fourth type of system (1962: 97).

Williams imagined this fourth kind of system, the democratic, but he could not find any well-developed existing examples. As a consequence, the democratic communication system existed only as a rather vague set of guiding principles, rather than as concrete proposals based on the weight of accumulated experience. It was, however, grounded in a well-worked out theory of the nature of human communication, whose elements can be shown to have permeated Williams's overall project (Sparks, 1993).

As can be seen, there was at least some degree of common ground between the two Western positions: both were clear, for example, that in contrast to the capitalist media the prime aims of communist media were symbolic rather than economic. On the other hand, they had different prognoses for the future. For Schramm and his fellows, the system followed logically from the theory, and so long as the theory remained the same there could be no substantial evolution of the system. Williams made less definite claims: his account of both authoritarian and paternal systems stressed how they could have different mixes of direct repression and relative freedom at different times. His real concern was with encouraging the construction of concrete examples of democratic systems as an alternative to all of the other three.

There was not, for Williams, any clear, hard and fast, line between different systems of media. Consonant with his well-known 'cultural materialism', the analysis of the concrete relations between media system and society always had primacy for Williams over any fixed schema derived from belief. The prognosis for the future of the communist media systems that one could derive from Williams would therefore tend to be much more provisional and flexible than those of the other camps: the 'authoritarian' could slide into, and out of, the 'paternal', and both could shade over into the commercial. One might even expect to find, at least in the nooks and crannies of all three systems, elements and sprouts of the fourth, 'democratic' system of communication. Indeed, one might reasonably suppose that, for Williams, it would be possible for any of the three anti-democratic forms to evolve into fully blown democratic systems without any particularly marked upheaval.

In terms of divergences between East and West, it is clear that the main division is located not along this geopolitical axis but within the Western 'camp'. Williams, both in terms of his method and his substantive conclusions, clearly inhabits a different universe of discourse than do the other two theories. For their part, Schramm and the 'Leninist theory of the press' have a great deal in common, both in how they think about the factors determining the nature of the mass media and their method of reasoning. We might broadly describe the differences between Williams and the other two theories as being derived from different conceptions of explanation. For Williams, cultural forms like the press, and the media generally, could only be understood with reference to their concrete historical circumstances of production. For the other two approaches, however, the decisive factor in determining the nature of a media system is the intention of its founders as derived from a study of the dominant value system. While it is perfectly understandable that Schramm should choose such an approach, which is after all consistent with his overall intellectual position, the fact that it is shared by the adherents of what called itself 'dialectical materialism' is rather more surprising. Perhaps it is one small piece of evidence as to the distance between the ways in which the representatives of communist societies thought about the world and the Marxist version of the critical project that the official spokesmen should have more in common with the US opponent than with a Western critic.

The obvious question that arises from this comparison is: how well did these different theories account for the nature of the actually existing communist systems in the period before the collapse of communism? It is tempting to say that, now the Cold War is over and the USA won, we know who, in Schramm's revealing phrase, had 'a weakness' in their 'national armour' and end the discussion there. This would be a mistake. We have an almost unique opportunity to examine how well two kinds of theories of the media, different both in their content and in their methodology, explained a major and important reality. Such chances are relatively rare and deserve close attention. The prognoses as to the potential for change and evolution present in all three theoretical systems may be tested with regard to the actual record of the decline of the communist systems.

The communist media before 1989

In the high period of Stalinism, which we might date from 1928 to 1956, it was possible to give numerous examples of the way in which there was a unified and orchestrated mass media responding directly to the latest political imperatives from the Central Committee, the majority faction thereof, or the Great Leader himself. We have already cited two such examples from an anti-Stalinist leftist, and it is possible to find numerous later publications from a variety of viewpoints that argue more or less similar cases even for much later periods (Lendavi, 1981). On the other hand, there are writers with direct experience of the system who argue that, in reality, the media of these countries fitted this model at best for a brief period and were, in fact, rather malleable from early on. Goban-Klas, for example, identifies four phases in the history of Polish media between 1944 and 1989, only one of which, between 1949 and 1954, really fits the Stalinist theoretical model at all closely (Goban-Klas, 1994: 250).

Whatever the longer-term reality, by the 1980s it is clear that this picture of a co-ordinated, univocal and propagandistic media was no longer adequate for the vast majority of communist societies. The situation in the various countries differed very widely. Just as there were differences in the level of economic and social development between, say, Czechoslovakia and Romania, and in political regime between Hungary and Poland, so there were differences in the kinds of media systems operating.

As an example of one extreme, there was the situation prevailing in Romania, where the main expert commentator argued that the Ceauşescu regime had instituted a media system that corresponded very closely to the classical model of communist media (Gross, 1990). Political control of the media was more or less total and more or less complete. The activities of all of the different media were co-ordinated and subordinated to the goals defined by the leadership. The economic situation was so serious that television broadcasting had been reduced to a very low level. Even in this instance, however, it is important to note that the close political control of the system was not a timeless features derived from some ideal model. There had, at an earlier stage, been a more 'liberal' internal regime, lasting from 1965 to 1971, which had been reflected also in the mass media (Gross, 1996: 9).

As an example of the other extreme, we may take the Hungarian system, in which the degree of direct control over all kinds of media messages was much smaller. Television, for example, broadcast large amounts of Western programming, and was at least partially oriented towards entertainment goals (MTV, 1991: 19). Once again, we should note that this relative liberalisation was not a permanent aspect of the system. On the contrary, while there was a long-term trend away from communist control in the aftermath of 1956, this was not uniform across the media, nor was it without upsets and setbacks (Kováts and Tölgyesi, 1990: 1–2).

If we look in more detail at the television systems of Poland, Hungary and Czechoslovakia, we can see clear evidence of the kind of uneven changes that were going on. There had been a considerable degree of what we may call 'pre-adaptation' before 1989. By this term, we mean that in important, but not central, respects the institutions of the Stalinist regimes had transformed themselves in ways that are characteristic of a commercialised broadcasting system. There had been changes to journalistic ethics, to the financing and to programming content, and in openness to Western influences. The extent of the changes varied from country to country, as did the nature of the pre-adaptation.

The television systems of the Visegrad triangle were moving away from the model of the politicised monolith towards a more open and commercial way of working. The speed of the movement was uneven between the different countries, with Czechoslovakia moving most slowly and Hungary most quickly. Nevertheless, the direction was clear and there is no evidence that any group in the bureaucracy attempted seriously to impede that progress in the name of communist principles, or of anything else. Here, at least, the leadership of what we may genuinely call the ideological state apparatuses appear to have decided that there was no future in the old system and to have begun to move cautiously towards a new order.

We can track this in more detail in a number of ways. All three broadcasting systems were already using Western programmes. Insofar as figures are available to us, they suggest that this openness to Western programmes had been a growing feature of all three in the 1980s. According to Varis's 1983 study, between 25 and 33 per cent of programmes broadcast in each country originated outside the 'Eastern Bloc' and, overall, '45 per cent of the aggregated total imports broadcast was produced in East European socialist countries, while 55 per cent was purchased from other countries of the world' (Varis, 1985: 32–5). There were, however, important differences between countries.

Czechoslovakia appears to have been the system least integrated into the world programme market, and most dependent upon Soviet material: its third channel was dedicated entirely to rebroadcasting programmes from Russian TV. Even in this tightly controlled country, however, Western entertainment programmes found a substantial outlet. In 1983, Czechoslovak TV imported 24 per cent of its overall programming, of which 50 per cent was from Eastern European socialist countries and 50 per cent from other countries. Forty-one per cent of its entertainment programmes and 36 per cent of its cultural programmes were imported. On the other hand, only 4 per cent of informational programmes were of foreign origin, but these latter figures are unfortunately not broken down by country or bloc of origin (Varis, 1985: 34). By 1986, 26 per cent of total broadcast time was accounted for by foreign acquisitions, originating in some 46 different countries. There was still a heavy preference for material from other Eastern Bloc countries:

As for the structure of TV programmes in terms of their provenance, the richest source of exchange of TV programmes is the socialist countries, which is reflected in the programming. Over the past five years (1982–87) the average ratio between socialist countries' production and those from the non-socialist states has been 66::34 in terms both of the number of programmes and programme hours. . . . The statistics show that, in 1986, Czechoslovak TV viewers were offered programmes from 16 European non-socialist countries, of which three dominate: France (24 per cent), Britain (21 per cent), and West Germany (20 per cent). (Tesar, 1989: 138)

When we consider the smaller Slovak Republic in isolation, we find that in 1980 29 per cent of programmes broadcast were imported, 10.6 per cent of the total were from 'non-socialist' countries (CST, 1980: 82). By 1985, the 129 hours of Western programmes broadcast accounted for only 4 per cent of the overall total. This fall in Western imports has to be seen in the context of a general decline in the international trading of Slovak television. Eastern Bloc imports fell to 13 per cent of the total and there was a sharp fall in programme exports at the same time (CST, 1985: 57, 120).

Similarly, Poland had been increasing its Western imports in the course of the 1970s. Precise data do not exist for television, but it has been argued that Western commercial productions were 'predominate'. This was curtailed from 1982 onwards, when the rapid import of Western series was reduced and repeats became much more common. Apparently, this was not simply a response to the introduction of martial law but:

. . . the inevitable result of the financial difficulties suffered by the TV network. An over-generous financial policy up to 1981 led to a need to reduce financing radically and to do this programming increasingly utilized items which did not require dollar expenditure (or other convertible currency). (Pomorski, 1988: 182)

Within these financial constraints, Poland was characterised by an almost complete openness to foreign entertainment programming. By 1986, 42.8 per cent of feature films and 47.1 per cent of series shown on Polish TV originated in the 'Western countries' (Jakubowicz, 1989: 148–64). News, on the other hand, continued to be tightly controlled during the first part of the decade. After 1987, however, there was a significant decrease in the propaganda content of the news, marked by the introduction of programmes like 'Panorama of the Day' and 'Tele-express'. Significantly, these programmes did not run against each other, so viewers could if they so chose continue to watch television while avoiding the official news programmes, which were themselves officially 'relieved from the duty of educating society' (Jakubowicz, 1989: 161).

Hungary was probably the most open system with a substantial part of the broadcast output, both factual and entertainment based, purchased from a range of Western sources. In 1986, MTV (Hungarian Television) purchased 601 programmes from Western sources out of a total of 864 foreign acquisitions. The largest supplier of programme units was Britain, accounting for 228 items. West Germany accounted for 122. The largest Eastern supplier was the USSR with 116 items (MTV, 1991: 19).

Jakubowicz argues that, with regard to Poland at least, this situation represented an attempt by the bureaucracy to come to terms with the reality of its position in the country. Faced with the evidence, in every form from mass strikes to the results of opinion polls, as to the deep failure of its attempts to win the ideological struggle for the hearts and minds of its own population, the regime retreated. It no longer believed that it was possible to use the mass media to mould the consciousness of the population to acceptance of the desirability of the communist order. It did not think that it could make enthusiastic participants in socialist construction out of the Poles. It allowed, indeed encouraged, the development of entertainment programmes, which were clearly at least acceptable to the mass of the population. Since these were best and most cheaply acquired through purchases from the West, they were quite prepared to accept such imports. After all, if one's population already holds to an alien ideology, and rejects your own attempt to persuade them otherwise, there can hardly be any objection to allowing them to enjoy the more harmless manifestations of their preferred belief system. On the other hand, the regime retained quite firm control of the news, since it aimed to demonstrate that its rule was at least inevitable if not beneficial. Like some other politicians in quite different systems, it sought to present only its own picture of that narrow and immediate area of experience covered by news and current affairs. By the late 1980s, however, the character of this definition had changed from an emphasis upon the positive achievement of socialist construction towards a much more pessimistic picture of reality. The people of Poland were no longer being asked to express enthusiasm for the triumphs of the socialist system, or even to believe in the socialist system: they were expected only to endure it.

The other major elements of pre-adaptation to the market system were more nationally specific. Television in Hungary already carried extensive advertising, but the other countries had not developed this to the same extent. The separate advertising department of Polish television only opened in 1990, but from 1984 onwards the International Trading and Investments Corporation in Warsaw produced commercials for Polish Television and, by 1987, 2 per cent of total broadcasting time was commercials (Jakubowicz, 1987: 16–17; Mrozowski and Pomorski, 1989: 12; PRTV, 1989: 20). Czechoslovak TV had carried some advertising in the past, but this had ceased to be significant as long ago as the early 1970s, probably as part of the termination of the country's 'premature' attempt at market reforms. For Slovakia, 'reklama' (advertising) constituted 0.7 per cent of broadcasting in 1980, but there is no figure for any of the succeeding years (CST, 1980: 84). It is fair to conclude that advertising was not a significant part of television either in terms of broadcasting output or the finances of the system.

Hungarian broadcasting had for long been more open to advertising. Hungarian radio had, in the late 1980s, set up a quasi-independent station, Radio Danubius, which, although wholly owned by the state broadcaster, depended entirely for its revenues upon the sale of advertising, from which it derived considerable profits. With regard to television, it is striking that the events of 1989 produced singularly little change in the amount of advertising material. MTV recorded a constant 3 per cent of advertising from 1980 to

1991. In more detail, the two MTV channels carried 262 minutes of advertising per week in 1989; by 1991 this had risen to 353 per week. This rise of 35 per cent is considerable, but it has to be set against a rise in programme output from 134 hours per week in 1989 to 181 hours per week (for the first 11 months alone) in 1991; this was a rise of more than 35 per cent (MTV, 1991: 12–15). As we shall see below in the discussion of the media wars, there were specific reasons for this absolute increase after 1989, but on this evidence we can hardly see 1989 as the decisive turning point.

The final area in which the systems departed from the classical stereotype was in their openness to foreign signals. The communist countries had long histories of attempting to jam the radio propaganda broadcasts of their foreign enemies. They persisted up to 1989 in this practice. According to Radio Free Europe, which had some direct experience of interference, television seems never to have been jammed, even when Western signals were quite widely available. In Hungary, where 30 per cent of the population is able to receive terrestrial Austrian and Yugoslav signals, there had never been any attempt to prevent reception. In mid-1980 there were some attempts to restrict the community reception of satellite signals. The Press Act of 1986 officially ended MTV's monopoly and confirmed the right of cable systems to produce and distribute their own programmes (Clarke, 1987: 22–3). At the end of April 1988 the Hungarian Post Office had licensed 62 cable systems, and by this time approximately 120,000 households were able to receive foreign satellite signals (Szekfü, 1989). This option was taken up by many people. According to one source, during the first half of the 1980s,

> The share of those who watched foreign TV programmes increased from 19 to 31 per cent and – within this – of those who frequently (several time a week) watched foreign stations, trebled. (Szecskö, 1986: 16)

In the case of video, there were no political moves to control the import either of Western technology or programmes, although the customs service operated tariffs that had the effect of rationing such items through price rises. Nevertheless, in 1984, according to official sources, between 500,000 and 600,000 people out of a population of around 10 million had access to video recorders, although some estimates were for a much lower figure of around 120,000 adults with recorders in their own homes (Pogany, 1988: 223–4; Szecskö, 1986: 15). By 1987, there were said to be 200,000 video recorders in Hungary (Clarke, 1987: 23).

The Polish system, likewise, eventually permitted reception of Western satellites signals (and even gave up jamming most Western radio broadcasts in the mid-1980s), but were more persistent than the Hungarians in placing bureaucratic obstacles in the way of ownership. According to Jakubowicz, up to 1984 the law was silent on reception devices, but in that year a new law on communications banned the possibility of radio and television 'for other than ordinary uses'. This made it illegal to use a satellite dish. However, in 1986 rules were laid down for obtaining satellite permits, which were obtainable from the Ministry of Telecommunications and approved by the police.

The issue of permits began in March 1987 and by the end of the year between 2,000 and 3,000 people had been granted permits. It was at this time that SMATV systems began to appear, the first in Ursynow in Warsaw. As of November 1988, permits for group reception were granted, and by the end of the year the requirement for police approval had been dropped (Jakubowicz, n.d.b: 12). This obstructionism had its effect: official figures record 0.1 per cent of the population as using such devices in 1989, rising to 10 per cent only by 1991 (TVP, n.d.).

Video recorders do not appear ever to have been illegal in Poland. The restriction on their ownership was largely economic. To buy them required a large sum of scarce convertible currency. Apart from authorised outlets, they were often acquired as an investment by Poles travelling abroad, who then resold them inside the country at a profit (Pomorski, 1988: 184–6). It is, however, rather difficult to specify exactly how many people had access to these devices. Jakubowicz cites three conflicting sets of figures for the 1987–8 period: the Centre for Public Opinion Research reported that in 1988 there were 120,000 recorders in Poland; *TV World*, in May 1988, reported that there were 500,000; an article in the then official Polish newspaper *Polityka*, of 12 March 1987, reported that there were 700,000 recorders in Poland (Jakubowicz, n.d.b: 8). The major area of conflict was over the control of distribution outlets and involved a three-way tussle between the central state, local government and private entrepreneurs. The issues, however, were not political control and censorship of Western material, but the enforcement of international copyright conventions and the sharing of new revenue streams. Before 1984, there were about 100 private video rental shops. The Ministry of Culture and Arts wrote to local government, which had authorised these shops, complaining that they had legalised systematic piracy. Consequently, some of the shops had their licenses withdrawn. The directive was ineffective because in 1986 local government rights to license such shops were suspended. The law on cinematography of July 1987 led to the confiscation of tapes and the birth of several hundred illegal shops, as against 20 legal state-run shops. The majority of videos sold by the illegal shops were foreign-made (Jakubowicz, n.d.b: 11).

In terms of their structure, the different systems had already begun a process of internal reform that was to give them an organisational structure which in some cases has survived intact up to the present. In the case of Poland, television, from the start of the 1980s, did not escape the general economic crisis that gripped the whole Polish economy. This was exacerbated by the year-long strike of actors and directors in 1982–3, which meant that there was no home-based supply of programmes and that substitutes had to be purchased from abroad (Goban-Klas, personal communication, 1992). In response to these difficulties, Polish Radio and Television (PRTV) became a 'state enterprise', meaning that it became responsible for its own finances, rather than being paid out of the state budget (Jakubowicz, personal communication, 1992). From that time onwards, there was a trend towards reducing the dependence upon subsidy by increasing licence fees. Reflecting the general uncertainty about the future direction of Polish society, television was subject to a veritable barrage of different, and often contradictory, legal and quasi-legal instruments. For example, in 1984, the Polish Press Law of 26 January introduced a Press Council and internal charters for radio and television. The internal financial structure of PRTV was reformed in 1985 by Directive No. 146/85, and a major review of the structure was initiated in 1987 by Directive No. 202/87. A special commission was set up to reform television, with a directive to 'make it more like the BBC' (Goban-Klas, personal communication, 1992). The driving force behind these attempts to alter the structure of television, in Poland as elsewhere, was economic rather than political.

The final major element in the decay of communist control over the symbolic environment of their states was the emergence of oppositional material, most often illegal publications. These are best known by their Russian name of *Samizdat*, but in fact were probably more developed in Poland than else-where. Beginning in the 1970s, there were by the time that Solidarity became a mass movement literally hundreds of such publications, and even a couple of intermittent radio stations. Although martial law led to a sharp clamp-down, within months a new and increasingly vigorous illegal press was developing. Once again, there were hundreds of different, often ephemeral, publications that put a wide range of oppositional voices forward. In practice, despite the efforts of the police and the censors, the communists were no longer able to ensure that the only sources of information and opinion were under their own control (Goban-Klas, 1994: 165–79, 186–91).

The variety of communist media systems

By 1989, the evidence is that the media systems of the communist world dis-played a wide variety of different states. There were those systems which, according to the most expert observers, retained at least the main features of the classical Stalinist communist model. Romania is by far the clearest exam-ple of this type of system, although even this was relatively open to foreign radio and television signals. There were others that displayed a considerable degree of what I have termed pre-adaptation to the Western model. Hungary is the most notable example of this kind of system.

Between these two extremes lay a number of countries that displayed dif-ferent combinations of control. East Germany, for example, had a relatively high level of political control over the media system, but was, for geographi-cal and linguistic reasons, extremely open to foreign signals. Just before its collapse, one expert wrote that: 'in the GDR "media pluralism" in the bour-geois sense does not exist and is not wanted'; nevertheless 'the decisive feature with regard to communication culture in the GDR is that two opposed media systems are in operation' (Hanke, 1990: 185). One was that of the communist GDR, the other that of the continent's strongest and most successful capi-talist state, the Federal Republic of Germany.

It seems clear from the evidence that these features of the communist media system cannot be explained by reference to the kind of positions advanced either by the official apologists for communism or by Western writers like Schramm. In their account, communist ideology had a definite view as to what the nature and position of the mass media were in a communist system, and that ideology directly informed the actual workings of the media. If, and only if, the central tenets of that ideology were to change would we expect to find changes in the media systems themselves.

The evidence that would best support the Schramm view would be the gradual relaxation of the media in the USSR as a result of the policy of *Glasnost* in the mid-1980s. Here, there were indeed changes in the sort of expectations that were placed upon the media by the ruling group, which in their turn produced a marked difference in the nature of the media themselves. By the later 1980s, Soviet scholars were trying to find ways of theorising the new conditions:

> Basically, Glasnost means having ready access to various facts of life and an open, public discussion of these questions. . . . The process of openness is not related to individual or small group information, but above all to public information. . . . Greater openness will have a profound effect on the relationship of the mass media and public opinion. . . . Making mass media part of the process of greater openness will oblige them objectively to get rid of political pompousness, general phrases, and makes it impossible 'to varnish' different aspects of life. It is known that 'communication reality' differs from actual reality. The range of difference may vary significantly. In the course of restructuring the conditions for approximating 'communication' image of man's environment and reality are being built up. . . . Our press is taking various steps to orient journalists to a more accurate reflection of reality. (Korobeinikov, 1988: 7–9)

This commentator goes on to give examples both of the attempts being made to render Soviet journalism less an instrument of 'varnishing' reality and of hostility to such efforts. The argument, however, is made in terms of a need to depart from the actual practice of the Soviet media, and to return towards a closer rendering of the theoretical goals of the system in giving 'a more accurate reflection of reality'. On the then-Soviet account, the process of *Glasnost* in the media was necessary because the mass media did not in practice follow the goals outlined in the 'Leninist theory of the press'. It cannot, therefore, be the case that the ideas and values held in society determine the nature of the mass media.

It appears on the basis of the evidence put forward by Gross that the situation in Romania also corresponded more or less exactly to the prescriptions of the Schramm theory. Even in this case, however, as Gross himself admits, the situation was far from static. There had been an earlier period in which the Romanian mass media were more liberal. In the 1980s, alongside the political repression, the other notable feature of the Romanian system was that it was contracting:

> After 1985, the domains of social, economic and political life were subjected to huge cuts in money and personnel. Romanian national radio – which began to broadcast in 1928 – reduced by half its transmission time. The number of

newspapers dropped from about one hundred to around forty. The worst situation was that of Romanian television, which nearly ceased to exist, broadcasting only two hours a day. (Marinescu, 1995: 82)

It is extremely hard to see how this contraction might be explained within the framework of either Schramm's or the orthodox communists' theories. Both recognised an important, indeed vital, contribution on the part of the media to securing social consent and it is therefore fair to say that they accorded the mass media a relatively high priority – higher than many other obvious consumer goods, for example. There are two possible explanations as to why the mass media in Romania contracted. The first is that there was a change in the role the ruling ideology accorded to the mass media. This seems unlikely since, if Gross is to be believed, it more or less directly reproduced Schramm's account. The second is that the mass media were subject to the overall economic calculus that was applied to the system as a whole and that, as the crisis in Romania deepened, so the media contracted along with everything else. This seems much more probable but, in furnishing a rather crudely 'materialist' explanation for one prominent aspect of the Romanian media, it casts considerable doubt upon the overall validity of a theory based on the premise that it is the ideas that people have about the function of the media that determines their nature.

At the very best, faced with evidence of this kind, we might want to argue that theories of this kind articulate the intentions of the dominant groups in societies rather than describe the actual practices of the media themselves. The intentions that dominant groups have about the media, and what their theoreticians claim they intend to do, are not, however, an adequate basis for understanding what actually occurs in a given situation. Quite apart from issues of self-deception, the wishes of a dominant group, and the values to which they adhere, are subject both to constraint and to contestation. The mass of the population proved by their deeds, in 1956 and on many later occasions, that they were very far from blank sheets of paper upon which the *nomenklatura* could write what it wished. The central values of the dominant group were contested, sometimes hotly, sometimes silently, from below. The dominant group, too, was not 'building socialism in one country' in an economic vacuum. It was attempting to maintain its rule in a hostile and predatory world and that task imposed great economic constraints upon the rulers' freedom of action. The media systems of the region were not the direct result of values and policies, but the consequence of struggle and compromise.

An explanation that begins from the concrete material circumstances in which these societies found themselves, and which traces the way in which the different situations of the mass media were the result of the working out of these forces would offer a much better explanation of the ways in which the media were differently run in the various societies. For these reasons, Williams's version of media theory is a much better starting point for understanding the evolution of the communist media systems in the 1980s. The gradual relaxation of party control over the media, the increasing commercialisation of the system, and the willingness to permit the audiences access to different interpretations of the world than that preferred by the *nomenklatura* are better understood if we see the mass media as responding to a range of pressures, originating both inside and outside the specific societies in question.

From this perspective, there seem to have been three major factors that influenced the general situation of the mass media in any particular country: external pressures from the economic and political structures of an increasingly globalised economy, internal opposition from a variety of dissident groups, and élite divisions within the *nomenklatura* itself as to the future of the societies they controlled. Obviously, in reality all three of these were so interconnected that it is difficult to distinguish them, but in principle they can be seen as distinct.

The most obvious and persistent of external pressures was that of the Soviet Union, which acted as a control over the fissiparous tendencies of its various satellites and as a guarantor of the local communist regimes against internal dissent. Starting with Yugoslavia in the 1940s and continuing with China in the late 1950s, this control was often challenged even by the local communist regimes. In a number of cases, most obviously Hungary in 1956 and Czechoslovakia in 1968, military intervention was employed to ensure continued loyalty. The other major form of external pressure was from the competitive demands of the world market. Even though the initial idea of the communist model had been autarkic national economic development, the price of this attempt was first and foremost the deployment of massive resources into the military machines of the communist bloc. From the 1970s onwards, however, most notably in Poland and Hungary, this pressure also took a direct economic form through loans, trade and attempts at membership of the International Monetary Fund (IMF). The pressure of the world economy on the Soviet Union and its allies increased as their growth rates slowed down, although it is important not to exaggerate this tendency. Contrary to the dominant mythology after 1989, complete economic stagnation was not the central characteristic of these economies. Up to around 1975, the command economies had 'worked' at least as well as their free-market competitors, both in terms of crude growth and in terms of measures like life expectancy (Szelenyi and Szelenyi, 1994: 212–21). Even in 1986–8, the years both of the terminal crisis of communism and a great boom in Western capitalism, the growth rates in centrally planned economies were comparable to the Organization for Economic Co-operation and Development (OECD) average. During those years, the OECD average was 3.5 per cent per annum economic growth, while Poland grew annually at around 2.4 per cent, Bulgaria at 4.2 per cent, and Romania at 5.1 per cent per annum. The major exception appears to have been in the performance of what were, overwhelmingly, the largest economies in each bloc, the USA and the USSR. In 1981–5, the USA grew at 3.0 per cent per annum, while the USSR grew at 3.2 per cent. In the 1986–8 period, the figures were 3.6 and 2.8 per cent respectively (Kolodko, 1993: 125–6).

The response to these different kinds of pressures was one of the main

factors influencing the standards of living of the population. The overall figures for growth conceal the fact that the main destination of these rises in
output was the military machine, and that on a wide range of indicators
living standards in communist countries remained well below those of the
West. The inability of governments to satisfy the immediate consumption
needs of their own populations was, at least indirectly, a factor increasing the
possibility of the various oppositional groups gaining a mass audience. Mass
opposition to the communist regimes can be dated back at least to the 1953
Berlin Rising. In Hungary in 1956, mass discontent was great enough to
bring down the existing order, which was only re-established by Russian
tanks. In the other great recent example, that of the rise of Solidarity in
1980–1, the very fear of Russian arms was enough to cause the movement to
hesitate in mounting a direct challenge to the Polish state.

The presence of such large-scale opposition naturally influenced the extent
to which the media system was open to other perspectives than that of the
party élite. In the extreme case of Solidarity, the mass media themselves were,
at the high point of popular mobilisation, the subject of direct negotiation
between the regime and its opponents, and the communists were forced to
agree to the principle of allowing oppositional voices in the official media
themselves. After the imposition of martial law, 'order' was restored in the
official media, but the regime was unable to stop the production and distribution of large numbers of illegal and clandestine newspapers, and even
occasional radio broadcasts.

Where the regime was able to exert renewed control, as in the case of
Hungary after the Russians crushed the 1956 revolution, the strategy for
ensuring the continuation of that rule involved a gradual and limited process
of liberalisation, which meant that living standards were allowed to rise
slowly and dissenting opinions were not so rigorously persecuted and marginalised as had earlier been the case.

The pressure of the opposition was a factor in determining the degree of
unity of the communist élite themselves, as was their relative dependence
upon Soviet arms. Thus, while division within the communist élite in the
Prague Spring of early 1968 permitted an efflorescence of different opinions
in the mass media, the Russian invasion of August of that year marginalised, jailed and exiled the liberal communists and installed in power a
group that owed its position entirely to the Russians. Part of their attempt to
hold on to power was a reimposition of complete and direct control over the
mass media.

In the course of the 1980s, all three of these factors came together with particular force in the Western outposts of European communism. On the one
hand, Gorbachev made it clear that the USSR was no longer willing or able
to intervene to re-establish orthodoxy in other countries. On the other hand,
the pressure to integrate into the world economy grew ever greater, particularly as the burden of debt incurred in the 1970s began to impact on the
living standards of the population.

Although only Poland had recent experience of mass opposition, the lessons of Solidarity were learned better by the communist rulers throughout the region than by the oppositions. As Bauman put it:

> It was the Polish *Men of Iron* who made the Czech revolution so *velvety*, while sparing the Hungarians even the trouble of night vigils at Vaclavske Namesti. (Bauman, 1992b: 117)

A policy of concession and retreat seemed the only feasible one in such circumstances. Under these pressures, the élites in some countries split into conservative and reform wings. In what was then Yugoslavia, the divisions were further exacerbated by the different nationally based sections of the bureaucracy fighting each other for shares of the federal resources. The overall consequence of these factors was that the bureaucracy was no longer either interested in exerting, or even able to exert, a direct control over the media. It had effectively abandoned its attempt to construct a new world, and one wing wished only to negotiate the terms of their full readmission to the world order.

The divisions within the bureaucracy meant that there was less agreement on the desirability of repressing oppositional voices, or of controlling completely the output of the mass media themselves. Indeed, there was a positive advantage for some of the reform-minded communist bureaucrats in the existence of a relatively greater degree of freedom in the mass media. It allowed the mobilisation of public opinion behind their versions of desirable change, as when the Slovenian leadership allowed increasingly 'nationalist' voices to develop in the media in order to bolster its opposition to Belgrade. The existence of oppositional media was also to the advantage of the reforming communists since it both gave a voice to the people with whom they wished to negotiate and allowed their emergence as a stable political force capable of entering into negotiations.

The conclusion that a review of the evidence with regard to the explanatory power of different theories of the mass media in communist societies, and indeed of the underlying social theories upon which they were based, thus demonstrates that the more 'materialist' views are superior. They allow an understanding both of the variety of existing 'communist' systems and the changes that specific systems had experienced over time. The policies of the *nomenklatura* towards the mass media were the product of a range of different forces, in which their publicly held views and beliefs about the proper place and function of the media were only one set of influences alongside others.

Conclusions

If, then, we adopt Williams's categorisation rather than Schramm's or the orthodox communists', it is legitimate to ask whether the gap between the communist media systems and those of capitalist countries was in fact as wide as is often supposed. We may consider the media systems of the communist countries in the 1980s as occupying varying positions between the authoritarian and the paternal, and shifting between them depending upon the extent to which the dominant wing of the bureaucracy remained committed to the idea of the construction of a communist society. There are, of course, other media systems, both today and historically, of which we may say they are either authoritarian or paternal.

While the most obvious candidates are the numerous undemocratic regimes that still endure today, relatively repressive media forms have not all existed in dictatorships. A contrast between the media system in France during the 1960s and that of the waning communism is instructive in this context. If we consider the broadcasting system in isolation, then there are strong similarities with the mass media of the later period of communism in, say, Hungary or Poland. Broadcasting in de Gaulle's France was completely politically subordinated to the politics of the president and his political party. The government interfered in all aspects of broadcasting: finance, personnel, programming. The aim of that interference was to establish as much as possible that the output of broadcasting supported the policies of the president and denigrated his opponents (Kuhn, 1995: 113–28; Thomas, 1976: 11–23). Certainly, there was a very wide divergence between the sorts of relatively balanced coverage operating in broadcasting in Northern European and North America and those pursued by the Office de Radiodiffusion Télévision Française (ORTF). From this perspective, the media system of communism appears as one version of a more general category of authoritarian and paternal regimes that rest upon a variety of different forms of social organisation and political philosophies.

On the other hand, we should remember that this similarity is not an identity. France under de Gaulle was a bourgeois democracy, albeit a rather tenuous one, not a dictatorship. For broadcasting, this meant that there were formal rules that permitted the opposition access to political programming during election periods and undermined its complete subordination to the government.

Second, and more importantly, French society was a bourgeois society in the sense that large parts of capital, and in particular the press, were independent of the state machine. As we have argued above, the different sectors of the ruling class are, in this sort of society, relatively loosely articulated. The government did not control the press and oppositional forces, including the communists, were able legally to publish their views in newspapers and magazines. The independent voices were not only those of the political left, but also of sections of the commercial press which for one reason or another did not support the Gaullist project. De Gaulle himself is alleged to have said: 'My enemies have the press. I have television.'

In the case of the communist societies, their very totalitarian nature meant that there was no possibility of such stable oppositional forces emerging and sustaining themselves over long periods of time. The plurality of voices that existed in those societies towards the end was a symptom of their decline and decay rather than a feature of their structure. There was, in principle, no independent organisation of economic or political power that could sustain such oppositional media. In practice, it is true that organisations like the Catholic Church in Poland were able to sustain legally sanctioned media, but these were the result of a compromise by the regime, which was forced to admit the failure and limitations of its totalitarian programme.

In the case of the mass media, then, the concept of totalitarianism, particularly as modified to exclude an overemphasis on the role of the individual leader, arbitrary rule and systematic terror, and a stress upon the concentration of power in the hands of a political élite, is useful in that it enables us to distinguish clearly between the kinds of media systems operating in communism and those present in other kinds of societies. We need to be clear, however, that these differences are differences in the extent of the control of the political élite over the mass media. Communist societies were not unique in that they repressed oppositional media. They were not unique in that they attempted to control the output of broadcasting. Such efforts can exist even in bourgeois democracies. What was unique was that the élites attempted to extend systematic control over all areas of the mass media.

As the systems declined and decayed, so their ability to exert this control weakened. The reality of their symbolic landscape became, to a greater or lesser degree, more pluralistic. It did not, however, become any more democratic. While the communist media systems changed considerably, particularly in some of the countries of the western edge of the communist bloc, they remained communist media systems in which power resided in the hands of the *nomenklatura* alone.

In reaching such a conclusion, however, it is important to bear in mind two important qualifications. The first is that the three examples of ways in which the communist media adapted to the decline of their system were not unique to such systems. The struggle between national broadcasting systems and the world market is a well-researched phenomenon. The degree of closure achieved by Czechoslovakia, the most unreformed of our examples, was very far from exceptional by world standards. Japanese Television (NHK), for example, almost certainly still has a far higher proportion of internally generated programming than did Czechoslovak Television (CST) in the 1980s. Indeed, one might argue that the figures for total imports even in this case are directly comparable with those for British terrestrial broadcasting and much higher than for the US networks. So, too, with advertising. Although the level, and nature, of the advertising carried on these systems before 1989 was small, its most striking feature was its very existence. It represented a departure in principle from the idea of a symbolically driven broadcasting service. The notion that it is the programming that comes first in a broadcaster is very far from extinct. In the 1980s it proved impossible to introduce advertising into the BBC, for example. The communist media were engaged with a similar problem, but they found a more commercial solution than did the government of Margaret Thatcher. Third, the idea of using the power of the state to exclude undesirable symbolic materials was hardly the special province of the communist states. In fact, they proved less able in the 1980s to exclude matter they might have found offensive than did some Western governments.

The British government, during the 1990s, has four times acted to close down satellite channels that were beamed into the UK from foreign countries. Admittedly, this action involved pornography rather than political information, but the principle is similar. In none of these cases, then, were the situations that the broadcasters confronted and the changes that took place in the media systems of the Visegrad countries wildly out of step with more general tendencies in the industry.

The fourth point to note, however, is that these problems and changes, however familiar in their details, took place within systems that were structured differently to their Western cousins. While we might say that the broadcasting organisations of the communist countries came in some ways to resemble our own rather more closely, they remained radically distinct. The strongest that can be said of these changes is that they can be seen as 'pre-adaptations', strictly speaking evolutionary assets created for one function in one environment that find a different function in another. They are not evidence of 'convergence'.

We may summarise the distinction that we wish to make by saying that the material pressures that confronted the broadcasters of the communist world during the 1980s were ones that forced them to make considerable changes to their systems. They accommodated to political changes, to popular discontent, to official cynicism, and to plain old penury, with a considerable degree of adaptability. What, however, remained completely off the agenda, and for which there is no evidence whatsoever that it even began to take place, was any change of the system. Even MTV, liberal, almost pluralistic, in its programming, habituated to advertising and competing with equanimity with foreign signals, remained essentially a communist broadcaster. The other broadcasters of the region fitted that model even more exactly. There was no internal logic whereby the system could reform itself into something different and better.

4

Negotiated Revolutions

In this chapter, I first consider the question of whether the changes that took place in Central and Eastern Europe in 1989 and the immediately succeeding period may properly be called 'revolutions'. I demonstrate that there is no serious theoretical obstacle to using that term, provided it is defined with sufficient clarity. The question of whether the events themselves did actually display the kinds of characteristics that would warrant use of the term is thus an empirical one.

I then review the four main theoretical accounts of 1989, ranging from those that stress the total, complete and epochal character of the changes through to those that find some difficulty in considering the events as sufficiently thoroughgoing as to warrant the use of the term. Although most of these grand theories are rather remote from concrete claims about the nature of the mass media, I attempt to extrapolate from their general claims to concrete predictions about the nature of the transition in the mass media.

The evidence as to the changes in television and in the press is then considered. While these appear at first sight to offer support to radically different theoretical accounts, I argue that in fact they can be seen as constituting evidence for a particular kind of continuity. In this context, the two cases, the GDR and Czechoslovakia, in which the negotiated transfer of power broke down, are seen as particularly important, if brief, interludes in what was otherwise a revolution in which the masses were at best supporting players whose role was to applaud and confirm the actions and decisions taken by others on their behalf.

In the immediate aftermath of the events of 1989, it was widely agreed that what the world had witnessed was a series of revolutionary changes. As one observer put it: 'Everyone in the West was clear . . . concerning the events of 1989 in Central and Eastern Europe . . . there has been a revolution (or revolutions)' (Kumar, 1992: 309). The titles of the host of books and articles on the subject also bear eloquent testimony to the commonplace nature of this conception. Amongst others, we find: *Reflections on the Revolution in Europe* (Dahrendorf, 1990); 'Revolution in Eastern Europe – revolution in the West?' (Kux, 1991); *After the Revolutions: East–West Trade and Technology Transfer in the 1990's* (Bertsch et al., 1991); and so on. Almost overnight, an old and established order, which had survived all sorts of historical shocks, including war and armed revolt, was destroyed and replaced with a new and different one. Events of this pace and magnitude must, it seemed, have been revolutions in the proper sense of the term. As one journalist put it:

> Nobody hesitated to call what happened in Romania a revolution. After all, it really looked like one: angry crowds in the street, tanks, government buildings in flames, the dictator put up against a wall and shot. (Ash, 1990: 20)

Subsequently, doubts have come to be expressed on this judgement. Some of the objections are no doubt based on the observation that the term 'revolution' is dripping with all sorts of high modern, indeed Marxist, connotations. To admit that it was revolution that brought down the dreadful tyrannies of Stalinism would be to give credence to the idea that the world can be improved by this kind of action.

Other commentators have more substantial reasons. The processes themselves were in fact very varied, ranging from bloody street fighting in Romania to comfortable negotiations in Poland and Hungary. The outcomes appear to have differed widely: the old parties, in different camouflage, continued in power in Bulgaria and Serbia; new parties, publicly aligned with the West European right, took power in the Czech Republic and Poland. In some countries, most notably Poland and Hungary, the second round of democratic elections led to the return of the successors to the old communist parties to power, albeit in a new, social democratic, form (Coppieters and Waller, 1994; Mahr and Nagle, 1995). The pace of change, in the media as much as in the wider society, was very uneven in different countries. It seemed to make little sense to lump all of these different events and processes together into one single term.

Some observers, looking at the scope and extent of change, particularly in the Balkans and much of the former USSR, were persuaded that the most striking feature of the new societies was the degree of continuity with the past. Since so many of the structures and personnel were identical with those of the communist regimes, it was tempting to conclude that there had been no substantive change at all. To speak of a revolution was ridiculously to overstate the scope and importance of the events.

In the case of the mass media, if one restricts one's view to broadcasting, it can be argued that the changes in some countries were relatively small. As we have seen, there had already been quite extensive changes to television in some of the countries of Central and Eastern Europe which, it can be argued, rendered them similar to some forms of broadcasting existing in the West. Perhaps the changes subsequent on 1989 simply represented a continuation and acceleration of these reform tendencies that were already present under communism. If this were the case, then clearly there would be no grounds for claiming that anything like a revolution had taken place.

Let us take a single example. It is often argued that the mass media of the communist epoch were characterised by personnel policies that privileged political loyalty above professional competence. Since, as we shall see below, in the case of Hungary during the 'media wars', there were quite large-scale sackings of journalists purely on the grounds that they did not follow the line laid down by the post-communist government, then it would be possible to argue that nothing fundamental had changed in the running of broadcasting. Indeed, since the scale of the purges exceeded anything in the recent past, it might seem to be the case that there had been a reversion to an earlier model of political control rather than some real improvement.

The question of whether the end of communism was actually consummated by events that we may term revolutions can thus be seriously challenged. If we look in more detail at the case against regarding the events of 1989 as revolutions, we find that there are, in fact, two quite different positions being argued. The argument that the detailed evidence suggests that the degree of continuity in these countries was so great as to render the use of the term 'revolution' inappropriate is one thing. It is concerned with measuring the extent of the changes issuing from a set of events and judging that they were so small as to render the events themselves of minor importance. There is, however, another argument that claims that there were central features of the events themselves that renders the use of this term quite wrong. This is an argument about the nature of the events themselves, and involves a theoretical rather than an empirical discussion. In this chapter, I first review what is at stake in the term 'revolution' and discuss whether it is appropriate to apply it to the end of communism. This is the theoretical argument. I further ask what was the nature and character of these events, particularly with regard to changes in the nature of the media systems. This is much more of an empirical argument, although it leads directly to the consideration of theoretical questions concerning the nature and character of the events themselves. Even if the events of 1989 are found to constitute a revolution, it still remains an open question as to what kind of revolution they actually were.

What is a revolution?

The term 'revolution' is so widely used as to be notoriously an almost meaningless banality. There is an information revolution. There are revolutionary new washing powders. The implications of some new idea will revolutionise our thinking. The list could be extended endlessly. It is therefore worthwhile asking whether the term means anything useful any more. Certainly, since it is applied to such a wide range of events, processes, ideas and products, any attempt to use the term would need to be rather precise about the exact sense intended in a particular context.

I want to argue here that the term remains a useful one for the study of the way in which human societies change, although it is essential that in so using it certain common assumptions about the nature of revolutions are discarded, since they obscure the important and substantial point of employing the term. At the most general level, many definitions stress that the primary characteristic of a revolution is that 'change' is 'fundamental' and 'sudden', and that it is qualitatively distinct from other processes in that it is 'an acceleration of previously existing rates of change' (Kumar, 1971: 10). Galtung's definition seems to summarise this issue very clearly: 'A revolution is a fundamental change of social structure brought about in a short period of time' (Galtung, 1974: 9).

This definition is intentionally broad, and encompasses many different kinds of processes. If we restrict ourselves to the study of change in human societies, one valuable distinction that can be made is that between systemic transformation and the aggregative change to a continuing system. Systemic transformation involves an alteration to the basic ways in which a particular aspect of social life is organised. Aggregative change implies that the balance of elements within a given structure of social organisation alters. Following a well-established distinction in politics, the former of these kinds of change is what I understand as a revolution, the latter what I understand as reform.

Even if one accepts the general utility of the term 'revolution', it might still be the case that it is, more or less a priori, inappropriate for the analysis of the events of 1989. In the study, or rather reporting, of the changes in Central and Eastern Europe there has been an attempt to coin the hybrid term 'refolution' to describe a process that is alleged to share elements of both polarities. Ash, for example, followed the passage cited above with precisely such a qualification:

> It is, however, a serious question whether what happened in Poland, Hungary, Bulgaria or even Czechoslovakia and East Germany, actually qualified for anything but a very loose usage of the term 'revolution'. This doubt was expressed by several intellectuals in the countries concerned. Should popular movements which, however spontaneous, massive and effective, were almost entirely non-violent, really be described by a word so closely associated with violence? Yet the change of government, no, the change of life, in all these other countries was scarcely less profound than in Romania. By a mixture of popular protest and élite negotiation, prisoners became prime ministers and prime ministers became prisoners.
>
> This sudden and sweeping end to an *ancien régime*, and the fact that it occurred in all the countries of Eastern Europe within the space of a few months, may justify the use of the word 'revolution'. . . . (Ash, 1990: 20)

For Ash, it seemed that the character of the events, and in particular their non-violent nature, cast very considerable doubt over the validity of the general term 'revolution', while the depth and extent of the changes rendered the term 'reform' quite inadequate to describe what had happened. He therefore coined the term 'refolution'.

This seems to me a particularly unsatisfactory evasion of the central issue at stake. No revolution supposes a complete, total and sudden transformation. All involve the setting in train of a process of cumulative change. Events like the Russian Revolution did not lead to an immediate and total transformation of society. The seizure of power did not immediately result in peace, nor did the landlords disappear, nor hunger vanish. Certainly, no new socialist Utopia emerged one November morning in 1917. Such a judgement is quite independent of one's assessment of the nature and importance of those events. One can construct the outcomes quite differently while retaining the same intellectual point. If one accepts the conventional argument that Stalin, The Plan and the Terror were the natural and inevitable outcome of 1917, they still lay more than a decade in the future. They were distinctly not born the instant the cruiser *Aurora* opened fire. Similarly, no reform, by definition, leaves the system that it alters in the exact same state. The very use of the term implies some change to the existing order. The British Labour government of 1945 was determinedly not revolutionary – indeed, in many parts of the world it was actively counter-revolutionary – but it did achieve some very important, and quite long-lasting, changes to the ways in which people in this country lived. The opposition between 'reform' and 'revolution' is not one between change and stasis. The fundamental difference is that reform takes place within a framework constituted by a revolution. It is revolutions that set and establish those frameworks (Luxemburg, 1970: 77). On those grounds, the events of 1989 may certainly be considered as revolutions.

The line of reasoning behind the assumption that 1989 did not change the framework is based on a shallow objection concerned with the character of the events themselves. Because these differed one from another, and not all of them were marked by blood in the streets, then they could not all have been examples of 'revolution'. In that respect, the hesitation about 1989 is part of the more general confusion about the nature of revolutions.

The weakest and most trivial argument against the use of the term 'revolution' in this context is to assert that most of these events could not have been revolutions since they were not marked by the use of political violence. The underlying mistake here, frequently repeated in more general theoretical studies, is to imagine that violence is both a distinctive and a necessary aspect of any revolutionary change (Calvert, 1990: 15). There are two flaws with this argument. The first is a negative one. Violence saturates political life in the modern world. Wars, insurgencies, civil disturbances, revolutions and counter-revolutions are the commonplace of news reports. Parties and movements of almost all political persuasions use violence in attempts to achieve their objectives. Violence in the pursuit of political ends cannot therefore be considered as specific to revolutions. The most strongly one could state the case in the light of this evident fact is that it might be the case that all revolutions use violence, but the use of violence is not a peculiar and distinguishing characteristic of revolutions.

The second flaw is a positive one, and undermines even that attempted defence of the position. There are numerous examples of rapid and complete change, which it is difficult not to consider as revolutions, that involved no violence whatsoever. A relatively recent example from Western Europe was the 1974 fall of the long-established fascist regime in Portugal. This was achieved overnight by a military coup that involved no reported violence at all. The political structure inherited from the days of Salazar was swept away, a colonial empire was liquidated, major social upheavals followed, and eventually a stable bourgeois democracy was established. Admittedly, if one considers the process as a whole, there was indeed some violence. Internally, there were two small risings by the right and a final confrontation between the social democrats and the far left. The liquidation of the colonial empire also eventually involved very much more substantial violence, particularly as a result of US and South African intervention in Angola, and the Indonesian occupation of East Timor. The actual transfer of power itself, however, was almost entirely peaceful. The serious violence associated with the process in the long term was the direct result of the actions of established state machines, rather than insurgents. It would be foolish to deny that these massive political and social changes, spread around the world, did not constitute a revolution. If that is the case, then the evidence demonstrates that revolution is not necessarily linked to violence. The strongest defensible case is that revolutionary changes, like many other political phenomena, frequently involve violence. It follows logically from this that the absence of violence does not automatically disqualify a particular change from being considered a revolution. There are therefore no grounds for considering the relatively peaceful nature of the many of the transformations of 1989 as an obstacle to them being revolutions.

In the concrete case under consideration, the equation of revolution with violence leads to absurd conclusions. Social and political change resulting from substantially internal political factors in the former communist world has probably progressed furthest in the Czech part of what was, in 1989, Czechoslovakia. The 'velvet revolution' in Prague was, famously, conducted without any violence. There were mass demonstrations and strikes, and it was early on mistakenly alleged that the secret police had murdered a protesting student. The old regime, however, was quite unable to find the political will to use the considerable repressive forces at its disposal to crush its opponents. On their part, whatever their views on the place of violence in social change, the opposition found that the collapse of the old regime meant that they had no need to confront the issue. The most far-reaching of the outcomes of 1989 was not the result of violence.

On the other hand, there can be no doubt that change in Romania has been extremely slow to come, and very limited in extent, yet the overthrow of the Ceauşescu regime was accompanied by street fighting, large-scale killings, the storming of public buildings, and the more or less public execution of the former tyrant. The change of regime had all of the drama and horror that are commonly imagined to be essential to revolutionary change. The outcomes of all of this have been much more modest than in the most peaceful case.

If one believed that the presence or absence of violence was the determining factor in deciding whether an event was a revolution, then one would be forced to conclude Romania had experienced such an event and that Czechoslovakia had not. It would therefore follow that a revolution had achieved relatively little in the way of change, but that whatever it was that took place in Czechoslovakia had achieved far more. Unless one holds as an article of faith that revolutions change nothing, this is clearly a ridiculous position and must be rejected.

A more intellectually substantial objection to the claim that these events constituted revolutions is that the pace and extent of change, even in the most advanced cases, has been so slow as to render the concept of revolution meaningless. It is certainly true that there have been significant continuities between the last years of the communist regimes and the first years of the new order, and these are quite clear in television. The theoretical issue at stake here is the level at which change has taken place.

In terms of the distribution of public power in society, we can, at least analytically, distinguish two different levels at which it is organised – the narrowly political and the more diversely social, of which economic power is one major factor. As we concluded in our discussion of totalitarianism, it was a distinctive feature of communist societies that these two aspects of power were very closely connected. Indeed, in principle, they were fused. There can be no doubt that the political system in all of the former communist countries, even those like Serbia, where the Communist Party and its immediate successors have maintained an unchallenged grip on the state apparatus throughout the period of change, has undergone a radical transformation. Put very simply, the matter is one of transition from a dictatorial to an electoral system. In the old regimes the leadership of the communist parties had an effective monopoly of political power that they exercised independently of even formal popular sanction. In the new order, the holders of political power are everywhere subject to election and re-election. This process took place extremely rapidly and has fundamentally altered the nature and scope of political life.

It therefore seems sensible to retain the notion that, whatever other continuities we detect in these societies, they all experienced what we may term revolutions. The fact that these changes have been most immediately marked at the level of the political life of the countries in question, and that we can find substantial continuities in other areas of social power, might lead us to conclude that these were limited revolutions. It might, for example, prove valuable to pursue the distinction, made famously by Trotsky, between the relatively narrow political revolution and the broader social revolution that transforms the whole of social relations in a country. One of the major questions to be explored below is precisely the extent and limits of the revolutions that did take place in the media.

The final objection to use of the term revolution is a relatively technical one concerning the question of agency. It is conventionally thought that revolutions are 'made' by a particular class, social group or political party, which may be termed the 'agent' of revolution. It is often claimed that it is difficult to identify such a force in the case of Central Europe. Given that the outcome of the revolutions is likely to be the institution of fully developed market economies throughout the region, it must be the case that a class of capitalists will be the ultimate beneficiaries of the process. These did not exist to any significant extent prior to 1989. We therefore seem to have had a revolution in which the putative beneficiary was absent, and the actual agents of change were acting in such a way as to ensure their own subordination. The problem of 'reforming the economy [entails] the creation of an entirely new class of entrepreneurs and owners' (Offe, 1991: 868–9). The masses who made the revolution will not reap a reward for their efforts (Bauman, 1992b: 170). The answer to this problem seems to lie in the fact that the concept of agency, as used in this context, conceals within itself three distinct elements: the group that leads a revolution; the group that makes up the base of support for a revolution; and the group that benefits from the outcome of the revolution. In the classical Marxist theory of the socialist revolution, which is where the idea of 'agency' is most fully developed and which clearly influenced the thinking of both the writers cited above, these three groups were considered to be identically represented by the proletariat. There seems no compelling theoretical reason for generalising this aspect of a particular social class in what Marxist theory itself considers to be a unique kind of revolution. In the case of Central Europe, we might identify the largely intellectual groups of dissidents as those who led the revolution, the bulk of the population, particularly the urban working class, as the base of support for the revolution, and that section of the *nomenklatura* that has managed to adapt to the new conditions as the group that has benefited most directly from the revolution. In this sense, the revolutions were much more like the great French Revolution, in which the role of the bourgeoisie as such was overlaid by the actions of peasants, plebeian radicals and intellectuals, than the proletarian revolutions envisaged by Marx.

All of the above suggests that it might be entirely reasonable to call the events of 1989 'revolutions', since they are not disqualified in advance by the absence of violence, the extent of the continuities, or the lack of apparent agent from being thus categorised. The question of whether they actually were revolutions, and if so what kinds of revolutions, is an empirical one. In order to assign them to that category we need to look in detail at the kinds of changes that were involved, and the elements in society that were affected by them. If we can show that these changes were indeed systemic rather than cumulative, we would be justified in using the term. In the case of the media, we need to investigate the actual processes of change in order to reach a conclusion. In discussing whether the events of 1989 were properly to be called revolutions, we therefore have to consider how far they constituted changes *of* the system rather than simply changes *to* the system.

Four theories of 1989

While there is no a priori reason why we should not use the term revolution when discussing the end of communism, to say that an event has been a 'revolution' does not close the question of its nature and character. Unless we suppose that society is a single unitary whole, as in the famous caricature of the 'expressive totality' attributed to some Marxist writers, which can only change completely and all at once, then it is perfectly possible to have different kinds of revolution. Although the communist societies had, we have argued, a 'totalitarian' character, and were thus much more highly unified than is the case in the Western bourgeois democracies with which we are more familiar, it might still be the case that what we are discussing are systemic changes, which only affected some parts of society, rather than immediately transforming the whole.

One influential review of the end of communism distinguishes two major positions, defined by their relative assessment of the implications of 1989 for the 'debate' between Marxism and liberalism (Held, 1992: 20–8). Such a juxtaposition, however pedagogically useful, is, in this instance, even more contrived intellectually than is usually the case. As we shall see, it is perfectly possible to find both self-professed 'Marxists' and self-professed 'liberals' holding quite different positions on this issue.

A much better way of starting to think about the questions involved is to begin by observing the two general trends in analyses of the changes. The first of these tends to stress the depth of the changes brought about by 1989. These are theories of discontinuity, and they are therefore in no doubt as to the empirically revolutionary nature of the events in question. The other major grouping consists of those writers for whom the most striking feature of the changes is the degree of continuity between the systems existing before and after 1989. For them, the revolutionary nature of the events is at best partial and at worst non-existent.

We can go beyond this simple polarity and identify four kinds of theories about 1989, differentiated by their estimation of the nature and extent of the changes brought about in the fall of communism. The first of these, which we may term the 'total transformation' school, is in no doubt about either the revolutionary nature of the events or the fundamental discontinuity between the two systems. The second school, which we may term the 'social (counter-) revolution' school, argues that while there may be strong continuities in some areas, there has indeed been a revolution at the level of economic organisation that has been of a fundamental nature. The third school, which we may term the 'political revolution' school, argues that the change is to be identified primarily at the level of the organisation of political life, and that in other areas there remain very substantial elements of continuity. The fourth school, which we may term the 'what revolution?' school, argues that, in all essential areas, there has been a striking degree of continuity between the systems existing before and after 1989, and that it is therefore illusory to speak of there having been any change sufficiently substantial as to constitute a revolution.

Within each of these, there are important differences of emphasis and interpretation, but they remain sufficiently distinguishable to warrant treatment as distinct groupings. None of the different schools belongs exclusively to one or other political interpretation of communism, although it is possible to discern clear 'right' and 'left' preponderances, at least in the first two versions. We will review the main theoretical propositions advanced by all four schools. Unfortunately, we are here dealing with a level of social theory for which concrete evidence is of secondary importance, and the structures of the mass media frequently irrelevant. I have therefore attempted to extend what seem to me to be the logical consequences of each theoretical position to formulate propositions about the nature of the events and their outcomes, and then to concretise these into assessments of the likely changes to the media, and to broadcasting in particular.

Total transformation

The 'total transformation' thesis about 1989 is certainly very well represented
in the literature. The dominant view in the West is that the revolutions
involved profound changes at all levels of society from the spiritual to the economic. This is the view articulated most famously by Fukuyama (Fukuyama,
1992). It is, however, accepted even by many of his sharper critics, like
Dahrendorf (Dahrendorf, 1990). According to this line of thinking, the events
constituted both political and social revolutions. This is also the dominant
popular account present in the press, and we may almost call it the official
version of the story. It is shared by those former admirers of Stalinism like
Eric Hobsbawm, who see in the collapse of communism the end of any possibility for human progress.

In this version, the old order was entirely communist, indeed totalitarian.
The economy was entirely directed by the arbitrary planning decisions of the
central apparatus. Political power was concentrated exclusively in the hands
of the Communist Party. Social life was regimented by the 'mass organisations' constructed and controlled by the party. A dreary equality of misery
and uniformity of life was imposed upon a cowed population. There has
been both a political and social transformation in which the ruling order
was swept away in its entirety and replaced by a new order. This new order is
essentially Western-style, liberal, democratic capitalism. Ernst Kux, writing a
leading article in the official US journal *Problems of Communism*, summed up
the perspective thus:

> Democracy with a separation and control of powers replaces the 'dictatorship of
> the proletariat'; the monopoly of power of the party can no longer withstand the
> plurality of interests. The socialist planned economy, which is actually nothing
> other than control of production and consumption by the party, is yielding to the
> free market economy. This is the historic success of the revolution in Eastern
> Europe. (Kux, 1991: 2)

This proclamation of victory had a certain irony. So complete has the change
been, so successfully has the US version of the good life triumphed over all of
its historic opponents, that the eager intellectual warriors who had fought so
well for the West found themselves in that worst of capitalist limbos: they
were now surplus to requirements and faced redundancy.

The majority of the proponents of this view are convinced that this change
has been wholly positive, in that they believe that there is an automatic and
necessary connection between the market economy and political democracy.
As one writer, after reviewing the case for an authoritarian political solution,
concluded:

> Democracy, rather than being a luxury that the Eastern European countries can
> hardly afford in their economic transformations, is perhaps the single most impor-
> tant pre-condition for successful economic reform. (Pickel, 1993: 160)

This line of thought prefers to ignore the very considerable historical evidence
of the happy co-existence between a market economy and the most blood-
stained forms of dictatorship. The proponents of this view share the belief

that capitalism in Eastern Europe will follow the best features of the US model rather than the worst features of, say, Chile.

The reasons advanced for the historic collapse of communism have a considerable variety. According to Fukuyama, basing himself on what seems to me to be a very tendentious reading of the famous 'master and slave' passage from *The Phenomenology of Mind*, the fall of communism arises from the essential human struggle for 'recognition', which can be most fully realised only in the conditions of individualism prevailing in a capitalist democracy. For others, more impressed by von Mises's critique of socialism, the failure of communism was due to the inferiority of The Plan to the price mechanism in allocating scarce productive resources effectively. What the advocates of these views all seem to share is a retrospective confidence in the inevitability of the downfall of communism.

One of the major unresolved issues within this school of thought, particularly evident in differences between Eastern and Western proponents, is the extent to which they believe the process of transformation to have been completed. For Fukuyama, in his self-proclaimed philosophical idealist mode, the realisation of the promises of 1989 may be somewhat delayed, but the essential spiritual revolution has already been so well accomplished that 'we cannot picture a world that is *essentially* different from the present one, and at the same time better' (Fukuyama, 1992: 46). Eastern European proponents of this view like Kornai and Klaus, who tend to cite Hayek rather than Hegel as their intellectual reference point and are thus much more 'materialistic', take a view that the process is still radically incomplete and that it requires political action in order to accomplish the economic and cultural tasks of the revolution (Klaus, 1991: Kornai, 1990).

Social (counter-) revolution

Less sweeping is the 'social (counter-) revolution' view. This was theorised by the late Ralph Miliband, and by a number of people traditionally holding a range of independent and critical positions towards 'actually existing socialism'. It is possible to find this position lurking behind many of the 'left' criticisms of the aftermath, for example those collected by the *New Left Review* (Blackburn, 1991). In this version, the old economy was essentially socialist, but political power was held by a bureaucratic caste. The horrors of the old order, for which the position makes no apology, were the product of this alien encrustation upon an essentially healthy body. In its classical formulation, this caste was 'the organ of the world bourgeoisie' in communist societies, but in other accounts it was simply a 'deformation'. The (counter-) revolution is in the process of sweeping away the old socialist economy and transforming the bureaucratic caste into a true capitalist class. As one writer, working within categories recognisably derived from orthodox Trotskyism, put it:

> The ideological about-face in 1989 was not a radical departure for the nomenklatura. It could afford to abandon a Marxism it always scoffed [*sic*]. What drives

it is not ideology but opportunism. The main present concern of the bureaucrats is to preserve their domestic political position and to receive the protection of international capitalism against the people they have been persecuting . . . a new business class is emerging on their side. (Meillassoux, 1993: 34)

Although various other versions of the precise mechanisms of the counter-revolution are possible, this school of thought is usually concerned to stress that there has indeed been a sharp discontinuity at the level of the economic structure. In this version there has been a social but not a political revolution.

It is often also the case that the outcomes of the revolution are not seen as uniformly beneficial to the mass of the population. As Miliband put it, the old order may have suffered from a tyrannous political form, but it issued from genuine popular sentiments and embodied real social gains:

> What is at issue here is nothing less than the complete undoing of the social revolutions which occurred in these countries after World War II. That such social revolutions did occur may be obscured by the fact that most of them, in Eastern and Central Europe, were imposed from above, indeed from the outside, and that the regimes issued from them turned out as they did; but this does not negate the immense, revolutionary changes, good or bad, which they all experienced . . .
>
> For a short couple of years after 1945, and before the imposition of the Communist monopoly of power, there was hope, nurtured in the terrible years of war, that there might be built a democratic and egalitarian order . . . [but] . . . it was quickly snuffed out by the onset of the Cold War and the imposition in all countries of the Soviet sphere of influence of the Stalinist model of political rule and economic organisation, with the Communist monopoly of power and the stifling of all dissent, and the imposition of the command economy over all aspects of economic life. (Miliband, 1991: 376–7)

The change in the political order has provoked a wave of 'capitalisation', in which a leading role will be played by members of the *nomenklatura*, who are in the process of transforming themselves from bureaucratic parasites to private capitalists. This involves a transition from socialist to capitalist property forms and production relations, and, given the nature of capitalist social relations and the extremely unfavourable social and economic circumstances in which this transformation is taking place, Miliband is extremely pessimistic about the prospects for the long-term health even of the formal gains of democratisation:

> The revolutions of 1989 were largely fought in the name of freedom and democracy; and enormous efforts have been made by a multitude of official and unofficial sources in the West to persuade ex-Communist countries that the essential, indispensable condition of freedom and democracy is free enterprise and the market, in other words, capitalism. In fact, a capitalist restoration is much more likely to produce conditions where free enterprise does indeed flourish, but where freedom and democracy would be severely curtailed or even abrogated altogether. (Miliband, 1991: 385)

Although probably most attractive to those few Western leftists who wish to hang on to some positive view of the old order, this position is not unknown in the former communist countries, either amongst the voting masses or amongst intellectuals (Bihari, 1991; Kowalik, 1991). There are also some

Western non-leftists who, while welcoming the overthrow of the communist order, question whether the task of constructing a capitalist economy in conditions of severe social crisis can best be achieved by a democratic political model:

> Paradoxically, democratic states are not necessarily the best states for a transition phase, as the case of Chile demonstrates. To manage social conflict, one needs both a democratic and a strong state. Our logic leads us back again to the restructuring of the state to make it stronger, for the state is the key to a successful transition. (Haye and Shi, 1993: 489)

Authors in this tradition are much more willing than those in the first group to face up to the issue raised by 'transitology' (Bunce, 1995; Schmitter and Karl, 1994; Terry, 1993). At stake in this hotly debated matter is the extent to which it is possible to build up a general body of comparative knowledge about the transition to a democracy, and to a market economy. If such a procedure is possible, then obviously the repressed issues of the historical relationships between capitalism and dictatorships enters the debate, and once one admits such evidence then the simple belief that the transition from communism is necessarily and eternally a democratic one becomes rather more problematic:

> Recent research on the politics of economic reform suggests a need to insulate key economic management functions from direct political pressures and at the same time to improve the channels for ongoing consultation between the government and concerned interest groups on other aspects of economic policy and reform. But what aspects of economic policy can appropriately be insulated in a democracy? (Nelson, 1993: 460)

While usually recoiling from directly recommending a dictatorial solution, writers from this perspective clearly see the task of economic restructuring as more important than political forms. For them, the political outcomes of 1989 are contingent; the central question is the social transformation.

Other writers are sceptical about the democratic promise of the transformation because of the specific features of post-communist societies. George Schöpflin argues that, while the economic changes that are underway in Eastern and Central Europe are part of an irreversible progress to market capitalism, the nature of the inherited political culture is much more problematic. Not only did communism provide a long apprenticeship in anti-democratic practices, it also failed to complete the modernisation of the economy. There remain large strata, particularly in the countryside, who are socially resistant to the conditions of modernity and to the democratic practices that follow from this (Schöpflin, 1993). The likely outcome of these forces is a specific kind of political and social formation called 'post-communism':

> The essence of post-communism . . . is that it now constitutes a *sui generis* system which is marked by some democratic practices, with stronger or weaker commitments to pluralism, so that both political and economic competition have become a reality. At the same time, anti-democratic ideas and practices are also current and have some roots in society as well as legitimative discourses to back them up. These latter, when coupled with the structural obstacles to democracy, imply that the

road to the construction of genuine democracy will take a fair period of time.
(Schöpflin, 1995: 63–4)

While the future is therefore likely to be capitalist, the political forms by
which that is accompanied are much less predictable.

For most of the leftist representatives of this school of thought, the basic
reason for the collapse of the communist system was the incompatibility
between its rational socialist economic basis and the distortions imposed
upon it by the bureaucracy. As the clearest theorist of this analysis of communism, the late Ernest Mandel, put it when writing about the USSR:

> Only the material interests of the bureaucracy became the motor for fulfilling the
> plan. Thereby, the power and the privileges of the bureaucracy as opposed to those
> of the mass of both the workers and the peasants, became rigidly institutionalised
> through the economic system and society as a whole. Stalin's total political control
> at the top crowned a complex system of levers and incentives to ensure a minimum
> of operability of the planned economy which was thereby, from the start, a form of
> planning managed by the bureaucracy in the interests of the bureaucracy. (Mandel,
> 1991: 206–7)

According to this position, the essential feature of the revolutions of 1989 lay
in the new impetus they gave to economic organisation. Political changes, if
any, were entirely secondary: the case of China would appear to indicate that
they were quite unnecessary, at least in the short term. The new order will be
marked by the privatisation of the means of production and the creation of a
new and recognisably capitalist system with a new and recognisably capitalist ruling class.

Political revolution

Elements of continuity are much more evident in the final two positions. The
view that there was indeed a revolution, but that the changes were far from
fundamental, is best theorised by the philosopher Alex Callinicos, identified
by David Held as: 'one of the most vigorous defenders of classical Marxism
today' (Held, 1992: 25). In this version, the old order was essentially capitalist, albeit 'state-capitalist'. Both economic and political power was held
collectively by a bureaucratic capitalist class, roughly identical with the
nomenklatura (Cliff, 1974). The revolutions constituted changes in the political order, but at the social level there is a recomposition of the capitalist class
from a collective to an individualised form:

> The social meaning of the East European revolutions was obscured by their most
> visible aspect, the collapse of the Stalinist one-party states. But an economically
> dominant class must be distinguished from the specific political form through
> which it both secures its own cohesion and establishes its rule over society. . . . The
> relationship between ruling class and political regime had been especially intimate
> under Stalinism – the very name often given that class referred to the *nomenklatura*
> system through which the party leadership made appointments to key positions.
> Nevertheless, the one-party state provided the political framework through which
> the dominant class of bureaucrats, managers, generals, and secret policemen exer-
> cised their social power. . . . The substantial continuity both in the core apparatuses
> of state power and in the personnel of the ruling class itself indicates the limits of

the political upheavals in Eastern Europe. They represented a change in political regime rather than in social system. (Callinicos, 1991: 57–8)

In this version there has been a political, but not a social, revolution. While 'democracy' is evidently not an integral feature of capitalist societies, the importance of the shift to democratisation in these specific cases was that it was the sole political form that could allow the recomposition of the ruling class to take place. It is not possible to speak of a social revolution from this perspective, since the actual social relations of production have in no fundamental way been transformed, even in those industries that have been privatised, and the central institutions of the state like the army remain more or less intact (Hardy and Rainnie, 1996; Haynes, 1996). Much more fundamental for this account is that the fusion between political and economic has been broken. Under certain conditions, that can lead to recognisably democratic forms, since this kind of political order allows different strategies to be debated and adopted at a minimum social cost. However, in situations of extreme social tension, these forms are not essential to the new order: since there are now a plurality of interests, there will necessarily be a plurality of interest groups that can articulate different strategies. What is certainly the case, however, is that the mechanism for totalitarian rule no longer exists in these countries. That is not to say that it could not be rebuilt, perhaps in a radically different form, but that, while it is absent, overt political struggle of a kind not present in totalitarian countries will be possible. No matter how undemocratic, indeed dictatorial, the post-communist countries might become, they will not have the same political dynamics as in the past.

What revolution?

The final position argues that the collapse of the communist regimes, although visibly dramatic, did not in the end constitute any serious transfer of political or social power, and thus cannot really be termed a 'revolution'. The proponents of this position, which we may term 'what revolution?', argue essentially that the power structure remains identical in substance despite the appearance of change. Writers in this vein are prone to consider the differences between different forms of class rule, for example between bourgeois democracy and totalitarianism, as being relatively minor questions.

The most important version of this position argues that the main characteristic of the transformation is that popular voices were excluded or marginalised. The change was one in which the élite recomposed itself without experiencing any serious challenge to either its political or economic power. A version of this thesis is advanced by Norman Petras:

Eastern Europe did not experience a revolution insofar as the popular mobilisation was never institutionalised, but circumvented. What occurred was a circulation of élites and, in a few cases, not a great deal of circulation (at least not from the bottom to the top). Power was not transferred downwards but laterally – from the party élite to the managers, intellectuals, property owners, investors. . . . Élite substitutionism involved the replacement of a collectivist bureaucratic élite linked to the East by a privatising intellectual élite dependent on the West. (Petras, 1993: 21)

Here, the lack of popular mobilisation, or the ways in which popular mobil-isation was channelled or controlled, combined with the fact that there was considerable continuity of personnel before and after the events of 1989, are taken as token that there were no revolutions.

In particular, it is argued, the new regimes do not constitute any serious democratic advance on the old order. Both constitute deeply élitist forms of rule, although the modalities through which this rule is exercised might differ widely:

> Instead of a transition from authoritarianism to democracy, it will be argued that what East Europe is undergoing is rather the transformation of a Marxist–Leninist type of authoritarianism into a 'populist' or 'liberal' one; in other words, not a tran-sition from one system to another but a transformation, mutation or metamorphosis, of a system that is basically continuing in its essential features. From this it will be concluded that an essentially authoritarian, collectivist, and cor-poratist system is likely to prevail over the forces of democracy, capitalism, and the market. (Lomax, 1993: 50)

According to this kind of account, the differences between Western capitalism and Eastern state socialism are secondary to their common dependence upon excluding the populace from any serious role in government. This is monop-olised by what, in some versions, is called a 'New Class', a 'managerial bureaucracy', which controls political and social life equally exclusively in both the USA and the communist and former communist countries (Piccone, 1988: 19; *Telos* Staff, 1991: 7).

Changes to society and changes to the media

As remarked above, these different positions are usually argued at a fairly high level of abstraction, and are therefore general statements about the nature of change. One can examine their theoretical standing and internal coherence, but if one wishes to consider them with regard to their ability to explain the evidence, then it is necessary to construct what seem to be the con-crete consequences of each view. This necessarily involves something in the way of extension and speculation, particularly when we come to the question of specific changes to the mass media. In attempting to do this, I have tried to show as clearly as possible the intermediate steps through which I have passed in order to arrive at the concrete propositions that will be interrogated against the evidence. We may briefly outline the conclusions of each theory with regard to general social issues as follows:

1   Total transformation: It follows from this position that, since these trans-formations were so deep and so extensive, research would expect to encounter radical discontinuities of structures and personnel in all aspects of life, particularly in the most important economic, social and political organisations.
2   Social (counter-) revolution: Research would expect to encounter radical discontinuities of economic and social structures, but not of personnel.

While there might be a change at the political level, this would not be an essential element of the revolution and would very likely prove transitory.

3 Political revolution: Research would expect to find continuities of social and economic structures and personnel, but these changes would not necessarily be replicated in the political sphere, whose internal organisation would very much be the product of prevailing circumstances.

4 What revolution?: Research would expect to find very strong evidence of continuity both in the political and economic structures of society. While there might have been some small changes, investigation would show that these were superficial. Some of the changes that are to be observed have a negative consequence for the subordinate groups.

The first two of these positions take the view that the societies of Eastern Europe were radically different from those of Western Europe and North America, and that since 1989 they have started to become much more similar. Consequently, they tend to stress discontinuities between the past and the present. The third position sees the Eastern European societies as having been special variants of a general capitalist model, and thus stresses their continuities. The fourth sees Western European societies, and Eastern European societies both before and after 1989, as essentially variants of the same repressive type of social system, typically some form of bureaucratic new class. In abstract form, we may represent the four positions by means of Table 4.1, in which the key elements of difference in their accounts of the old societies, the nature of the change and the emerging system are placed one against another.

Table 4.1   *Different theories of the nature and extent of the revolutions of 1989*

Theory	Old economic system	Old political system	Nature of revolution	New economic system	New political system
Total transformation (Fukuyama)	Socialist	Totalitarian	Political and social	Capitalist	Democratic
Social (counter-) revolution (Miliband)	Socialist	Totalitarian	Social	Capitalist	Indeterminate/ authoritarian
Political revolution (Callinicos)	(State) capitalist	Totalitarian	Political	(Private) capitalist	Indeterminate/ democratic
What revolution? (Lomax)	State socialist	Marxist–Leninist authoritarian	Illusory	Collectivist and corporatist	Populist or liberal authoritarian

If we further narrow the scope of enquiry to the question of television broadcasting, we are forced to speculate even more as to the practical implications of the different theoretical positions. Despite a growing number of detailed studies, there are, as yet, singularly few writers who have attempted to give theorised accounts of the role of television broadcasting in the collapse of Stalinism and its aftermath. We cannot, unfortunately, point to a developed body of writing that locates itself self-consciously within any of the general theories that we have considered above. Despite the obvious importance of the nature and role of the mass media to the resolution of any of the more general questions, it is striking how little of the specialist literature in the field of post-communism even discusses this issue. We can, however, repeat our deductive effort above in the special circumstances of television broadcasting.

In this case, it is possible to make a rather crude division between the 'social' and 'political' aspects of the question and assign questions of finance, organisation and regulation to the former, and questions of executive personnel and policies with regard to political power to the latter. It is necessary to enter a small reservation with regard to the personnel. Obviously, under any of these theoretical frameworks, we would expect to find considerable continuities amongst the creative and technical personnel, partly since these groups implement but do not determine broadcasting policy and partly because they have, in the short run at least, a quasi-monopoly of scarce skills that are necessary to any television service. However, at the senior and editorial level at least, we would expect the appointment process to be influenced by the nature of the transformation. Within those limits, however, the division considered for the transformation process as a whole may be applied to this special case.

Total transformation

In the case of theories of total transformation, we might then expect to find that, at the economic level, the old state socialist system of television was replaced by a new commercial system. At the political level, the old, party-directed policies and party-approved personnel were replaced by independent, commercially oriented policies and that staff were appointed on a non-political and purely professional model. The broadcasting system would be, in principle, plural with regard to party political issues.

There is in fact some writing that fits itself directly and self-consciously into this line of thinking in the area of television. In the immediate aftermath of 1989 two reports were produced. The first, by Diana Lady Dougan for the US State Department, was rather ominously titled *Eastern Europe: Please Stand By*. Apart from the title, and the call for a 'cadre of economic green berets', the report notes that:

> While the horizons for private broadcasting may be limited, even government television has airtime to fill. Some countries seem prepared to go beyond the safe European models and are particularly attracted to American news and public affairs programmes. Western Europeans, especially Germans, are quickly positioning themselves. By contrast the presence of American broadcasting interests or expertise is minimal. (Dougan, 1990: 5)

The report foresaw cataclysmic changes in broadcasting and was concerned to make sure that US companies took full advantage of the opportunities. The second, by Everett K. Dennis, for what was then called the Gannett Foundation Media Center, was titled *Emerging Voices: East European Media in Transition*. This suggested that there was a rapid, complete and unprecedented change going on in all of the media, in particular in television, and that the task of the US government was to move rapidly to ensure that the emerging institutions and practices were based as closely as possible on American models.

There are a number of intellectual representatives of this position in the former communist countries. One is Oleg Manaev, from Belarus. Like the advocates of the more general theoretical position residing in the former communist countries, Manaev and other writers tend to stress the need to complete the transformation, as against the Western tendency to imagine that everything is already decided. Influenced directly by Hayek, Manaev argues that the only way to ensure freedom is through a break-up of the single 'subject' constituted by the totalitarian state. It must be replaced by a plurality of 'subjects', which 'may be represented by individuals, social groups and institutions . . . [that have] . . . political and economic independence' (Manaev, 1993: 119–20) It follows that the best guarantor of freedom of expression and thus democratic political life is through the immediate and wholesale privatisation of all the channels of communication, since state control leads inevitably to 'serfdom':

> Now the question is: what can stimulate the changing of the social role of the media in the transitional society – especially its rethinking by the main actors of mass communication – most effectively? . . . [I]n those concrete historical conditions that Belarus faced after the collapse of communist power and ideology and the disintegration of the USSR, the most effective mechanism of changing the social role of the media . . . is expansion of free enterprise, including the privatisation of state media and the foundation of private enterprise. (Manaev, 1995: 61–2).

A similar view of the main objective of media policy is advanced by other writers (Androunas, 1993: 107–29). Marinescu, writing about Romania, argues:

> Given the double objective of Romanian society at present – the installation of a democratic political system and the development of a free-market economy – it is obvious that the dispute 'Public vs. Private Property' in the audio-visual sphere is linked to that of the 'single political party vs. pluralism' issue on the political stage. The establishment of private ownership in broadcasting stations constitutes the only alternative to the 'communist-type regime' – because . . . the increase in the number of independent channels in a society means, in fact, an increase in the opportunities for different groups within it to make public their ideas, opinions, and views. (Marinescu, 1995: 95)

In case it should be thought that this view is only held by writers from those parts of the ex-communist world in which change has been very slow, one can also identify Mihály Gálik, writing about the Hungarian experience, as in this camp (Gálik, 1992).

Social (counter-) revolution

In the case of social (counter-) revolution theories, we would expect to find that, at the economic level, the old state broadcaster, characteristic of a socialist system of television, was replaced by a new commercial system. At the political level, there would tend to be a continuity of senior personnel. These would now pursue a professionally determined set of policies commensurate with the shift towards a market economy. The broadcasting system might, depending upon prevailing conditions, be plural or highly controlled.

The writer who comes closest to this view of the nature of changes in the media is Slavko Splichal. In his view, the former socialist system is being replaced by a system that is both commercialised and highly politicised. This he terms 'Italianisation', drawing a direct parallel with the media relations in that capitalist democracy (Splichal, 1994: 145–8). While the end of communism has meant that there are now private broadcasters, these permit no greater voice to the public than did the old communist organisations:

> The new model of mass media in Slovenia largely favours the interests of the political, commercial and professional élites and enables them to transmit their ideas, attitudes and instructions to the people. The media are often used as the battleground of party élites tending to maximise their political power and to change the political map. (Splichal, 1995: 113)

In addition to the persistence of political intervention in the mass media, both state and private, there is now the additional danger of the development of a private monopoly in broadcasting, which could have serious political consequences, as exemplified by Berlusconi.

Political revolution

In the case of Callinicos, at the economic level we would expect to find important continuities between past and present, given that state-owned and regulated broadcasting is not specific to communist countries and has indeed been a central feature of Western European reality for many years. On the other hand, the fragmentation of the old ruling class might lead to those sections who found themselves excluded from personal control of broadcasting attempting to institute a commercial system. There would tend to be continuity of personnel, who already performed a 'professional' function with regard to broadcasting. As with the previous system, relations with political power would be contingent upon circumstances.

A number of East European writers on television fall within this general category, particularly Prevrátil, Jakubowicz and Kováts. They would, almost certainly, have considerable reservations about being identified with this explicit theoretical position, but their concrete analysis of television broadcasting does seem to provide unwitting support to Callinicos. Prevrátil, for example, writes that in the former Czechoslovakia: 'The old élites lost most of their direct political power but remain in important positions in management, economy, some political parties, local administration and elsewhere', including broadcasting (Prevrátil, 1993: 6). Jakubowicz, summarising the outcome of six years of the Polish experience, wrote that despite considerable progress towards permitting private broadcasting:

... as far as Polish Television is concerned, a question mark hangs over the depth of change actually achieved. The fact that its programme and information policy is, if its critics are to be believed, partly subordinated to a political goal, and that democratisation has made little progress, means that change may be more superficial than real. Fascination with Poland's robust and chaotic political life, pursuit of political goals in programming and a tendency, resulting from a reliance on advertising revenue, to show as much foreign and preferably American fiction and entertainment programming as possible has meant that during the evening Polish Television is a politics – and entertainment – oriented medium. That is not really different from the situation in the past, e.g. in the 1970s, when the Communist rulers sought both to propagandise the population and to offer American entertainment in order to create a sense of well-being and buy social peace. (Jakubowicz, 1995: 76)

While changes to the economic structure are well underway, it seems that the degree of political interference, and the basic structures of state broadcasting, remain remarkably similar to those of the communist past.

What revolution?

As regards the account that argues the absence of revolution, the expectation is that there has in fact been no substantial change in the mass media. Before the 'revolution' these excluded all who were not members of the élite. Today they do the same. I have not been able to find any writer who advances this view systematically with regard to the media as a whole, although logically those who identify themselves in the tradition of Horkheimer and Adorno should hold to this position, since for them the distance between totalitarian and democratic broadcasting is so slight as to be invisible. There are, however, those writers who argue that, while the change should involve a new kind of media, in practice television at least remains completely unreconstructed:

The 'restructuring' of Bulgarian TV within the limits of changing the leadership has become so routine that one can barely expect to see any legislative steps taken. A number of strong applicants are pressing the release of state monopoly over this major national medium to private television. Politicians, however, still believe that this media stronghold can be kept as a means to influence public opinion. It seems that the current socialist government will be reluctant to release the monopoly over the national broadcasting space. (Iordanova, 1995: 29)

Evidently, the differences between this position and the one argued by Marinescu are relatively limited, and influenced as much by the peculiarities of national experience as by differing theoretical positions. However, to the extent that this latter position does rely upon a notion that there is a possibility of 're-communisation' in the region, it is a view that tends to state the limited and fragile nature of the change very strongly.

Following the attempt, which we outlined in our discussion of the general theoretical frameworks, to construct comparable categories testable in each case against concrete evidence, we may schematise these propositions for each theorist at the level of the television systems in Table 4.2.

The writers we have discussed above are only, or mostly, concerned with the central television broadcasting institutions in the countries under

Table 4.2   *Different theories of the nature and extent of the changes to media*

Theorist	Old structure	New structure	Old personnel	New personnel	Old politics	New politics
Fukuyama	State	Commercial	Political	Professional	Dependent	Independent
Miliband	State	Commercial or mixed	Political	Professional	Dependent	Contingent
Callinicos	State	State or mixed	Professional	Contingent	Dependent	Contingent
Lomax	State	State or mixed	Élite	Élite	Élite	Élite

consideration. For a number of reasons, these do not constitute the whole story about the likely future of television broadcasting, but they were the central, indeed the only, official structures in the old regime, and it is from the changes they have experienced that we must begin our attempt to understand the nature of the overall change. This is consonant with the central concerns of this book, but we must note that the press has been relatively neglected in discussions about the transformation of the media. As we shall see, the process there was rather different from that in broadcasting, and any adequate accounting for the change must certainly at least include some discussion of the issues it raises.

Degrees of negotiation

In the last chapter, we saw how broadcasting had, to different degrees in different countries, already begun to develop away from any resemblance it may ever have had to some pure Stalinist model. If we consider the more general evolution of the communist countries, we find substantial evidence that 1989 itself needs to be understood as a part of a process of a historical development, rather than as an isolated event to be understood only in its own terms.

Some writers have used the differences of historical trajectory to argue that there were distinctly different types of transitions in 1989 (Banac, 1992). Certainly, there were differences from country to country, but the variety of these events should not obscure a certain common element. The most remarkable fact was that the old regimes, or at least their decisive elements, did not present any sustained resistance to the revolution. Only in Romania did any major section of the regime, the notorious secret police, have serious recourse to arms, and they were defeated by that other central state structure, the army itself. Elsewhere, no faction of the old regime was able to muster the political will to defend itself militarily against its opponents.

There is only one possible explanation for this extraordinary series of examples of an entrenched and undemocratic élite surrendering power without serious resistance: the majority of the ruling groups in the various communist regimes knew that the old ways could no longer be sustained and accepted the need for a change in the system. Although mass independent opposition movements had appeared nowhere outside Poland, the scale and power of the working-class opposition in the early days of Solidarity was sufficient to impress upon the rulers of all communist countries that a serious attempt to repress their populations did not provide a solution. Any regime that knows that it cannot rely in a crisis upon its own repressive forces – and after Gorbachev's declaration that the Soviet Union was not prepared to intervene militarily, there were no available outside forces – is bound sooner or later either to need to win popular consent or to negotiate its own exit. It was the latter path the communist parties ended up following.

In fact, if we can trust the limited evidence, the communist regimes, while far from enjoying popular support, were in some cases less unpopular than Cold War ideologues might have suggested (Kurant, 1991). One pre-1989 Polish study, for example, found that, during the high period of Solidarity, there had been very egalitarian attitudes, particularly amongst blue collar workers. As the decade progressed, these were progressively weakened, but there was no evidence that they were replaced by enthusiasm for the market economy (Kolarska-Bobinska, 1988). Another study, using data from 1984, found that only 18 per cent of the population were against any form of socialism, which was only slightly more than the 16.5 per cent who supported the Polish version of 'Real Socialism'. Only 11 per cent were in favour of the private ownership of the means of production. The author concluded that 'the idea of social ownership and a planned economy enjoys popular support' (Ziółkowski, 1988: 155). Overall, there seemed in the dying years of communism to be a contradictory social consciousness dominating in Poland. There was some empirical evidence that suggested that 'social consciousness already reflected some change in the political domination over the economy, but there was no strongly marked desire for an heroic rising to overthrow communism' (Kolarska-Bobinska and Rychard, 1990: 306; Marody, 1988). Data from 1985 for Hungary suggested that public opinion was equivocal about the future, but generally favourable to political changes (Bruszt, 1988). We can find no comparable material for other countries, but given the intensity with which the opposition had confronted the regime in the early 1980s in Poland, it is likely that elsewhere there would have been even less critical consciousness. The regimes therefore could not expect to be loved, but they did enjoy sufficient social space to try to negotiate their own demise (Poznanski, 1993: 3).

The nature and extent of the negotiations into which the various regimes entered varied according to three basic factors. One was the extent to which the communist regime had already permitted 'liberalisation'. While it was still possible, as late as the spring of 1989, for Western (pro-Stalinist) observers to point to Bulgaria and the GDR as examples of successful, unreformed central planning, elsewhere there had already been a move away from this rigid model (McIntyre, 1989). In the case of Hungary, for example, there had been a long process of retreat from the command model of economic and social life, beginning perhaps as long ago as the aftermath of the 1956 Revolution and accelerating under Kadar in the years following 1968. In other cases, for example Czechoslovakia, the process of economic liberalisation that took place in the late 1960s was cut by off the Russian invasion of 1968 and a new version of the command model was installed. There, the communist leadership had no serious reform programme (Reiman, 1989).

The second factor, which was clearly closely related to the first, was the degree to which the leadership of the Communist Party itself was united. This, too, varied from country to country. Again, Hungary provides an example of one extreme, with an established reform communist wing present in many parts of the state machine, including the mass media. A study of the local party cadres, fortuitously undertaken in the period immediately prior to the negotiations that ended communist rule, found a collapse of belief in the system even on the part of people whose lives were bound up with its maintenance (Horváth and Szakolczai, 1990: 300). In fact, the social decomposition of the *nomenklatura* was already so well advanced before 1989 that one prominent Hungarian sociologist claimed that there was already a 'grand coalition' between the old oligarchy and middle bureaucrats on the one hand and 'new capitalists' on the other, and provided a vivid imaginary picture of how this coalition hung together:

> If the daughter of a (former) top party or state apparatchik owns a fashionable boutique downtown, if his son is the Hungarian representative of a Western company, if his son-in-law is the president of a holding, his grand-daughter studies at Oxford, and his mother-in-law has a small hotel on lake Balaton, then the grand coalition can already meet around the family tree on Christmas eve. (Hankiss, 1990: 255)

The obvious extreme contrast was Romania, in which power seems more or less to have been concentrated into the hands of the Ceauşescu family itself, and in which any opposition either from inside or outside the party was dealt with extremely severely. The other countries lay somewhere in between.

The final factor was the presence and size of the opposition. Here, Poland provides the exemplary case. Solidarity was a highly developed opposition movement which, even when illegal and bitterly repressed in the aftermath of martial law, commanded widespread influence. Although the experience of martial law had resulted in profound changes in Solidarity, it was still a major alternative pole of attraction to the party and state (Ost, 1989: 69–74; Ost, 1990). In other cases, Czechoslovakia for example, there existed a well-developed oppositional movement, but without the same history of mass involvement as marked the Polish case (Selucky, 1989). In the case of Hungary, some observers argued that there was not really a distinct oppositional movement at all. Rather, many people existed in the official 'first society' for part of the time and in the oppositional 'second society' for part of the time. These were not 'two distinct groups of people . . . [but] . . . two dimensions of social existence' (Hankiss, 1988: 21–2). Finally, as in Romania and Bulgaria, there were cases in which there appear to have been no developed internal oppositional movements at all.

The various combinations of these factors meant that, in some countries, most notably Poland and Hungary, it was possible for the reform communists and the non-communist opposition to negotiate agreements for changes to the system. In the case of Poland, while the final cause of the collapse of the old regime was undoubtedly the strength and organisation of Solidarity over nearly a decade of legal and illegal existence, negotiations between a reform-minded wing of the bureaucracy and a wing of the Solidarity leadership had been going on since the wave of strikes in 1987, which signified to everyone that martial law had failed to crush working-class opposition. The transition was eased and directed by a series of 'round table' negotiations between representatives of Solidarity and the government, covering most of the major areas of social life including the mass media. The initial intention was to negotiate a compromise that would allow the Communist Party to share power with Solidarity, and it was only after the latter's overwhelming triumph in the elections that the deal broke down and it became clear to everyone that the former trade union would have to form the basis of the new government (Wesołowski, 1990: 440–1). In Hungary, by 1985, a clear reformist current had emerged within the ruling Hungarian Socialist Workers' Party (HSWP). The first independent political opposition parties began to emerge publicly in the course of 1987–8, and swiftly commanded substantial support (Urban, 1989). There was a protracted series of internal disputes over the nature, pace and objectives of change preceding the opening of genuine dialogue with the opposition and the eventual realisation of free elections (Bruszt, 1989; Körösényi, 1992a). The actual transition was again managed by 'an informal alliance between reform Communists and the organized forces of civil society' (Bruszt, 1992: 57). In other cases, where there was a much less developed opposition and a more unified ruling group, the changeover did not have the same character. In one case, Romania, it involved considerable violence. In another, Bulgaria, it was wholly peaceful. In both of these examples, however, what seems to have taken place is that one wing of the *nomenklatura* replaced another.

The case of Czechoslovakia was different again. There was little evidence of élite negotiation before the fall of the communists. This was partly because the reform wing of the bureaucracy had been ousted from power after 1968. Contact between the official world and the opposition certainly existed throughout the period, although it was mostly amongst intellectuals that such contacts took place. These were accelerated by the turmoil in the leadership of the ruling party in the late 1980s, but never played the same sort of formalised negotiating role that characterised other countries. Wolchik writes that:

> Although certain individuals . . . attempted to serve as mediators, the Communist Party's options were limited by the fact that, in contrast to the situations in Hungary and Poland, where communist reformists helped to ease the transition to multiparty rule, there had been no clearly identifiable reformist faction in the leadership in Czechoslovakia for over 20 years. (Wolchik, 1991: 49)

This meant that there was no faction internal to the ruling élite that could come forward and offer a settlement to the opposition. The terms of the transfer could only be worked out after the end of the regime. But confronting this forcibly unified ruling élite was an opposition which, while large and diverse, had nothing like the same history of mass involvement in political struggle as did the Poles. When the change came, then, while the top level of the old élite was swept away, more junior elements immediately began to accommodate themselves to the new situation.

What has been described as an 'élite' model of the transfer of power is one of the most striking features of the revolutions of 1989 (Misztal, 1993: 464–5). In none of the cases we are here centrally concerned with was the actual transfer of power accompanied by any serious popular mobilisation. The leaders of the reform communists and the leaders of the opposition, or the leaders of different wings of the communist party itself, agreed, with a greater or lesser degree of friction, the rules of the new game. At no point were the basic structures of society challenged.

As we shall show in more detail below, there were two very important exceptions to this general picture: Czechoslovakia and the GDR. In those cases, the popular mobilisation preceded the political changeover, and in some ways went beyond the limits of simple political change. Even here, however, the degree of popular mobilisation was much lower than that which had accompanied earlier crises in communist countries. The year 1956 in Hungary saw a mass rising, the destruction of the secret police apparatus, the arming of the population, and a bitter military struggle against the invading Soviet troops. In Poland in 1980–1, there were repeated mass strikes, workers' councils, and a year-long struggle that mobilised almost the whole of the population. If the population of Eastern Europe were to be freed in 1989, it seemed more or less universally agreed by both the communists and their opponents that this would have to be done on the behalf of the people, rather than as the result of their own activities.

Controlling media change

The starting point of the negotiations in Poland and Hungary, in which it is fairly clear in retrospect that at least the reform communists were looking to reach some kind of accommodation with their opponents, was that the communist party would continue to be the dominant political force in society. It was only in the course of negotiations, and in particular after the outcomes of the elections, that this compromise fell to pieces. The debates over the control of television need to be seen very much in this light.

In Poland, the transfer of power in broadcasting was begun through 'round-table' negotiations between the communist government and the Solidarity-led opposition in early 1989. The 'sub-table' on the media, which opened on 12 February 1989, was taken very seriously by both sides. The government sent the well-known spokesperson Jerzy Urban and Solidarity sent two of its most important public figures, Adam Michnik and Tadeusz Mazowiecki. The two sides began with rather different conceptions. The communist authorities proposed some easing of controls over the media, including the legalisation of the underground press, but its plans included continued Communist Party domination over radio and television. For its part, Solidarity had moved back from its earlier desire to establish direct 'social control' over broadcasting. It now proposed a three-stage plan, starting with the setting-up of Solidarity departments in radio and television and the observance of rules governing fair and equal air time for the main political forces, to be followed in stage two by the transfer of one national TV and one national radio channel to 'social groups and forces'. In the third phase, a National Broadcasting Council, a non-governmental body with a variety of different representatives from both political and social movements, would take control of policy and supervise all broadcasting matters (Jakubowicz, 1991). This was completely unacceptable to the government and Solidarity quickly backed down and demanded the right to broadcast its own short programmes on the government channels. An agreement was eventually reached in March 1989, which gave Solidarity an autonomous production department with the right to broadcast programmes once a week of between 30 and 45 minutes. Censorship, however, remained in force. The elections of 4 June were conducted under this agreement, which allowed all social movements and parties the right to their own broadcasting slots. The government kept to some, but not all, of the 'round table' agreements. Solidarity was allowed to broadcast, but its time was very limited compared to the deluge of pro-government propaganda (Goban-Klas, 1990). In response to this, and bolstered by its electoral victory, Solidarity, in July, changed its demand to control over the news and current affairs programmes on the second national television channel and a change in the composition of the Polish Broadcasting Council in line with the new balance in Parliament (Jakubowicz, 1991: 169). In the event, once the new Parliament met and Solidarity entered into government, there were no immediate structural changes to television. Tadeusz Mazowiecki, the new Prime Minister, said in an address to the Sejm on 12 October 1989:

> There must be an open flow of information between the government and the people. The right of access to radio and television must be equal for all. Television and radio must be pluralistic in character. (Mazowiecki, 1989: 163)

There was little immediate action to realise these noble sentiments. Some senior managers, and those journalists most closely connected to the old regime, were purged, but the numbers involved were relatively limited. One of the heads of agreement in the 'round table' talks had been that there should be no 'anti-communist witch-hunt', and the first post-communist head of broadcasting, Andrzej Drawicz, upheld that agreement. According to one writer: 'Very few individuals have lost their jobs and certain presenters who were strongly associated with martial law have stopped appearing in front of the camera but retain back-room jobs' (Witkowska, 1990: 14). A special commission, chaired by Karol Jakubowicz, was established by the Committee for Radio and Television in October 1989 and was charged to consider the future of television and to prepare a report to the Senate, but no immediate structural changes were implemented (Jakubowicz, 1992: 5–8). Even three years later, Leszek Wasiuta, then head of Channel One of Polish Television, was able to say that: 'The structure is the same as under Communism, because it is a very good structure and it works equally well under Communism or Capitalism' (Wasiuta, personal communication, 1992).

The two important changes that did take place very quickly both had far-reaching but rather different implications. The first was the abolition of censorship in broadcasting. This took place in January 1990. The last remaining element of censorship, the requirement of a licence to publish, established by the Press Law of 1984, and which really only applied to the printed media, was abolished by Amendment No. 181 in the Press Law of 5 August 1991. This clearly represented a major change in the legal conditions under which the Polish mass media operated, and its effects rapidly became apparent, notoriously in the flood of new pornographic printed publications and videos that had been strictly illegal under the old regime.

The second change, which had implications running counter to the ending of censorship, was an alteration in the position of the Roman Catholic Church with respect to broadcasting. The Act on State Relations with the Roman Catholic Church in the Republic of Poland, dated 17 May 1989, had recognised the right of the Church to have access to the airwaves. This was interpreted in an agreement between the Church and the Radio and Television Committee, then headed by Jerzy Urban, as allowing independent organisations run by people appointed by the Catholic bishops to work inside radio and television (Goban-Klas, personal communication, 1992). The new Mazowiecki government modified the Act on State Relations by means of the Post and Telecommunications Act of 23 November 1990, Article 88 of which read:

1 The Church has the right to broadcast through the mass media the Holy Mass on Sundays and holidays and its programmes, particularly on religious, moral, social and cultural issues. . . .

3 The Church has the right to install and operate radiocommunications equipment for broadcasting radio and television programmes and to the allocation of the necessary frequencies for this purpose. (Poland, no. 504, 1990b)

As a result of this change, by September 1992 there were 18 radio stations and one local television station run by the Catholic Church. Thus, the extent to which the immediate aftermath of 1989 opened broadcasting to forces other than the existing state-run institutions was extremely limited. While it is true that the Church had been a focus for opposition to the communist regime, and a powerful support for Solidarity, the hierarchy had always been able to reach an agreement with the *nomenklatura*: Church and state worked together after 1956 and Poland in the 1980s witnessed both martial law and a wave of state-approved church-building. The first break in the state monopoly of broadcasting was, therefore, only a partial shift in the relative power of two of the dominant structures of Polish society.

The case of Hungary was, in the first instance, even more gradual than in Poland. The grip of the HSWP on the media began substantially to relax after the fall of Kadar. In August 1988, the Central Committee dissolved its Department for Agitation and Propaganda. In January 1989, the Minister of State, Imre Pozsgay, gave an interview to Hungarian Radio that neatly expressed the contradictions and uncertainty in the HSWP position:

Radio and Television, albeit operating under the direct supervision and orientation of the government, should serve and express the entire public sphere of society of the nation. This means that the government does not consider these media exclusively its own political instrument; in the programmes the most varied social views and efforts could be expressed. The government must take care of keeping this expression of views within the constitutional limits in accordance with the press law stipulations. (Pozsgay, 1989)

Clearly, at this stage the leadership of the HSWP wished to try to hold on to as much of the old broadcasting order as possible, while opening it to the opposition as much as was necessary.

The pace of change quickened in March 1989, when the 'list of competencies' – the basis of the *nomenklatura* system establishing whom the Central Committee thought was fit to hold senior posts in the media and elsewhere – was abolished. In the same month the opposition conducted a 'symbolic seizure' of MTV. The Trilateral National Round Table negotiations between the government and opposition, conducted during the spring of that year, formed a sub-group on the mass media. Three main positions were put forward. The government wished to keep television under state control but was prepared to loosen its grip by allowing what it called a 'responsible social body' to exercise some influence. The main opposition party, the Hungarian Democratic Forum (HDF), also saw TV as essentially a non-commercial organisation. While it was prepared to consider the possibility of private television channels, it saw MTV as a 'national institution' under the control of the government. Amongst the main tasks of broadcasting, it identified the task of reaching the large numbers of ethnic Hungarians outside the national boundaries. The third main position was that advanced by the Alliance of Free Democrats (AFD). They proposed that MTV should remain a non-commercial organisation, but argued for a greater degree of self-government, and accepted the need for other forms of broadcasting organisation, some of them commercial (Kováts and Whiting, 1992).

No easy agreement could be reached on these policies, or upon the thorny question of the role of broadcasting in the forthcoming elections in March–April 1990. Eventually, a moratorium on changes to broadcasting was agreed, and each of the 54 registered political parties was granted the right to broadcast on the main TV and radio channels during the first round of the elections. However, the distribution of results meant that only 12 parties gained the right to national lists and thus to broadcasts during the second half of the campaign (Körösényi, 1992b: 76). The third major point of agreement was the classification of the projected new media law as one of that class of fundamental laws that required a two-thirds majority in Parliament for their adoption (Varga, personal communication, 1992). This decision was to have very important consequences later on in the struggle over the control of Hungarian television.

The elections produced a government dominated by the HDF. In negotiation with the AFD, they discussed the basis for amendments to the constitution. Among the points agreed was the need to 'aim for the establishment of party-neutral national media' (Bozóki, 1992: 69). As a step towards this, Law LVII of 1990 specified that the heads of state television and radio should be appointed by the President of the Republic (under the constitution necessarily a representative of the opposition) on the nomination of the Prime Minister (speaking, of course, for the government). The new director-general of television, Elemer Hankiss, was appointed under this law.

Part of the agreement leading to Hankiss's appointment was that he would retain senior staff loyal to the existing regime, in particular the editors of the main news and current affairs programmes. He embarked upon a top-down restructuring of television that did not involve any very extensive purges of staff held to be implicated in the running of the old system. As Hankiss put it, his aim was 'to destroy the old power structure without a witch-hunt' (Hankiss, personal communication 1992). The main aim of his plan, as we shall see, was to transform the efficiency of MTV rather than to build a radically new organisation. Even in this, it has been persuasively argued, he was not embarking on any radically new course of action, but continuing efforts that had been made in the past by his loyally communist predecessors (Kováts, 1995: 48–50).

Overall, then, the nature of the transition in these two countries, at least insofar as broadcasting was concerned, was the replacement of one set of directors with another.

The major contrast to the picture of a controlled transition was formed by Czechoslovakia and East Germany. In both of these, the old regime had no liberal wing that was ready to enter into negotiations, and the oppositions were not prepared to engage in the sorts of dialogues that took place elsewhere. In both of these cases, it was popular mobilisations that drove the communists from power.

The mobilisations had considerable importance for the structures of the media. There was a sharp break in Czechoslovakia where the system was most rigid and had made least pre-adaptation. According to Jaroslav Kostal, head of audience research for Czech Radio, there had been some small changes in the internal atmosphere of radio and television prior to 1989, although from his perspective the only concrete evidence he could produce was that his department had been allowed to purchase computers for research purposes in 1985 (Kostal, personal communication, 1992). What took place there was much more like a 'real' revolution (albeit a 'velvet' one) than what occurred in the Poland and Hungary. Even then, the events in Prague seem to have been much more spontaneous than in Bratislava. The view of Petr Malec, then director-general of Slovak Television, was that: 'The revolution in Bratislava was not entirely spontaneous. There were some machinations from outside' (Malec, personal communication, 1992). In Prague, however, the change in television certainly involved a direct challenge to the existing structure and there was a direct mobilisation of the workforce in the struggle against the old regime. The party leadership retained complete control over broadcasting right up to November 1989. When the 'velvet revolution' began, the refusal of the existing management to broadcast reports about the demonstrations in Wenceslas Square led directly to the setting up of a strike committee (called 'The Garage' after its main meeting place, which was the large garage under broadcasting HQ, in which the outside-broadcasting and other vehicles were kept). On 22 November, some television employees managed, despite the efforts of the party hardliners, to broadcast 5 minutes of one of the rallies. By 24 November, with the resignation of the Communist Party's Central Committee, 'The Garage' took effective control of programming. They broadcast live programmes of the demonstrations, including the appearance of such different oppositional figures as Havel and Dubček (Kaplan and Šmíd, 1995: 33–4). The directly elected management council, however, did not survive as an independent force. The leaders merged with the old 'trade union' structure and helped to initiate the reform of the system. The changes led to the replacement of senior managers, and some 60 per cent of journalists, but the basic structure remained more or less intact (Šmíd, 1992: 2–5). Within a fairly short period, at least the substantive body of the old hierarchy had managed to re-exert its control over broadcasting. According to Milan Jakobec, then secretary of the Czech Broadcasting Council, 'There have been some changes in TV management, but mainly it is the same people. . . . The same mafia are still running things' (Jakobec, personal communication, 1992).

The example of East Germany was even more interesting. The collapse of the old order was protracted, and there was no ready-made opposition waiting to step out of the wings. The leadership of the Socialist Unity Party (SED) continued to believe up until the last moment that their relative economic success would insulate them from the turmoil in other communist countries. When the cracks first began to appear, first as a result of the mass emigration to the West in the summer and then with the string of huge demonstrations, journalists, television workers and citizens' committees effectively took over the media. Many of the older editors, the worst collaborators and the secret policemen were driven out and, for a relatively brief period, there was an explosion of media freedom. The citizens' committees attempted to construct a new legal and social framework for the media, and were encouraged in this by the provisional government. On 5 February 1990, the Volkskammer passed a resolution guaranteeing freedom of expression, which included the entitlement of a wide range of political, religious and social groups to representation in the media. This effort was terminated by the process of unification. As part of the treaty, the East German government accepted that the West German model of broadcasting would be imposed on the East. The establishment of the new system involved the destruction of the temporary civic control of broadcasting and the importation of West German right-wing political figures as the controllers of most stations in the run-up to re-unification. These new managers carried out a thorough purge of anyone suspected of having been a supporter of the old regime, and even of many who were simply independent. The broadcasting system that emerged after reunification was almost wholly West German, indeed Bavarian, in structure and politics (Boyle, 1994; Kilborn, 1994).

A study of broadcasting thus suggests that those theories that stress the sharp discontinuity between the communist past and the world emerging in 1989 cannot be sustained. Rather, theories that accept important elements of continuity obviously command greater empirical support. It might, however, be reasonably objected that the narrow focus on broadcasting has given a distorted picture of reality, and that if interest were broadened to include the press, a very different picture would emerge. Despite the fact that the main focus of this book is on broadcasting, it is obviously essential in the interests of intellectual honesty to take such an objection seriously and at to consider, at least briefly, the changes in the printed press.

These certainly presented a very different pattern than that of broadcasting. We may determine three main trends in this field. The first was the rapid establishment of literally hundreds of new titles. In the tiny new state of Slovenia, for example, the number of daily newspaper titles doubled, from three to six, in the period following national independence (Novak, 1996). In Poland, between June 1990 and December 1992, new titles were being registered at an average of 100 per month. It was estimated by early 1993 that more than 7,000 newspapers and periodicals had been registered (Giorgi, 1995: 89). The explosion of numbers took place both in the newspaper and magazine sectors.

Many of the more newspaper-like titles were the organs of political groups and parties, and as these latter proliferated, so did the number of newspapers. In some prominent cases, particularly in Poland, these papers were effectively the new, legal and overground manifestations of well-established oppositional currents, edited and run by the dissidents who had kept them alive in the underground. The best-known examples of there were *Lidové Noviny* in Prague and *Gazeta Wyborcza* in Warsaw. There were, however, many purely commercial publications, aiming at the same kinds of diversified tastes as exist in the normal Western capitalist media market. These were set up by entrepreneurs of all sorts of backgrounds, sometimes with no prior record of opposition, sometimes with personal histories deeply entwined with the previous regime. The most notable of these latter is probably Jerzy Urban, the former spokeperson for the communist government, who set up a major Polish satirical publication.

The second kind of publication was that directly set up by foreign, usually Western, media corporations, who wished to take advantage of the new market. These direct, start-up investments were relatively few in number, although they contained some titles, like *Blesk* in what was to become the Czech Republic, that were to be very important in the emerging press market. These kinds of paper were, from the very beginning, essentially local copies of established Western media. They were an attempt, and often a quite successful attempt, to export an advertising-funded, profit-oriented business model to a new market.

The third kind of printed publication was not really new at all. It was a continuation of the existing press. One group of such publications is the Catholic press in Poland, but in general this group is the old party-dominated press under new ownership and with a new editorial direction. This new ownership was sometimes the senior employees of the papers and sometimes a foreign media corporation. Very often, it was some combination of the two. Hungary provides the best-known examples of these processes. In the course of 1989–90 all the Budapest daily press received injections of foreign capital, from Maxwell, Murdoch, Bertelsmann, Carlo de Benedetti, Bonnier, Springer, Hersant, and some other less well-known, mostly Austrian, media companies (Giorgi, 1995: 45–6). This process of internal takeover involved the semi-official government newspaper *Magyar Hírlap*, whose journalists did a deal with Robert Maxwell, and the party paper *Népszabadság*, whose journalists came to arrangement with Bertelsmann AG (Jakab and Gálik, 1991: 21–8). Even more notorious was the process of the privatisation of a group of local, party-owned newspapers by Springer. This was agreed between the Springer representatives and the editorial staff, completely bypassing the apparent legal owners of the papers (Giorgi and Pohoryles, 1994: 29–30). The effective seizure of party assets in 'wild privatisation' was also a feature of the immediate post-revolutionary phase in the Czech press, where the first phase after 1989 was 'a period of spontaneous transformation with regards to patterns of ownership occurring within a void in respect to legal regulation' (Giorgi and Pohoryles, 1994: 154). Poland, where the majority of the press was in the hands of a state combine (RSW), presented a different picture. There, a Liquidation Committee was appointed on 12 April 1990, by the first post-communist government. It divided the spoils between journalists' co-operatives and the new political parties. Care was taken to avoid too much foreign ownership, and that which was permitted was largely French. The new ownerships that emerged, however, were often in weak financial positions, and very soon found themselves forced into associations with various foreign investors (Giorgi, 1995: 75–80, 90–4; Goban-Klas, 1994: 221–4).

Irrespective of the nature of the titles or their ownership patterns, however, a common thread in the new press situation was the very rapid development of a commercial press model. Certainly, subsidised papers remained, but the bulk of the press quickly became a business enterprise. This meant that the content and the size, not to mention the stability, of titles underwent a rapid change. The number of papers and magazines founded was very large indeed, but the number that survived was very much smaller. The normal workings of the capitalist market were ruthlessly effective in this field.

Conclusion

There appear to be two distinct trends in the nature of the change in the mass media, depending upon whether we focus our attention on the press or on broadcasting. In the former case, the old media system fragmented very quickly and was replaced almost immediately by a new, market-oriented system, which rapidly began to integrate itself into the world media market. In the case of broadcasting, and particularly television broadcasting, the most striking feature of the period after 1989 is the degree of continuity of the system. There were some changes, particularly at the very top, but the institutions remained fundamentally unchanged.

In terms of the theoretical perspectives on the nature of the transformation, these shifts would seem to support quite different perspectives. The situation in the press apparently gives credence to the views of post-communism that stress radical change: there has been a total and complete transformation of the system. The old non-market, communist model has been replaced by a market-oriented system that is comparable to that in the West. The situation in broadcasting apparently gives support to the views that stress the limited nature of the changes. In terms both of structure and of personnel, the television system appeared to survive the change more or less intact. There was no sharp disruption of the way in which television was organised such as we would expect to find in any fundamental social transformation.

On closer consideration, however, these apparent differences emerge as two aspects of the same process. In both press and television, while individuals who were particularly committed to the old system were driven out of office, the bulk of the senior staff remained comfortably in post. Even when the journalists were seizing newspapers that were legally the property of the Party, there was no serious opposition. On the contrary, the Party leadership seems positively to have encouraged the process. The journalists and other senior staff developed new political positions and guided their organisations in different directions, but they retained control of the institutions. While it was true that some members of the *nomenklatura* lost their social role, the *nomenklatura* as a whole retained its grip on society.

The corollary of changed political conditions after 1989 is a degree of social continuity. That is clearly present in broadcasting, in which the old structures and personnel manifestly survived the changes. In the press, however, the general tendency was for most journalists, excluding those most compromised with the old regimes, to have an important role in the fate of the publications, either seizing them for themselves or negotiating terms with new owners. It was precisely the political guarantor of the old order, the Communist Party as a collective organisation, that lost out in this process: most members of the *nomenklatura* and their journalistic servants made the transition to the new conditions without serious upheavals.

These two different trajectories can thus be seen as the two sides of the one process of political transformation. The broadcasting institutions were so large, and so politically sensitive, that they could not simply be seized by one group or another. Their fate and position demanded a political agreement between all of the political forces in the new arena. They were not candidates for immediate, unregulated privatisation and there was a powerful example, in Western Europe, in which broadcasting continued to be state-owned even in democratic capitalist countries. Newspapers, on the other hand, were individually much smaller and could be seized piecemeal and either sold off or continued as private operations. In the case of Poland, where the ownership structure of RSW made this expedient impossible, the press process was much more orderly and bore similarities to the politicised decisions about broad-casting. In both cases, it was the old senior employees who benefited from the changes. The political colouration of the new media might be different, but they remained controlled by more or less the same people. There was sub-stantial social continuity in media institutions from before to after 1989.

The fact of this continuity is well illustrated by the only case in which there was indeed a radical transformation: the former GDR. Here, the destruction of the old system, and the widespread replacement of the senior figures of the old systems by new faces, was achieved not as a result of an internal process but through the imposition of an outside force: the West German state machine and the politically committed personnel of its dominant party.

This case is notable in that, in the GDR, and to a much lesser extent in the case of Czechoslovakia, there was indeed a fundamental challenge to the existing hierarchies of power and control in the mass media. These consti-tuted a genuine attempt at constructing an alternative method of running a society and a media system, and were based on quite different principles than either the old communist system or the new, capitalist one. The brief, and ultimately fruitless, attempts to establish a different way of running the media that flickered in these two cases are of extreme importance in under-standing 1989. They are concrete evidence that there were indeed social issues as to who should control the mass media, and how they should relate to society, that were not exhausted by the apparently painless death of the old order and the birth of the new, familiar, private capitalist one. They showed that there was indeed a third way, quite different from either form of social domination. It was in the interests neither of the old *nomenklatura* nor of their new Western friends that this sort of example should be allowed to flourish and establish itself. There is no clearer mark of the degree of social continuity between communism and private capitalism than that both sys-tems were completely uninterested in, and hostile to, any schemes that might subject the media to democratic control, either by the people who worked in them or by mass of the population.

The overall meaning of these changes is thus that the end of communism and the birth of capitalism were characterised by a change at the level of political life but a marked continuity at the level of social structure. It is per-fectly legitimate to call these changes revolutions, in that they involved a sharp break with the past order and the establishment of a new set of funda-mental social rules. In this, they differed qualitatively from the kinds of incremental changes we saw were taking place before 1989. The revolutions were not, however, total ones. On the contrary, alongside the changes we need to place very substantial elements of continuity. In terms of the theo-retical frameworks we have outline above, what happened fits most closely with Callincos's view that what took place were political, not social, revolutions.

Those views that stress discontinuity, and in particular the official Western version as promulgated by Fukuyama and other writers, bear no relationship whatsoever to what actually occurred. There is singularly little evidence that there was anywhere a complete and total transformation following upon the end of communism. The elements of continuity are too obvious, and too central, to be dismissed. In terms both of structures and personnel, the media show singularly little transformation, and what there has been is best understood as a mechanism for ensuring social continuity in the face of political change. It is, of course, possible that the elements of continuity constitute what we may term historic 'hangovers', part of the unfinished business of the revolutions. Given the nature and scale of these hangovers, this is on the face of it extremely unlikely. Whether this is the case or not, however, can only be really settled by examining subsequent developments.

A similar extension of the enquiry is necessary to settle the status of those theories that stress complete continuity. While the evidence reviewed so far tends to support the Callinicos case, it does not rule out the possibility of a much greater degree of continuity than that theory allows. We cannot resolve the issue between the two contrasting views of the extent of continuity without looking beyond the negotiated revolutions and considering the future evolution of the system, and it is to that we must now turn.

5

The Fate of Civil Society

The groups that came to office in the first wave of democratic elections in and after 1989 were led in Poland, Czechoslovakia and Hungary by people who had long records of opposition to the communists. Many had been jailed for their political views. In some other countries, notably Romania and Bulgaria, it was parties that were only lightly camouflaged successors to the communists who quickly won out, but in the Visegrad countries the initial political leaderships came from quite different political traditions. Although the speed of the transition from marginal opposition to government was so great that the structure of the victorious parties was everywhere uncertain, and all were soon to experience significant splits as internal differences became irreconcilable, there were some definite points of agreement amongst the new governors. They had ideas and policies developed over many hard years, and in government they found a chance to implement them in practice.

The politics of the opposition

These ideas were far from uniform, since the opposition to the communist regimes contained a wide variety of different intellectual currents. The differences between an Alexander Solzhenitsyn and a Jacek Kuron, in terms of social and intellectual background, political orientation and vision of the future were perhaps wider than those between many oppositionists and the regimes themselves.

The differences that emerged after 1989 were partly intellectual and partly social. Many of the better-known oppositionists were prominent intellectuals. Indeed, it has been argued that the revolutions themselves were primarily the work of, and firstly benefited, a section of the intellectuals (Bayard, 1993; Zubek, 1992). Only in Poland did any large number of manual workers come to prominence as leaders of the opposition. The parties that the former opposition led after the fall of communism, however, made an appeal to many strata of society, and the intelligentsia itself was far from unified. There was perceived to be, for example, a wide gulf between the young, urban, internationalised intellectuals of Budapest, and the older, provincial intellectuals based in the countryside and smaller towns. Intellectually, the inspiration of the oppositions varied between versions of religious ideology, outright pro-capitalism, reform communism, social democracy and, very occasionally, thoroughgoing left–Marxist critiques of Stalinism. Once out in the open, and subject to social pressures, these difference were bound to lead to the fragmentation of the formerly united opposition.

If we look for those factors that held the opposition together before 1989, we can quickly identify the more or less indiscriminate hostility of the regimes to any form of political diversity as the major objective factor. Faced with a massive and repressive state apparatus that was prepared to engage in a high level of persecution against all and any of its critics, it made a great deal of sense for the disparate opposition groups to hang together. Long-term disagreements about the future could reasonably be suspended in order to mount a joint assault on the common enemy.

There were, however, two important positive factors that united most of the oppositional groups and individuals. The first of these was nationalism. In all of the European communist countries, apart possibly from the former Yugoslavia, the evident reality was that the regimes had come to power more or less directly as the result of the victories of Soviet arms in 1941–5. That is not to deny that there were indigenous anti-Nazi opposition movements, nor that the communists had usually played a leading and heroic role in building them, at least after the Nazi invasion of the Soviet Union in 1941. It was also true that in many countries the communist parties emerged as a large political force in the post-war settlements. However, they eventually came to power not as the result of any indigenous and spontaneous risings by the local proletariat but essentially as the result of bureaucratic takeovers of governments that already rested on a state apparatus that had been thoroughly subordinated to the Communist Party (Harman, 1983: 20–41).

The regimes had been placed in power by Soviet tanks; their evolution had also been deeply dependent upon external forces. In the late 1940s and early 1950s, the leaderships of the local parties were thoroughly purged in order to ensure complete loyalty to Moscow (Harman, 1983: 50–60). The Soviet Union continued to maintain vast armies in the territories of the Warsaw Pact, which were directed at least as much against the local populations as against the Nato threat. In 1956 and in 1968, it was Russian troops who bloodily put down local movements that threatened the continuing grip of Moscow, if not of communism itself.

Consequently, in most countries, the regime appeared to the majority of its opponents as a foreign import. The communists were seen as having betrayed the nation to the Russians. This image was particularly potent partly because it held a large measure of truth, and partly because, in much of the region, it harked back to a much longer series of struggles against domination by supra-national empires, notably that of the Tsar. The liberation from communism thus had much of the unifying appeal of a national liberation struggle. Against Brezhnev's notorious slogan of 'proletarian internationalism', coined to justify Soviet military intervention anywhere in their sphere of influence, it seemed natural to stand for the interests of the nation.

It is important to enter two qualifications to this observation. It was never true, apart perhaps from the great crises of 1956 and 1968, that any of the regimes rested solely on Soviet arms. The communist project of industrialisation had radically altered the social structures of most countries and had produced new and large privileged layers who owed a major social debt to the regime. The struggle was, therefore, never in reality one of 'the people' against an alien oppressor and its clique of clients. The communist regimes, even when backed by Soviet tanks, could not have lasted 40 years without some substantial social support.

The second qualification is that, whatever may have been the truth about their original dependence upon Moscow, the local communist regimes certainly presented themselves in strongly nationalist colours. Positively, the communists were keen to encourage their own version of the national culture. The indigenous film industries that flourished up until 1989 in many countries, admittedly with variable aesthetic results, were impossible without massive state support and entered crisis after that protection was withdrawn (Folger, 1994; Macek, 1994; Raycheva, 1994). Negatively, the regimes were keen to denounce those whom they claimed to be disloyal to the nation. In particular, the regimes were not above using the vilest anti-Semitic jibes against the proponents of what they termed 'cosmopolitanism'. These tended to surface in moments of crisis, as in the aftermath of the Prague Spring and the Polish March events, both of 1968, when the rulers needed to grasp any ideas, no matter how disgusting, to win themselves popularity. In Poland in particular, of course, anti-Semitism had a long and foul history, and the communists adopted all of the traditional rhetoric in their campaigns (Goban-Klas, 1994: 133–46). The idea of the 'nation' has always exercised an evil attraction for the left, and the communist regimes of Eastern and Central Europe were only too happy to embrace it.

The line between opposition and regime on the question of national identity was thus a great deal less clear than it has sometimes been subsequently presented. The communists fostered their version of nationalism rather than attempting to eradicate it root and branch. As the regimes fell apart, it was often recently communist leaders and journalists who became the most vocal proponents of the new nationalism. Slobodan Milosevic is only the best known of an army of former communist bureaucrats and functionaries throughout the region who made the transformation to nationalist demagogues without the slightest difficulty.

The tragic consequences of these nationalist currents for many of the post-communist countries are well known. The division of Czechoslovakia into separate Czech and Slovak Republics, which increased the number of states upon which this study is focused from three to four, was the most peaceable and least barbaric of the new divisions of the region. We do not here need to expand upon the horrors that have taken place elsewhere. In the narrower context of the media, we will have occasion to note, both in the discussion of the legal arrangements for broadcasting and in some of the disputes over the political direction of post-communist television, the ways in which this general nationalist climate has influenced debates.

The second unifying feature of the opposition is more central to our current concerns. Where the communists emphasised unity, the opposition emphasised diversity. Where the communists emphasised the state and the party, the opposition emphasised the private actions of ordinary people. These ideas were formulated in various ways, but the common theme was an 'anti-politics' that embodied a rejection of the dominant discourses of political life as it was then experienced and stressed the empowerment of everyone:

> Yes, anti-political politics is possible. Politics 'from below'. Politics of people, not of the apparatus. Politics growing from the heart, not from a thesis. It is no accident that this hopeful experience has to be lived just here, on this grim battlement. In conditions of humdrum 'everydayness', we have to descend to the very bottom of the well before we can see the stars. (Havel, 1988: 398)

In this particular case, the formulation of the political perspective is understandably literary, and perhaps tinged with anti-modernism almost as much as anti-communism. In other cases, the same idea found a more philosophical formulation in discussion about the need to build a 'civil society'. This idea has been so widely diffused, and is so frequently invoked in discussions of the media around the world, that we need to give special attention to its elaboration and consequences.

The evolution of the concept of civil society

The use of the term 'civil society' was not specific to the opponents of communist states. It was used extensively in the struggles against the military dictatorships in South America and against the apartheid regime in South Africa. Subsequent to 1989, it has become very widely diffused in political and social theory, and has informed much writing about the media, including in the West. In all of these cases, it contains a common theme of the need to lay a stress on the empowerment of the mass of the population through the fostering of non-state organisation acting against those who dominate society, be they communist tyrants, military dictators, white racists or plain old capitalists.

Despite this widespread usage, the term had a special importance, and a particular difficulty, for the opposition to communism. Its provenance is usually dated to an essay by the Polish oppositionist Adam Michnik, written in the mid-1970s. This essay, or at least its English translation, does not actually employ the term 'civil society', but it clearly anticipates the central strategies of those who came to employ it (Michnik, 1985). Michnik rejected both of the existing strategies of opposition to the communist regime: that of attempting to influence the party leadership in desirable directions with a hope of reforming the system into democratic socialism; and that of attempting to organise the overthrow of the system and its replacement by some other form of social organisation. In its place, Michnik proposed an attempt to build alternative structures – associational groups, publishing enterprises, and so on – outside the official mass organisations of communist society.

In the short term, this perspective did not command enormous support, at least in Poland. Michnik and his interlocutors belonged to the intelligentsia and the dominant Polish tradition of opposition was large-scale proletarian protests like strikes and battles with the riot police. The extent to which these two currents were interlinked is much disputed, but it does seem that 'the roots of Solidarity were in the Baltic working class'. The intellectuals 'made a necessary but not a causal or creative contribution' to the massive strike wave and the foundation of Solidarity (Laba, 1991: 178). The high point of the union saw the discussion of proposals for immediate and radical changes in the society. The ideas current during the period when Solidarity was a mass movement went far beyond the much more cautious strategy mapped out by the oppositional intellectuals (Pelczynski, 1988: 376).

These ideas included proposals for a radical restructuring and democratisation of the mass media. The intention was both to free the media from the power of the Communist Party, to enable the citizens to receive accurate opinion and information, and to empower the citizens to articulate their views and opinions (Reading, 1994). In terms of the governance of radio and television, for example, these proposals involved the construction of a body of lay citizens to oversee its workings:

> Solidarity demands the abolition of the state administration's monopoly in running radio and television because it is contrary to the constitution of the Polish People's Republic. . . . Solidarity will take action to institute genuine public control over radio and television by appointing a managing and executive body representing government, political parties, trade unions, religious associations, social organizations, professional artists' unions, and self-management groups of the employees who produce and beam the programmes. (cited in Goban-Klas, 1994: 176)

This demand is one example of the expression of a desire for a thoroughgoing transformation of the mass media in order to bring them much more closely under the control of the mass of the population. It is a genuinely radical programme that bears close comparison with many of the ideas advanced in the West. To the extent that the term 'civil society' may be applied to this kind of programme, it means something a little short of the withering away of the state, but it implies a radical diminution of the power of the apparatus and a great increase in the ability of associations of ordinary people to control significant areas of social life.

Proposals of this kind were indeed seen as constituting a strategy based on the idea of civil society, particularly by expert expatriate observers in the West (Arato, 1981: 24; Bauman, 1981: 54). They constituted a programme of radical change to the communist order, but would be almost equally explosive if applied to societies based on private capitalism. In this conception, civil society had wide international appeal precisely because it seemed to offer an alternative to both state- and market-dominated models of the mass media. Unfortunately, the proposals did not have much chance to develop in Poland. After the imposition of martial law in December 1981, the opportunities for mass involvement in political life were destroyed. In their place, there was an enormous effort at the construction of underground and church-sponsored groups, meetings, publications and so on. In this situation, reminding one almost as much of the old nationalist slogan of the 'parallel society' as of any new thinking, the idea of the importance of *building* civil society gradually came to gain support. The foundations of civil society were already being laid in the web of illegal and semi-legal organisations, and these could continue to be expanded until such point as the regime was prepared to negotiate terms.

So long as the regimes, looking over their shoulders at the threat of Russian invasion, were not prepared to negotiate in any serious way, the idea of constructing civil society stood for a general range of oppositional activities, none of which could claim any particular priority or importance over the others. Within the forced unity of opposition, however, there was a series of different interpretations of what this new strategy might actually mean in practice (Kennedy, 1992: 29–63). In the course of this evolution, the radical edge that was present in the high period of Solidarity as a mass working-class movement was lost. The term 'civil society' changed its meaning, and came to stand for a number of different, and distinctly less far-reaching, strategies. In order to understand these, we need to examine the nature and a little of the history of the term in some detail.

The widespread use of the idea of civil society dates from the eighteenth century. Much of the subsequent discussion can be seen as part of the debate over the nature and meaning of the great French Revolution. In this context, the greatest and most systematic articulation of the idea into social and political theory was made by Hegel in his late and conservative *Philosophy of Right* (Hegel, 1967). Much later, the term was reintroduced into Marxist discussion, in a rather different sense, by Gramsci, but it is to the early nineteenth-century usage that more recent writers have generally referred (Bobbio, 1988).

In the lectures that made up his book, Hegel attempted to explain the necessary interdependence of three elements of social and political life: the family; civil society; and the state. The tripartite division of Hegel's political theory has often been overlooked, although it has recently been recovered by feminist critics of the patriarchal character of political theory (Pateman, 1988: 102–3). This division's importance for Hegel's theory is that it is only through the opposition of family and civil society that can we fully understand exactly what the function of the state is supposed to be. The fact that this dimension was dropped from most discussions of the question, and the family more or less unproblematically integrated into civil society, is one of the first theoretical problems with contemporary usages.

The family was the immediate site of natural affections. It was the world of the private. At the head of each family stood the father, subordinate to whom was the wife and the children. The model of the family was that of the small family firm, in which the father disposed of the family capital. Each family, through the activity of its head, entered into relations, which were primarily economic in character, with the heads of other families. This was the realm of civil society. If the family united people on the basis of love, then civil society divided them on the basis of self-interest. The role of the state was to reconstitute the unity of the home at the level of society as a whole: it was the state that produced ethical and political life (Sparks, 1994: 26–36; Sparks and

Reading, 1995: 33–9). In Hegel, the state, civil society and the family were necessary moments of the constitutional state, each of which was appropriate to a particular aspect of human behaviour. Despite the wild claims that have later been made for the necessary connection between the idea of civil society and democracy, for Hegel, the state was definitely not democratic in political form. On the contrary, one of the functions of the tripartite division of human society was to demonstrate how the ideal form of the state was necessarily a constitutional monarchy.

The important points in this extremely brief account are, first, that Hegel centred civil society on free and equal economic exchange: it was for him conflictual rather than associational. Those associative organisations that did exist in this realm, which he identified as guilds (trade organisations) and the police (by which he meant social services), were necessary only because of the accidental shortcomings of a system of exchange. They dealt with what Hegel termed 'contingencies' still lurking in the system. Second, he placed the family, in its familiar patriarchal form, outside the realm of civil society (Reading, 1994).

In modern usage, we can detect three mutations of Hegel's classical formulation. The first of these is the one closest to his own, in that it retains the tripartite structure of the original. On this account, the problem with communist societies is that the state has swallowed the family and civil society. The programme that follows from this is simple: the sphere of the state must be reduced and the family and civil society must be resurrected in opposition to the state. In economic terms, the state should be stripped of as much as possible of its economic role and the various activities privatised. In social terms, the family must once again become the centre of emotional and reproductive life. This was probably the most widespread view in Eastern European countries. As one commentator wrote of Poland before the transformation:

> By the mid-1980's, civil society came to mean for the Polish opposition precisely what Marx believed it meant all along – bourgeois society and nothing more. But whereas for Marx this meant the need for the destruction of civil society, for the Polish opposition it meant that the struggle to recreate civil society had to take the form of a struggle for bourgeois society. (Ost, 1989: 78)

As was pointed out by critics and proclaimed by some of its adherents, this was essentially a 'Thatcherite' programme for the urgent construction of private capitalism (Meiskens Wood, 1990). The radical intentions of the earlier discussions of civil society had more or less disappeared from this new account. This version of the idea of civil society was extremely 'materialist', in that it stressed that changes to the nature of economic and social relations were a prerequisite to the establishment of more 'civilised' ways of conducting political life.

Despite its closeness to Hegel's original formulation, however, in one important respect this version of civil society departed from his views. The programme of constructing bourgeois society, whether couched in terms of civil society or derived more brutally from Hayek, implied that the necessary consequence of achieving this goal was that there would be plurality and democracy. We should note that the distinction between plurality and democracy is one seldom drawn in this tradition, and whose implications are never explored. Building civil society, for this position, also meant building democracy.

Not all of the oppositionists in the communist countries, or their supporters in the West, were entirely happy with the prospect of overthrowing communism in order to build capitalism. After all, anyone could see that there was rather a lot wrong with capitalism. Instead, they looked to a third way, sociologically if not geographically somewhere between Sweden and the former Yugoslavia, which would encourage a benign form of civil society. The theoretical result of this was a revision of Hegel's model into a new tripartite form. On the one hand there remained the state, but this was now joined by the realm of the economy. On the other hand there was the separate and distinct realm of civil society. This latter consisted of voluntary organisations, associations, the family and so on. As two of its most distinguished Western theorists formulated it:

> We understand 'civil society' as a sphere of social interaction between economy and state, composed above all of the intimate sphere (especially the family), the sphere of associations (especially voluntary associations), social movements, and forms of public communication. Modern civil society is created through forms of self-constitution and self-mobilisation. It is institutionalized and generalized through laws, and especially subjective rights, that stabilize social differentiation. While the self-creative and institutionalized dimensions can exist separately, in the long term both independent action and institutionalization are necessary for the reproduction of civil society. (Cohen and Arato, 1992: ix)

We may consider this version of civil society as much more 'idealist', in that it is through the voluntary efforts of the mass of the population that the institutions needed to counter the power of the state and economic institutions will be created. In this account, the precise nature of the economic and state forms that prevail, whether socialist or capitalist, is secondary to the existence of countervailing power in the form of the voluntary associations of citizens.

Even this, however, did not quite satisfy all of the proponents of the term, since civil society in this formulation remains a category that could contain negative social forces and organisations as much as positive ones. There is nothing in the notion of the 'self-creative' nature of associations that assumes that they will adopt the side of freedom and democracy: after all, the hated communist parties of Central and Eastern Europe had mostly begun their lives precisely as voluntary associations formed under conditions of the most bitter persecution. The final, and relatively minor, reformulation was therefore to define civil society in terms purely of those associations to which it was possible to ascribe a positive dimension. This view was expressed most clearly by the Czechoslovak dissident Dienstbier:

> The basic aim of the self-organisation of civil society, of independent and parallel activities, is the preservation and renewal of normality, as we understand it in the European tradition. This means the renewal of civic awareness and interest in the affairs of the community; it means an appeal to the quality of work and decency in

human relationships; it means the attempt to maintain and expand awareness of one's legal rights, self-education and assisting in the education of others, writing books, publishing periodicals, putting on plays, holding seminars, exhibitions, concerts, etc. And it also means forming judgements, without emotion and with an effort to get as much information from as wide a variety of sources as possible, on various aspects of the domestic and international situation. (Benda et al., 1988: 231)

In this version, which we may term the 'poetic' account, the category of civil society effectively consists, not of the activity of people associated outside the sphere of the state, but solely of the activity of nice, educated, concerned, cultured and altruistic professional people associated outside the sphere of the state.

From these three, very different, theoretical conceptions of the nature of civil society flowed different strategies for the organisation of the mass media. In the case of the 'materialist' example, represented most clearly in media terms by Oleg Manaev, the mass media are no different to any other part of the economy. State ownership necessarily means dictatorship over the media and is incompatible with democratic political life. Following Hayek, Manaev argued that in any society there were active elements, called 'subjects', and those who were acted upon ('objects'):

Obviously the classical totalitarian society is monosubjective; only the State (parto-, theo-, or ethnocratic one) is a real free and actively operating subject in it. All the other elements of such a society are rather objects . . . of various actions of this super-monosubject. (Manaev, 1993: 120)

The best way to break this is to privatise as much of the mass media as quickly as possible. The existence of private media, whatever their limitations, mean that at the very least the views of several different social subjects are available to the mass of the population (Manaev, 1993: 147–8). The question of empowering society to control the mass media is solved by allowing society to own the media. But since, obviously, 'society' can't own anything, in practice individual members of society should be empowered to own newspapers, television stations and so on.

The idealistic version of civil society was by far the most widely diffused, being particularly strong in what was to become the state of Slovenia. The final years of communist decay saw the development of a range of different kinds of social and intellectual organisations that self-consciously represented themselves as 'civil society', as against the communist state (Splichal, 1994: 22–4). It found particularly strong support in the ways in which a number of journalists, and indeed publications, were able to articulate an oppositional position to that of the communist regime. In fact, due to the peculiar ways in which communist rule broke down in the former Yugoslavia, the most prominent of these publications were themselves more or less maverick publications formally owned by the dominant party itself. They were, nevertheless, the focal points, first for discussions and ultimately for popular mobilisation. They were the active constituents in the formation of what appeared to be a new and healthy civil society (Novak, 1996). Proponents of this view of civil society, like Slavko Splichal, had studied the Western media in some detail and were well aware of the problems involved in simply replacing the state with the market. Unlike the crudely materialist views of Manaev and others, they did not see the selling off of the mass media as any long-term guarantee that they would contribute to civil society and a healthy democratic polity.

Representatives of the poetic interpretation tended to stress the ways in which the relaxation of party control over the media allowed the representation of previously silenced voices and the empowerment of the citizens against large social organisations. As one observer wrote about the first days of the collapse of communism in Poland:

> Pluralization meant both the expansion of independent publishing by SDP (Polish Journalists' Union) members and continuing support for clandestine publishing, as well as ongoing attempts to bring institutions like Polish TV, which was seen as an instrument of social disintegration, or the publishing monopoly RSW Prasa-Ksiazka-Ruch, under social control. . . . Civil society is on the move. Hundreds of initiatives are springing up, from a Catholic Film Production Company sponsored by Andrzej Wajda and several other Catholic film makers, to a branch of SDP for high-school students. The unprecedented extent of decentralizing technologies such as audio-cassettes and VCRs, the backbone of independent culture for seven years, show no sign of abating, with three independent video producers in operation offering news, documentaries and films. The latter are preparing to sell both to the new television and to continue old channels of distribution through parishes and social networks of friends. Some citizens committees which organized the 1989 election on behalf of Solidarity are preparing to take over the bankrupt afternoon regional papers from RSW 'Prasa'. (Fedorowicz, 1990: 82–3)

The general hope was that all of this activity that developed underground in the years of opposition and which flourished as the systems entered terminal collapse would continue to provide the guiding principle for social communication in the new liberated environment. This very unleashing of popular energy and enthusiasm would in and of itself ensure that the new civil society was purged of all elements of domination and arbitrary power.

The idea of civil society thus evolved from a radical plan to transform the ways in which major social institutions like the mass media were controlled and divided into two major, and much less radical, strands. The first of these I have termed materialist, in that it stressed first and foremost the need to change the economic structures of society. The mass media were to be handed over to private ownership, and on this basis freedom and democracy would flourish. The second major strand stressed the need for strengthening voluntary organisations as the sole guarantors of popular rights. Within it, there was a spectrum from those who saw the existence of associational structures as a sufficient guarantee of a healthy civil society, whom I have termed the idealists, and those in the poetic tendency who saw the need to support only those associations that were filled with good intentions. The differences are summarised in Table 5.1.

Each of these different positions had implications for the ways in which the running of the mass media should be organised. The materialist explanation had the simplest answer: the maximum degree of privatisation would automatically ensure democratisation. Both of the other strands retained some

Table 5.1   *Different theories of civil society and the media*

Version	Key elements	Changes to media	General theorist	Media theorist
Radical	State/associations	Popular control	(Early Solidarity)	(Early Solidarity)
Materialist	State/civil society/ family	Privatise	(Hegel/Hayek) Kornai, Klaus	Manaev
Idealist	People/economy/ state	Empower associations	Arato, Cohen	Splichal
Poetic	Nice people/ power structures	Empower nice associations	Keane, Dienstbier	Fedorowicz

elements of the earlier radical project, in that they wished to ensure that ordinary people had some say in the running of media organisations, but they were far less clear about who was to be empowered, the exact ways in which this was to be organised, and the relationship between citizens and the basic economic and organisational structures of the mass media.

Testing the theories

The various different ideas of civil society and their implications for the mass media were very quickly put to what one might almost call an experimental test in the period after 1989. One of the main theorists of civil society argued: 'What was potentially new in the transformation of the East [was] the option of a self-democratizing civil society' (Arato, 1993: 612). It can seldom have been the case that apparently abstract ideas in political philosophy have been so directly related to the practical business of legislation and the exercise of executive power. Many observers saw the situation, particularly as regards the mass media, in almost experimental terms (Cohen, 1993). The outcomes of this natural experiment allow us to observe with particular, and decisive, clarity the utility of the different concepts that lie behind the term 'civil society' for the guidance of human affairs.

The old Stalinist state machine had had its own apparatus that fulfilled many of the functions of 'civil society', in the form of a vast mass of organisations designed to cater for every taste and social position. These, of course, failed the test of genuine independence and could not seriously be considered 'civil society'. They were, rather, a range of mass organisations controlled by the party. The best that could be hoped was that, as the bureaucracy split and argued amongst itself in the process of its final decay, spaces would open up for the use of existing organisations for the formation of at least the rudiments of the future civil society. This, in fact, was what occurred in the former Yugoslavia as the communist state gradually broke up along national lines, and the various sections of the bureaucracy attempted to strengthen their positions by allowing oppositional voices a hearing. In the long run, however, if civil society were to mean anything at all in connection with democracy, then the new social constructions would need to meet a number of criteria of difference. In particular, new organisations would need to be set up that embodied the principles of civil society and embedded them in law and social practice.

These organisations of civil society would need to be new, rather than simple continuations of the old order. They could not be red institutions painted white, as the phrase then ran. They would need to be constructed in such a way as to empower, rather than regiment, their participants. They would need to have structures that allowed their participants control over them, rather than being in reality organisations controlled and directed by an élite. They would need to exert real influence over the running of society and its major institutions.

In all of these aspects, the media were obviously of central importance. If civil society were to match up to the claims as to its central role in the construction of democratic society attributed to it by any of its three different versions, then this must involve a radically different set of relations between society and the mass media. Where the old relations had been 'top-down', then the new ones would need to be 'bottom-up'. Where the old relations had been ones of authority, the new ones would need to be characterised by thoroughgoing democratisation. Where the old relations had inscribed a discourse of arbitrary authority, the new relations would have to embody rational popular empowerment. Where the old relations had ensured the domination of an élite, the new relations would enable the people to make decisions.

In practice, these ideas proved to be completely illusory. In none of the mass media was any serious attempt made to 'empower civil society' in any sense other than the narrowest form of property ownership. On the contrary, a review of the evidence demonstrates that the élite control of the media, albeit in a rather different form, survived the transition barely reduced. There is no evidence whatsoever that any of the claims of the theorists of civil society to empower new groups of people were carried through in practice. When yesterday's persecuted oppositionist became today's minister, the drive to empower the mass of population disappeared almost immediately. The most that can be said is that, in the case of the printed press, there was a change in forms of ownership, often of dubious legality, which transformed this medium into a market-driven one. In the case of broadcasting, any attempts to empower civil society quickly evaporated and only the political élite gained a say in the running of television and radio. The quasi-experimental test of the various versions of civil society demonstrated quite clearly that they all offered an inadequate understanding of social dynamics and failed to act as guides to political practice.

If we consider the case of the printed press, we have already seen how change was characterised by a process whereby the bulk of the existing journalists, and often the existing editorial hierarchy in its entirety, simply took over the mass media. This was followed, or even accompanied, by a change in formal ownership in which large-scale media enterprises, often foreign owned, took a major or controlling interest in the papers. It cannot seriously be maintained that empowering a Maxwell, a Murdoch, a Bertelsmann, a Springer, a Neue Passauer Frei Presse or a Hersant constituted what anybody meant by 'empowering civil society'.

Even where the final ownership of the leading papers remained in the hands of the journalists, as for example in Slovenia and the Czech Republic, and in parts of the Polish press, the process of privatisation was not organised so as to ensure that, either internally or externally, there was any empowerment of civil society. When the press was privatised, either formally or informally, there was no insistence that a condition for legal recognition of that privatisation was the constitution of a democratic internal regime for the employees as a whole, or even for the journalists alone. Still less was it the case that there was any insistence that the papers find ways of enshrining the ideas of the readers in the direction of the paper through the construction of representative controlling bodies. Two Hungarian writers described very clearly the actual nature of the transfer of ownership in one part of the press:

> In early March 1990, a unique method of depriving a publishing house of its newspapers and periodicals was invented in Hungary. All the journalists and editors of the single national sports daily, the single women's weekly and all the satirical weeklies of the country abrogated their contracts of employment with the respective publishing houses on the same day and signed new ones with limited companies they had established collectively. They changed the names of the papers slightly and appeared on the market very soon. The papers of the new limited companies were delivered to subscribers without warning. (Gálik and Dénes, 1992: 11)

In such circumstance, the only form of 'control' over the papers exercised by their readers was their purchasing decisions, and in this instance even that was carefully limited by the new owners.

There was no attempt to ensure that the newly freed press was an embodiment of diversity either internally or externally. No law obliged the press to represent a variety of opinion within their own pages. No law contained provision to sustain press products putting forward minority views independently of the whims of the government of the day. While anyone was free to set up a newspaper or magazine, it was left entirely to the familiar processes of the capitalist market to determine which of these survived. No special encouragement was anywhere given to those forms of ownership, like readers' co-operatives, which might provide an alternative to purely market relations. However defined, a civil society, it might be thought, would be concerned to find ways of organising its press so that a range of views and opinions, particularly those from ordinary citizens, would find a voice in the press. Such a strategy was nowhere attempted. The press was simply passed over to the market, and moderated only by the political interests of the new governments.

The most vivid example of the way in which the shift in the press was undertaken without any serious thought for the development of civil society concerns the change in the Slovenian constitution. In the former Yugoslavia, the constitution included a clause that gave all citizens the right to express an opinion. Obviously, during the period of confident communist rule, this constitutional enactment was little more than window-dressing. In principle, however, it represented a unique democratic form.

Many, perhaps most, countries recognise the right to freedom of speech, but not all extend that right even so far as the right of a citizen to have a statement refuting an inaccurate report published. The UK, for example, does not. The US Supreme Court, in the famous Miami case, ruled that someone who felt aggrieved had no legally enforceable right to a reply in the same organ, since this would be a breach of the First Amendment conferring absolute freedom on the owner of a newspaper. What was unique about the old Yugoslav constitution was that it not only permitted a citizen the right to reply, but also granted the right of a citizen to initiate an article and to have it printed. Should a newspaper refuse to publish such an article, then the author had the right to appeal against the editorial decision to the court, which could oblige the paper in question to publish it.

In the early 1980s, as the Yugoslav regime began to break up, a Slovenian lawyer, and party member, started to try to exercise this right. He wrote a number of highly critical articles, including one that attacked the chief editor of the main daily newspaper, *Delo*. Initially, these articles were rejected by the newspaper in question and the lawyer's early attempts to force publication through the courts were unsuccessful. However, he persevered and in 1984 won a judgment from the Slovene Supreme Court that *Delo* was obliged, in the public interest, to print an article he had written; in fact, it was one that attacked the chief editor. This *Delo* eventually did.

There were one or two other successful cases during that period, but in essence this judgment had established the precedent that, unless a newspaper could show that the content of an article sent to it was trivial, it was obliged to publish it. In other words, 'civil society', in the oppositional sense, was granted direct and unmediated access to the main organs of the press.

The category 'civil society' was very important in the development of the opposition in Slovenia. The movement here was much larger and more sophisticated than in the other parts of Yugoslavia and it was in fact only in Slovenia that this legal position was ever established in practice. It was therefore surprising that, when this same civil society came to power after independence in 1990, the right was abolished in the new constitution. There was no public protest when it was argued that, while the right had been important and possible during the period when the media were 'social property', it was no longer appropriate now that the media were privately owned. The new government respected the right of property over the right to free speech. Civil society was no barrier against the power of ownership (Novak, 1996).

The case of television is a little more complex. Most of the systems that emerged have had, as we shall see, a strong 'European' dimension. That is to say, rather than privatising all channels and distributing frequencies to commercial operators, all states have retained at least one channel in non-commercial hands. There is, in Europe at least, a strong tradition that both public and commercial broadcasters are subject to some degree of external control. While it has generally been thought that the printed press can be left to pursue its own unsupervised ends, various arguments, of differing degrees of liberality, have been advanced and accepted as to why broadcasting needs to be regulated. There exists, therefore, a relatively powerful alternative to the market as a way in which broadcasting might be organised so as to broaden the range of opinion represented in its content and government, and this might be seen as the starting point for the institutional establishment of the powers of civil society as against the state. In the general European debate, this aspect of the media is usually referred to as 'public-service television'.

At its strongest, this term signifies a broadcasting organisation that is both independent of the market and the immediate pressures of the state. In reality, of course, not all of the broadcasters who tend to be grouped under this heading are in fact independent of either or both of these influences. Some of the models of regulation, for example the French Conseil Supérieur de l'Audiovisual (CSA), are clearly not concerned with empowering civil society and are explicitly concerned with legally regulating the differences of opinion that occur in a fragmented political élite. Others, like the British, empower a group drawn from a narrow range of the élite, but do not directly reflect party political power. The German model, which explicitly represents different political and social groups, might be taken as the nearest to a principle of the empowerment of representatives of civil society, although in practice this seems to mean that the political parties dominate broadcasting.

Imperfect though these various examples are, they do however suggest that the regulation of broadcasting might be constructed in such a way as to ensure the representation of groups other than the political élite itself, and to reflect a range of opinion rather wider than that of the currently ruling parties.

These examples exerted some influence on the legal regulation of broadcasting in the formerly communist countries, partly because they were well known to the experts charged with developing the new laws and partly because many Western advisers, particularly from the Council of Europe, promoted the idea of regulated public broadcasting quite strongly. The framing of the new legal situation clearly permitted an attempt to turn theories of civil society into the concrete practice of social control. Even if the argument of the need for freedom of property were decisive in the press and in commercial broadcasting, there still remained the possibility of constructing the governing councils of public television in such a way as to ensure that civil society was well represented.

There were, indeed, some attempts to ensure that it was not the state machine or the political élite that had the dominant say in the direction of television. The clearest example of this was the case of Hungary. Government policy was articulated in terms that clearly owed a debt to ideas of civil society. According to the Undersecretary of State at the Ministry of Justice responsible for broadcasting legislation: 'Institutionalised social control is an important element of the system of guarantees, which is aimed at ensuring that Hungarian Radio and Hungarian Television really function as public broadcaster' (Papácsy, 1992: 3). The supervisory body proposed in the 'first' broadcasting bill was based upon German examples, but an attempt was made to shift the balance away from the political party domination that was perceived as being characteristic of that model. From the early drafts of the Hungarian Broadcasting Bill, there was provision for up to half of the supervisory board to be nominated by political parties represented in the National Assembly and by the government (Hungary, 1991: Article 42). However, 'The number of members delegated and elected on the basis of Art. 42 may not exceed half of the total membership of the supervisory board' (Hungary, 1991: Article 43). Article 44 specified that the other delegates must come from 'organizations operating in [13 specified] spheres of interest'. The list of spheres included science, education, ethnic minorities, women, youth, sports, environmentalists and religious bodies. This formulation proved too imprecise, and the November 1992 draft of the Bill spelt out a principle of rotation in much greater detail. This attempt to find ways in which organisations not directly concerned with formal political life might have some say in the running of television obviously constitutes an attempt to enshrine the positive principles of the old opposition in statute (Hungary, 1992: Article 53). At this stage, there clearly was a genuine attempt to build into the governance of television a set of arrangements that would severely limit the direct influence of the political élite, empower non-state organisations, and thus try to ensure that broadcasting, while not reduced simply to private property, would be independent of the state.

The passage of a Broadcasting Bill in Hungary became embroiled in the notorious 'media wars', to which we shall return in the next chapter. Here, however, we need only note that the finally agreed Act modified the good intentions of the earlier drafts in ways that significantly strengthened the political élite. The 1995 Act gave the overall supervision of all broadcasting to the new National Radio and Television Board. This was empowered to licence new broadcasters, to regulate their activities, to operate a complaints committee, and generally to oversee all aspects of broadcasting. The members of this powerful body are 'elected for a four-year term by a single majority of all Members of Parliament'. They are to be nominated 'by the Parliamentary factions'. The chair of the board is 'jointly nominated by the President of the Republic and the Prime Minister' (Hungary, 1995: Section 33). There is, therefore, a finely tuned attempt to ensure that there is a balance on the new board, but it is a balance between sections of the political élite. Entirely missing from this body are the representatives of civil society.

Echoes of the old concerns do indeed find a place in the new law. Those broadcasters that are 'public foundations', primarily the new Hungarian Radio Public Foundation, the Hungarian Television Public Foundation and the Public Television Foundation 'Hungaria' (charged with broadcasting to Hungarians living outside the national borders), are governed by boards of trustees. The members of these organisations are appointed by two distinct methods. Eight members are elected by Parliament, from amongst individuals nominated by parliamentary factions 'in such a manner that at least one member nominated by all factions shall be elected' (Hungary, 1995: Section

55). These eight members are outnumbered by the 21 members delegated by a similar range of 'civil society' organisations to previous drafts. These include representatives of churches, minorities, sports organisations, old age pensioners, women, young people and so on (Hungary, 1995: Section 56. In the case of 'Hungaria', it is 23 representatives).

This arrangement appears to enshrine the principle of the empowerment of civil society at least in the management of the daily affairs of the public broadcasters. There are, however, a number of ways in which the detail of the legislation renders the powers of the representatives of civil society relatively less than they might appear. In the first place, the members nominated by Parliament are constituted as a distinct group, called the 'Presidential Body of the Board of Trustees' (Hungary, 1995: Section 55). The Presidential Body will meet at least monthly, while the whole Board meets only at least quarterly (Hungary, 1995: Section 61). It is the Presidential Body that runs the selection of the executive chairmen of radio and television, and has the initiative in dismissing them, although the actual election and dismissal are the province of the trustees as a whole. It is the Presidential Body that has the power to inspect the details of management (Hungary, 1995: Section 66). There is, in addition, a further and entirely separate body, the Supervisory Committee, that consists of three persons nominated by Parliament, which can report directly to Parliament in the event of a clash with the Board of Trustees. Unlike the other bodies, serving MPs may be members of this committee. It is notable that this body has, by law, a majority of opposition nominees (Hungary, 1995: Section 62).

It is quite clear, therefore, that the degree to which the representatives of civil society actually have any say in the running of radio and television is very limited. Their powers are carefully circumscribed by provisions that give considerable weight to people whose positions are entirely dependent upon the various factions represented in Parliament. Decisive power thus lies with the political élite rather than with civil society. It should, in addition, be noted that these arrangements are carefully contrived so as to attempt to ensure, not that the governing party is in possession of sole power of broadcasting, but that all the forces represented in the political élite are allowed a share of this control. The principle is thus clearly and indisputably one of empowering political society, as opposed either to the government or civil society.

A very similar conclusion was reached in Czechoslovakia. The October 1991 Federal Broadcasting Law established a Federal Broadcasting Council of '9 members from among experts, prominent personalities and public figures'. They were to be appointed one-third each by the Federal Assembly and the Czech and Slovak National Councils. While they would therefore clearly be political appointees, it is significant that a condition of membership of the Broadcasting Council was that they 'may not have functions in any political parties or political movements and may not actively and publicly appear in the name of any political parties or act to their advantage', nor represent any business interests involved in broadcasting (Czechoslovak Federal Republic, 1991: Article 18.3). The Czech TV law of 7 November 1991 specified a regulatory Television Council whose membership was designated by Parliament (Czech National Assembly, 1991: Article 4.4). In addition, a rather more open programme supervisory body, which included representatives of political parties and social, cultural and regional bodies, was set up (Czech National Assembly, 1991: Article 4.1). The chair of this body is the director general of Czech TV and the supervisory body has the power to appoint the editor-in-chief and directors of Czech TV. Similar provisions applied in Slovakia.

The split of Czechoslovakia into separate Czech and Slovak Republics, consummated on 1 January 1993, meant that the federal element of supervision became redundant. The national assemblies of both new countries had rapidly passed enabling legislation that permitted the restructuring of the former federal arrangements on to the basis of two distinct states. In the case of broadcasting, there was a very considerable continuity between the old and new systems (Johnson, 1993: 10–11; Kaplan et al., 1993: 12). What therefore emerged in the Czech and Slovak cases were broadcasting councils, responsible for the regulation of television and radio, that were directly accountable to Parliament and, as we shall see, directly subject to parliamentary pressure. There is, today, no sense in which the legislation empowers civil society.

The Polish case is, if anything, even more conclusive. There had been, as we have seen, a serious attempt made, in the early 1980s, to elaborate a genuine theory of popular control over the mass media (Reading, 1994). Although this was not couched in the language of 'civil society', the intent was clearly the same. As the situation changed, and as Solidarity modified both its aims and its practices, these attempts at a radical democratisation of communication receded into the background. In their place, a new and less extreme version of popular empowerment was developed. We can see this shift spelt out very clearly in an article written by Karol Jakubowicz in 1988, just as the Polish communist system was entering its final crisis. Jakubowicz argued that the existing theories of democratic communication, as much in the West as elsewhere, were no longer adequate. Developing the familiar distinction between direct and representative democracy with regard to different ways of thinking about communication, he argued that:

> Under ordinary circumstances most people would seem to be content to accept representative communicative democracy in the sphere of mass communication, so long as it is a diversified system corresponding to the differentiation of society, including broad participation in the formulation of communication policies, in the organization and management of the media and direct accountability of the media to society and the groups they represent. In representative democracy, decision making processes should take place in conditions of equality, autonomy, and adequate representation. If these conditions are met in the way media are organized and run, and in social communication itself, then representative communicative democracy has a chance of satisfying most of the expectation of a democratic-minded society. (Jakubowicz, 1993: 44–5)

Although the positive proposals of these formulations are ambiguous, they clearly represent a critique of any idea of directly empowering civil society. To speak of 'representative democracy' as having this key role is to envisage the political state as having a major role in the direction of broadcasting.

As we have seen, the interim arrangements for the media agreed by the 'round table' were conceived in exactly such terms: political influence on broadcasting was redistributed between the communists and their opponents according to a bargaining process. These, of course, were temporary measures produced by an exceptional situation, and one might expect to have found a more systematic attempt to realise some of the ideals of civil society in the considered legislation on broadcasting enacted by the new, freely elected, Parliament in which the former opposition commanded a clear majority. On the contrary, the issue of empowering civil society hardly ever enters into the debate. The sole reference to anything other than political appointees having any influence over the running of radio and television is in the 14 December 1990 Draft Broadcasting Law. In this draft, the National Broadcasting Board was to have 11 members nominated by the President and appointed with the approval of Diet (Poland, 1990a: Article 7.2). The National Board in turn appointed six members of a Supervisory Board. The seventh was to be appointed by 'the relevant employees' federations' (Poland, 1990a: Article 9.3). Even this minimal concession to social control had disappeared in later drafts (Poland, 1991). The law eventually passed simply has a National Council appointed by a combination of the two Houses of Parliament and the President of the Republic (Poland, 1992).

The reason for the elaborate system of appointment had nothing to do with the desire to open the control of radio and television to outside forces representing civil society. On the contrary, it was a product of the tense situation prevailing between President and Sejm, and represented an attempt to compromise between the powers of the different constitutional elements.

The extent to which any of the revised broadcasting laws have been prepared to widen the powers of ordinary citizens, rather than those of the political élite or its dependents, is thus everywhere extremely limited. Even in the case of Hungary, where the law as eventually enacted does indeed make some provision for such representation, the extent to which these formal provisions can actually be exercised in practice is uncertain. Given the weakness of the drive to establish such representation, it must be doubted whether it will prove effective. Elsewhere, even this dubious memory of the idea of empowering civil society is entirely absent. To the extent that the new broadcasting laws in Eastern Europe enshrine the principle of plurality in the governance of public broadcasting, it is a plurality for the political élite rather than for citizens.

Conclusion

In its earliest form, the idea of civil society represented a retreat from confrontation with the communist state. With the rise of mass working-class opposition to the system in Poland, the idea was to a considerable extent radicalised and became a programme for the transformation of social power relations. The defeat of Solidarity meant a retreat from those 'hot moods', and the idea of civil society underwent considerable revision. It split into three main currents. One, the most materialist, saw it as primarily another way of arguing for private capitalism. A second, the 'idealist', saw civil society as a sphere of voluntary associations separate from both the state and the economy, which would act as some sort of controlling or countervailing force over the anti-democratic elements inherent in those two power structures. The final version, termed here the 'poetic', retained some of the radical vision of the Solidarity phase, in that it hoped that the associations of civil society would be inspired by a democratic spirit and lead to new and positive forms of social life.

The general idea of civil society was an important unifying force in opposition. Opposition to a decaying but still totalitarian state system enforced alliances even on widely different currents. Once the communist states were overthrown, however, the pressures of different social interests acted to magnify differences. It rapidly became quite clear that civil society provided a very poor guide to the construction of a new order. The differing conceptions of civil society were exposed to the practical criticisms of political life, and two of them were clearly found completely inappropriate as guides for political action.

The 'poetic' version of civil society was the one that provided least purchase on reality. An extreme illustration of the inappropriateness of believing that 'civil society' can simply be defined as the activities of nice, civilised people is provided by the collapse of public order in many post-communist states. One obvious interpretation of the ethnically based civil wars in the former Yugoslavia is that they are struggles of civil society against the state, or struggles between different elements within civil society one against the other. It is quite clear that in practice 'civil society' is not made up of nice, tolerant people. On the contrary, it contains all the worst as well as all the best that contemporary society has to offer. In societies that have experienced half a century of continuous political repression and intermittent material hardship, and which are suddenly subjected to immense and unexpected social stresses, it is evident not only that there is a great deal of what is 'worst' but also that it is very bad indeed. Fortunately, in none of our central cases have matters come to such a pass. It is clear, however, that in the narrower scope of the future of the mass media, no significant forces were to be found prepared to act on the possibility that regulation could be based on civilised civil society. This interpretation of civil society does not bear further serious consideration, except insofar as its weakness illustrates an important loss. There was, we have stressed, a radical moment in 1989, most clearly in the GDR but also briefly in Czechoslovakia. No doubt a more extensive study would reveal other evidence of this potential. The 'poetic' idea of civil society, inherited as it was from the most substantial working-class mobilisation in Europe since 1968, carried with it some of that radicalism. To the extent that it embodied that positive moment, the term retained some value. On the other hand, it was formulated in such an intellectualised, one might almost say middle-class way, as to have very little purchase on the real lives of the people whose political activity would be essential if it were to come to have any real meaning. As a term embodying the dream of a world dominated neither by state nor capital, it had a real value, but its very ambiguity and abstraction, its remoteness from the real problems of daily life for the mass of the population, meant that it was quite unable to identify with the needs of the only potential agency that might achieve the kinds of change that its proponents desired.

The 'idealist' version, that there could be a civil society independent of the political and economic systems, which could exercise some sort of control over their actions, also proved an inadequate guide to practice. There was no attempt to introduce any degree of empowerment of this aspect of civil society in the press, and in at least one example, that of Slovenia, the shift towards privatisation constituted a retreat from an advanced position of empowerment to one less favourable to ordinary citizens. In broadcasting, there were one or two attempts to introduce elements genuinely representative of civil society into the regulatory bodies. In Hungary, the eventual legislation is a compromise that contains only a small element of the empowerment of forces outside the political élite, which remains the dominant force in controlling broadcasting. The other case is Slovenia, where the Broadcasting Council is constituted by elections by Parliament; but the Council of Radio-Television Slovenia, in daily control of the main public broadcaster, is indeed formally placed in the hands of what were self-consciously seen as the representatives of civil society. These representatives, however, turned out in practice to be responsive to pressures from political parties, which had 'succeeded in penetrating civic institutions and influenced the nomination of their representatives in the Council' (Splichal, 1995: 112). Elsewhere, there was either no attempt to carry through this worthy project, or else the attempt failed and there was a retreat into the standard model for the region.

This 'standard model' is one in which political society has been empowered. The new political élite has made every effort to ensure that broadcasting is run by bodies that are directly accountable to them. As we shall see below, these elements of accountability are frequently used by governments of different political colours to attempt to ensure that the news and current affairs output of the main broadcasters is suitably sympathetic to their activities and plans. A major difference from the previous regimes, however, is that the structure of the new governing bodies usually represents an attempt to balance the interests of the different major political forces, rather than directly to embody the control of the governing party. Insofar as this is effective, the new arrangements do indeed provide for a greater degree of plurality in the governing of television, but this has emphatically not been achieved at the expense of élite control.

The purchase on reality that this version of civil society gives us is thus very limited indeed. At best, its positive function is to identify an aspiration that was weakly present in one or two cases. It has a slightly greater negative function in that it focuses attention on two aspects of the transition that might otherwise be obscured. The evidence from Poland demonstrates that the opposition was prepared to retreat from the implications of the idea even before they entered into serious negotiations with the regime. Even those who had pioneered the idea of civil society found it an impediment to political action as they approached more closely to power.

Second, the example of Hungary demonstrates that there was no intrinsic link between the idea of civil society and the anti-communist opposition. The original plan to control television and radio by means of the representatives of civil society was one that was elaborated under the first post-communist government, dominated by the former oppositionists of the Hungarian Democratic Forum. They were unable to find sufficient political support to pass the Bill. The law that was finally passed found a majority in the second Parliament. This was differently composed. It had a heavy majority of MPs from the Hungarian Socialist Party, a successor to the communists, and it was these who pushed through whatever elements of empowerment for civil society remain in the final law.

The third, 'materialistic', version of civil society has come closest to accounting for the actual outcomes in the mass media. Civil society understood as private capitalism, pure and simple, has undoubtedly been initiated in the region. The press almost everywhere represents a triumph for this version of the theory, and at least a large part of broadcasting is in the process of becoming a private commercial operation. This model, of civil society as the arena in which individual economic actors enter into exchange and conflict, is one unburdened by any suggestion that other kinds of social forces should have representation in the running of the mass media. In a large number of cases, this is what has come to pass.

There was, however, an important point of difference between the classic theory of civil society and the way it is elaborated by its modern protagonists. In Hegel, as we saw, the existence of civil society was in no way connected to anything that we might wish to term 'democracy'. In the modern version, it was argued that there is a necessary link between civil society and democratic political life. If it turns out that the term 'civil society' is an exact synonym for 'capitalism', then there is no reason to suppose that there is such a direct and necessary link between it and democracy. The experience of fully capitalist societies has now endured at least 200 years, and has global extent. On that basis, there is no warrant for claiming any such link with democracy.

As we argued in an earlier chapter, there are indeed important ways in which capitalism can accommodate with democracy, other things being equal. In the case of the four countries that are the focus of our study, that accommodation has been general, albeit extremely strained, at least in Slovakia. To that extent, we may say that there has indeed been at least a conjunctural link between civil society in this very narrow sense and the development of democracy.

There is, however, an importance difference between the kinds of control exercised over broadcasting in these countries and that usually held, at least by the naïve ideologist, to be characteristic of democratic societies. The structure of control over all of broadcasting, and over the public broadcasters in particular, is highly politicised. There is no recognition in the formal structures of regulation for broadcasting to constitute a realm independent of politics. On the contrary, all of the efforts of legislators have gone to attempting to ensure that broadcasting is dependent on powerful political forces, while not being a fiefdom of any particular faction. There is clearly no one single model of the relationship between capitalism, civil society, democracy and the mass media.

If, then, civil society appears to be a relevant category of analysis only insofar as it is an exact synonym for capitalism, it is difficult to see how its continued use might be justified. It illuminates little that is new about the ways in which society may be organised, or about the mass media in themselves, or their relation to democratic political life. It appears to clarify nothing.

The only apparent function that it has is to obscure reality, which it does in three ways. In the first place, using the term civil society in this sense obscures the nature of the mass media that have actually been constructed. These are recognisably versions of the capitalist media. The critique of the democratic limitations of the capitalist media is so well known as to need no further elaboration here. Using the term civil society simply attempts to deflect such criticisms.

Second, the historical context of civil society was that of a society that could be thought to be characterised by a multitude of distinct, independent, small capitalists, including small media capitalists. It could plausibly be argued that such economic relations provided the possibility of a wide range of individual expressions of opinion. Those conditions clearly do not pertain in the epoch of the multi-national media corporation. To use the term civil society in this sense today is to obscure the reality of very unequal access to social communication.

Finally, because it is associated with other interpretations, the use of civil society in this sense obscures the extent to which the discussion is in fact about capitalism. The genuine, if misguided, democratic aspirations that are present in the other two uses of the term obscure the real debate over the democratic potential and limitations of capitalism.

In its only meaningful sense, the claims for civil society are claims for capitalism, in the media as much as in the wider society. In all of its other senses, the experience of post-communism has demonstrated that it was too unclear and too arbitrary a construction to be of any real use either in theory or in practice. In the post-communist countries, even its former protagonists are reconsidering their positions (Arato, 1994: 51). There seems little point in prolonging the use of such a concept in media theory elsewhere in the world.

The history of the concept of civil society in this context illuminates very well two important aspects of the transition that need emphasis. The first of these is the extent to which the eventual collapse of communism, although obviously predicated upon earlier, and very radical, mass upheavals, particularly that conducted in the early 1980s by Solidarity, represented a significant retreat from the goals of those struggles. The period of mass mobilisation and activity produced far-reaching plans for the complete restructuring of the media. The élite negotiations that finally resulted in the end of communism saw the opposition advancing far more modest proposals, none of which embodied the same radical image of society as was common in earlier periods. The ideas born of mass movements were kept out of the negotiating chambers as much in 1989 as they had been in 1945.

The second important point to emphasise is the fragmented character of the élite control that emerges from the transition. In the old order, there had been one single ruling group that, formally and informally, controlled all of the significant media. To the limited extent that there were different positions articulated in the media, these were the by-products of intra-élite struggles. They were thus particularly clearly present during the final decay of the regimes. While the dominant fact about the new situation in the mass media is that of élite domination, it is now a divided élite. The press and part of television is in the hands of the new capitalists, often in alliance with foreign businesses. The other part of television is, in practice, subordinated to the political élite. But in this latter case it is not simply the government that is empowered. On the contrary, the formal relationships themselves enshrine differences and conflicts between different political currents in the élite.

Taken together, these two factors provide powerful reinforcement for the theory of transition advanced by Callinicos. This emphasises the extent to which the fundamental transformation of social relations was absent from even the discourses surrounding 1989, while at the same time pointing to the far-reaching nature of the changes in the political structures that have in fact taken place. If it is as true after 1989 as before that the mass of the population are the objects of the mass media, without any formal mechanisms whereby they may speak for themselves, it is also true that today the voices speaking to them are many rather than one.

6

The Struggle over Broadcasting Law

The fact that the former opposition, for whatever reason, abandoned its leading ideas once in office meant that the radically democratic potential that was obscurely present in some of the ways in which the idea of civil society was formulated came to nothing. In those cases where there had been popular mobilisation – Czechoslovakia and, much more importantly the GDR – the flowering of popular democracy was quickly marginalised and eliminated. In most other places, the handover of power proceeded without even that degree of mass involvement. This inability to go beyond the very narrowest of political changes was one major shortcoming of 1989.

In the case of the media, the limited scope of the process meant that many changes that did take place were slow, tentative and not uniformly positive. Any changes to the mass media, and in particular to broadcasting, are closely related to more general social changes, and we begin this chapter with a brief review of these more general issues. It is against that background that the differences between different versions of 'continuity theory' are examined. It is argued that, while there was considerable continuity, there was also an equally important political change, and that those theories that claim that there has been no shift in the nature of power are mistaken.

The nature of the changes to broadcasting law after 1989 are then considered in more detail. Three major questions are here addressed: the time-scale of the changes; the nature of the emerging ownership systems; and what limitations were placed on the new broadcasters as regards ownership and programming. It is argued that the legal provisions put in place in the Visegrad countries were ones that saw broadcasting as having some kind of public, indeed public-service, role, rather than being simply extensions of the state or imitations of Western commercial models.

Social continuity in major institutions

As we have seen, the revolutions of 1989 did not have an immediate transformative effect upon the existing broadcasting institutions of Central and Eastern Europe. Rather, they remained in many important respects more or less intact. In this, broadcasting was not exceptional. Despite the changes to the political structures, there was considerable continuity in many aspects of social life. The major bureaucratic institutions in society, most notably the civil services, did experience some changes at the top, but overall there was a considerable degree of continuity. In the case of Hungary, one commentator wrote: 'In sum, no dramatic changes and no significant exchange mobility are expected at the top of the Hungarian social structure as a result of the latest regime transformation' (Andorra, 1993: 370). In the case of Poland, the transformation of at least the lower ranks of the bureaucracy into an expert, as opposed to a political, corps had begun in the early 1980s (Wasilewski, 1990: 744–5). Studies subsequent to 1989 have revealed strong continuities of personnel (Wiatr, 1995). Although some top functionaries have been removed, 'at the level of directors and professional experts, by and large the same individuals occupy the same positions now as they did before 1989' (Szablowski, 1993: 355). Even in the case of the Czech Republic, in which the government made much of its intention to purge society, and passed 'Lustration' laws to the effect that those compromised with the old regime were banned from certain posts, the 'grey zone' of experts who had at least passively collaborated constituted a major obstacle to implementing a purge (Šiklová, 1990; Šiklová, 1991: 771). In the event, the laws were formulated in such a way as to allow most 'collaborators' to survive (Kosik, 1993: 149). Prime Minister Klaus marginalised many of the former dissidents (Innes, 1993: 25). The changes were limited: 'Many if not most of this new élite has come from the lower ranks of the old élite' (Rutland, 1993: 106). Only in the former GDR does there seem to have been a very extensive purge (von Beyme, 1993). Even here, however, it was concentrated at the top as much as in the civil services as a whole in broadcasting. By 1993, in the state of Brandenburg, 51 per cent of the higher state officials were West Germans by origin, but only 3 per cent of the lower ranks (König, 1993: 391). Without a major social upheaval, the only possible source of such a layer of functionaries was from 'abroad', and this was only feasible in the special circumstances of German reunification.

The new entrepreneurs, who everywhere appeared in all aspects of economic life, were likewise very often familiar figures. We have already seen how some former communist functionaries in the newspaper industry were able to transform themselves into small-scale private press barons by dubious means. This was part of a wider process. In Poland, Hungary and the former Czechoslovakia, many of the new capitalists were the old managers, their sons and daughters, or their close relatives (Kiss, 1992: 1024–7; Kuczyńska, 1992: 160; Ost, 1993: 469; Poznanski, 1992: 648; Staniszkis, 1989: 43–4). One prominent observer, writing from a background in Western social science but very familiar with local conditions, summarised the main features of the formation of the new capitalist class in Prague as 'ill-gotten gains, and insider information, are used by the old apparat to turn themselves into the nouveaux riches' (Gellner, 1993: 189). The process detected by Hankiss in the period before the final collapse of communism was dramatically accelerated after 1989. What has been called the 'political class' proceeded to transform itself into an 'economic class' (Staniszkis, 1991: 38–69).

It has been argued that, beneath this institutional continuity, there has been a transformation of attitudes and values towards an 'individualist normative system' (Reykowski, 1994: 234). The evidence from empirical survey research appears to contradict these wild claims. In Hungary, there has been considerable continuity of values, and while there is strong support for democracy, there is only limited support for market reforms (McIntosh et al., 1994: 496–9; Simon, 1993: 236–8). In Poland, despite the electoral results, there were only slight changes to popular views of the political process immediately after 1989 (Marody, 1990). The next round of elections provided evidence to support the continuation of 'social democratic values' (Millard, 1994). Only in the Czech Republic does there appear to be a slight majority (of 50.1 per cent) supporting the free market (Mason, 1995). There is considerable evidence of the dominance of 'European', and more specifically 'German' or 'Swedish', as opposed to 'American', values and attitudes throughout the region (Rose, 1992). It should, however, be noted that US-type values are much more supported by the younger, better-educated and male sections of the population, and we might therefore expect to find an overall shift in the course of time.

Given these continuities of social structures and attitudes, the re-emergence as serious electoral contenders of 'successor parties' made up of large sections of the former communists comes as much less of a surprise. In general, despite the prevalence of 'social democratic' sentiments amongst the mass of the population, Western-inspired social democratic parties have failed to make any serious impact in most countries (Coppieters and Waller, 1994). In fact, 'the successor parties have effectively filled the socio-political niche which was expected to be occupied by the social democratic parties' (Mahr and Nagle, 1995: 397). Even the old unions have managed to survive as relatively stable organisations (Myant and Waller, 1994). Their most serious challenger, Solidarity in Poland, proved unable to sustain its unity in the course of the transition (Kloc, 1992).

As a result of all of this, there is much more continuity in the political trajectory of the post-communist societies than might appear simply by examining election results. These do indeed show the sharp growth, and then collapse, of substantial political parties like the Hungarian Democratic Forum (MDF), concentrated in a relatively short period of time. The early attempts at a very rapid transition from state to private ownership, which constituted the essence of the 'shock therapy' promoted by many Western experts, do not seem to have endured. Even in the Czech Republic, 'Despite priding himself on his Thatcherite convictions, Klaus's policies until now have more closely resembled those of a committed social democrat' (Mahr and Nagle, 1995: 404). The overall picture is of an élite consensus, extending from former dissidents to former communists, as to the need for a managed transition to a market economy. One observer, summarising the general experience, noted that:

> The occupants of prominent governmental positions are new, although the majority, as noted above, are not ex-dissidents or other 'outsiders' but come from the second group of the 'lower nobility'. The composition of the lower nobility itself, apart from the purge or retirement of the most notorious and least adaptable party loyalists and police informers, has changed little. (Bayliss, 1994: 325)

The new, post-communist, societies of Central and Eastern Europe remain dominated, to a surprisingly large degree, by the same individuals and institutions they inherited from the past.

In this case, then, as in so many others, broadcasting is an example of more general social developments, rather than representing some unique case that obeys laws different to the rest of society. Of course, broadcasting, just like health or the legal system, has its distinctive features, and therefore its experience of transition has unique aspects. One of them is that broadcasting was uniquely visible, and uniquely contested, but the basic nature of the process was one that displayed features similar to those of the rest of society. If there was no sudden change resulting from popular upheaval, it was the normal process of political and economic life that would determine the new shape of the media.

The transformation of the political landscape

While it is important to stress these elements of continuity, it remains important to recognise that the media, as with every other major social institution, were now operating in a system with radically different rules, and these were bound sooner or later to have far-reaching effects upon them. It is at this point that the analysis presented here diverges sharply from that of the pure continuity, or what was called in Chapter 4 the 'what revolution?', theorists.

Despite the strong evidence of continuity, there is a sharp difference between the condition of broadcasting before and after the fall of communism. In terms of the opposition used above, if the period before 1989 had been marked by a slow process of changes to the system, the events of that year marked what was undoubtedly a change of the system.

There was a political change in 1989. The new societies are everywhere, even in their most repressive form, characterised by a multiplicity of parties and by regular, and usually reasonably free, elections. A previously unified political élite has been replaced by one that is fragmented along party lines. The inevitable consequence of such a change was that the media became the sites of battles for political influence, in much the same way as they are in any multi-party society. It is true that the ways in which this took place, and its extreme virulence in some instances, were much more extreme than the norms prevailing in the bourgeois democracies of the West, but they were still much more like what happens there than they were like the monoliths of the past. There had, then, been a sharp change in the relationship between the media and the political élite. We might summarise this change by saying that the societies had become 'de-totalitarianised'. The process was not complete, in the sense that the fusion of the main centres of economic power into a single unit co-extensive with the state did not vanish overnight. Although the degree of co-ordination between the various elements of the 'plan' had always been much weaker in theory than in practice, and had been further attenuated by economic reforms in the last years of the system, the main industries still formally remained the property of the state, and their privatisation was one of the main political tasks facing the new governments. On the other hand, the political landscape had been transformed. The political élite was no longer organically connected to the economic élite, or the élite in any other major social institution. On the contrary, it was now only one source of social power amongst an increasing number. At the same time, the ruling class as a whole no longer laboured under the enforced unity of the single party. The political élite itself was bitterly divided, and it had both shed some of its former leaders and gained an influx of fresh forces, sometimes straight from jail. The structure of political life had been transformed, and the participants in part renewed, as a direct result of the revolutions of 1989.

One consequence, which was particularly evident in the media, was that, while to a large extent it was the same people who ran the factories and offices of the new economy, they now did so in a very different way than before. The social content of the relationship between employer and employed remained the same, but important aspects of its form shifted. The new owners are not collectively in possession of social capital but have divided it amongst themselves. They compete for markets and for revenue with each other. They have, more or less, abandoned the attempt to sustain economic development isolated from the world market. They compete with foreign capitalists for markets and for revenue, and, indeed, for the rights of ownership. The evidence of this is clear in the sudden increase in concern for the 'efficiency' of the workforce in broadcasting, and the subsequent threats and realities of large-scale sackings, not to mention the closure of numerous newspapers and magazines. It is also clear in the fact that, eventually, all of our focus countries have broken the state monopoly in broadcasting and introduced competing, commercially owned, channels. The dynamic of the media is today everywhere different than it was in the past. There is now a competition for audiences and for advertising revenue that has effects both upon the content and the structures of broadcasting and the press.

It is for these reasons that the general proposition that there was no revolution at all in 1989 has to be rejected. The evidence is that there were significant political changes that have had long-term consequences. Not only was broadcasting very different as a result of 1989, the pattern of its development is to make it ever more different. While these changes certainly do not correspond at all to the wilder claims of those who argued that 1989 represented a monumental transformation of the whole social world of Central and Eastern Europe, they were nevertheless sufficiently large both in their short-term effect and their ongoing potential as to constitute breaks of a revolutionary nature.

The slow process of passing new broadcasting laws

The restructuring of broadcasting that ensued from 1989 was not the spontaneous result of a popular upheaval. It also took an inordinately long time.

By the middle of 1990, there were stable non-communist governments in power in the then three Visegrad countries. It was more than a year later that the first, Czechoslovakia, passed a broadcasting law. The slowest was Hungary, where it took until December 1995. These long delays were remarkable in that freedom of expression was one of the key demands of all oppositional groups everywhere. The delays also had obvious consequences: the laws were implemented not against the blank background of a new epoch but in a set of circumstances where new habits and new patterns were already established. The protracted nature of the process is, on the face of it, something of a puzzle, since the new governments all professed themselves horrified by the practices of their communist predecessors, and determined to establish radically new information regimes as quickly as possible.

The business of changing the broadcasting laws was the product of the routine processes of parliamentary legislation. In many ways, this fitted the ideology of the revolutions. One of the benefits believed to flow from the establishment of civil society was the existence of a 'state of laws'. By this was meant a society in which duly enacted legal forms were in place for the running of public and private affairs, and in which the courts could be relied upon to enforce legal rights in the face of arbitrary, personal, or political power.

It is undoubtedly the case that this notion of a 'state of laws' was based on an overestimate of the extent to which social relations in most bourgeois democracies are, in fact, regulated by set legal forms, and an underestimate of the extent to which communist societies had developed legal systems of their own. Additionally, for obvious historical reasons, the proximate model for a state of laws was German, rather than Anglo-Saxon, and the culture of precise statutory formulation of the scope of social action was thus much more developed. However, it could reasonably be argued that, if freedom of expression were to be a reality in the new state, then it was doubly important that it should be enshrined in a properly established legal framework. Whatever one might believe about the political character of its successive historical transformations at the hands of the differently composed Supreme Courts, it is the legal character of the US First Amendment that stands as the central international symbol of free speech.

The need for legal sanction should not be taken too seriously as a reason for the delay in resolving the problems of broadcasting. As we have seen, the newspaper press in a number of countries was more or less seized, and deployed as their private property, by the employees. It was only later that legal changes legitimised an existing situation. In this respect, it is particularly noteworthy that the most notorious case of newspaper seizures was never challenged in the courts. The 1990 acquisition by Axel-Springer Budapest Ltd of the seven major Hungarian regional dailies, in circumstances of extremely doubtful legality, caused a major scandal. The legal owners of the papers, the Hungarian Socialist Workers' Party (HSWP), believed that it had been robbed of its property. Springer responded by arguing that it had not taken the papers over: it had simply launched new papers with very similar names and staff. This, obviously, is the kind of issue that law courts exist to settle. In fact, the question never came to court. Springer paid the HSWP some 200 million Hungarian forints, but refused to acknowledge any legal obligation. A private payment resolved what was clearly a matter of public law involving media ownership (Gálik and Dénes, 1992: 12). As in any other capitalist country, the 'state of laws' was moderated by the play of private interest.

One reason for the delay lay in the political circumstances of law-making, and the different interest groups that were involved in the media. It is here that we notice the first clear evidence for the impact of the political revolution of 1989. The plurality of political parties in the new legislatures, and their uncertain social bases, as well as the admirable degree of public concern over the future of broadcasting, meant that there were numerous opportunities for the various elements who had an interest in the future of broadcasting to find ways of having their views expressed in the general debate.

There were at play in this arena at least four different kinds of forces. First, there were the politicians, who everywhere seem to have believed that it was a matter of considerable importance for them to have direct control of broadcasting and to be able to influence at least its political coverage. The personnel in leading positions in broadcasting were changed with considerable frequency wherever the politicians found that they had the power to do so, although in few cases did changes in the leadership of broadcasting parallel political shifts quite as closely as in Bulgaria (Iordanova, 1995: 30).

This view of the relation between broadcasting and political power was often caricatured by critics as an instrumentalist hangover from the old ways. It was very easy to say that politicians were simply unaware of the scientific research on media effects, and therefore placed exaggerated importance on the need to control broadcasting. Similarly, it could be claimed that the urge to interfere was due to politicians' ignorance of the superior practices prevailing in capitalist countries. These arguments could not survive the 1994 spectacle of the political success of Berlusconi based, as it at least in part was, on a media empire. His electoral triumph reinforced the politicians' views, and discredited their critics.

In fact, it is much more plausible to argue that the urge to interfere with broadcasting was a necessary consequence of the new and unfamiliar political realities of post-communism. For all of the parties involved, the absence of a clear legal position meant that the powers of politicians to influence broadcasting were undefined. The government could use the time to try to ensure that it controlled broadcasting. The opposition could look forward to the next elections, a new government, and their own chance to subordinate broadcasting. The jockeying for position, both between politicians and between politicians and the other interested groups, was a structural consequence of the more general uncertainty about power relations in post-communist societies. There had indeed been a transformation of the political order, but the shift in the form of property ownership remained incomplete. To disentangle state property and convert it into private property requires political action, every bit as much as does the reverse process. Thus

all aspects of the emerging new order were saturated in politics, and broadcasting formed no exception.

A second group involved in these struggles was the leadership of the broadcasting institutions themselves and their professional advisers. These people
tended to have as an immediate goal the preservation of their own positions
and thus of the institutions upon which they rested. To the extent that they
had an ideology behind this ambition, they tended to hold to one or other
versions of the idea of public-service broadcasting. Many of the senior advisers on broadcasting in the former communist countries were thoroughly
familiar with, and admiring of, various aspects of West European broadcasting, particularly the BBC and Channel 4. It was their desire to sustain the
existing broadcasting organisations more or less intact, but to attempt to
distance them as far as possible from the influence of the political apparatus.
For them, a period of delay was one in which their relations to politicians
were uncertain, and often highly conflictual. They were therefore generally in
favour of a clear resolution to the problem as quickly as possible, provided
that it could be agreed on terms of at least relative independence.

A third group was made up of entrepreneurs who wished to exploit broadcasting as a business. Some of these were indigenous and some were foreign;
very often they were alliances of both elements. Some were former broadcasters and others simply businessmen. However, they all shared an ideology
of privatisation. Collectively, it was their desire to see as much of the broadcast spectrum privatised as quickly as possible and with as few licensing
constraints as possible. Individually, it was in their interests to ensure that
they themselves obtained one of a very limited number of franchises. This
could lead them to try to profit from delay. Nicolo Grauso, an Italian entrepreneur who invested heavily in local television stations in Poland, is an
example of how it was possible to use the legal vacuum to create a position
which, while not legally supported, was not actually illegal either. When the
legal position was finally clarified, it was to his disadvantage in that the new
Broadcasting Council refused to grant him a licence and he was forced to
close his putative network. The actual beneficiary of the first national television licence in Poland was an entrepreneur who had used the delay to
establish a satellite-based service that was to be transferred to the new terrestrial franchise. Delay, for the entrepreneurs, did not necessarily mean
inactivity.

The final group was made up of the employees, and in particular the journalistic employees, of the broadcasting institutions themselves. In their
majority, they certainly had an interest in the preservations of the organisations in which they had built their careers, particularly as unemployment
very quickly became a new, widespread and most unwelcome reality in the
region. More specifically, however, the journalists themselves had experienced the end of communism as a liberation from personal constraint. Their
immediate prior experience was of a journalism marked by self-censorship,
and occasional overt censorship. The ending of this produced a real sense of
liberation. It was, however, not necessarily a liberation into a new kind of

impartiality. On the contrary, the new period was experienced as one in which the journalists had great freedom from managerial constraints on their views, but also one in which they could pursue their own political tendencies in their professional work. Journalists in both print and broadcasting quickly, and often openly, developed political identifications with different parties and used their access to the media to advance such views (Jakubowicz, 1996: 63). For them, any new settlement would necessarily mean a strengthening of managerial control and an establishment of agreed limits to journalistic freedom. A legal settlement was thus a potential limit on their ability to advance partisan views of their own.

It was between these different groups, each with their own interests and each with their own ideology, that the struggle over the new broadcasting laws was played out. Of these forces, the politicians were decisive, and it was their failure to reach agreement on new regulations that actually delayed the process. It should not be forgotten, however, that the state of indeterminacy was in the interests of at least some of the other groups. There was no overwhelming consensus amongst influential social forces as to the way ahead that more or less forced the politicians to resolve the crisis.

The Hungarian 'media wars'

The delays allowed all of these different groups to pursue their interests and to attempt to establish patterns of behaviour that embodied their view of the desirable future position of broadcasting in its daily routines. The most dramatic example of the ways in which these different interest groups came into conflict was the Hungarian 'media wars', whose history is worth briefly recounting.

The 'media wars' consisted of a long struggle over the political control of broadcast news. It was not that the MDF government elected in 1990 was reluctant to control the mass media. Rather, the struggle arose because the interim arrangements agreed as part of the transfer of power made it extremely difficult for the government to implement the kinds of direct control employed elsewhere in the region. The political sensitivity of broadcasting was recognised in that an attempt was made to ensure that the election coverage in the first election covered a wide range of opinion (Körösényi, 1992b: 76). There had also been a general agreement that there would be no new terrestrial franchises awarded before a new broadcasting law was passed and that the passage of this law, which was considered to have almost constitutional status, would require a two-thirds majority in the Parliament in order to prevent any government manipulating the legal system to its immediate party advantage. The degree of freedom of any government was thus limited.

The power that did remain with the government was the ability to appoint the inaugural directors of the radio and television organisations. Since this, too, was perceived as a politically sensitive position, the precise mechanism was that the candidates were nominated by the Prime Minister, but actually appointed by the President of the Republic. The mechanism for the dismissal of these individuals was never clarified. In the rosy optimism that surrounded the outcomes of the first democratic elections, it was generally assumed that all men (and it generally was men) of goodwill would find ways of reaching a suitable compromise without recourse to such direct forms of pressures (Kováts and Tölgyesi, 1993: 40–4).

The Prime Minister and the President duly consulted and appointed a prominent journalist, Gombár, to the directorship of radio, and the famous dissident sociologist Elemer Hankiss to the directorship of Hungarian Television (MTV). The latter was not a member of any political faction, but was generally thought of as being close to Prime Minister Antall (Cunningham, 1994: 4).

Although the appointments were of an interim nature, designed to run the existing broadcasting organisations until such time as the new broadcasting laws came into force, the appointees were generally recognised as having a reforming role. Both were interested in the Western public-service model, and Hankiss at least was most impressed by the independent production system that he observed at Channel 4. Both wished to carry out quite extensive reforms, but were committed to change without any political witch-hunt of the existing staff.

Hankiss and Gombár soon came under sharp criticism from the governing party (the MDF) and in particular from its extreme right wing. The basic charge was that their coverage of Hungarian politics was insufficiently sympathetic to the policies of the MDF. This was compounded by the strong emphasis upon nationalism present in the MDF. The fit between state boundaries and ethnic groups is particularly poor in the case of Hungary. Perhaps 30 per cent of ethnic Hungarians in Europe live outside the boundaries of the present Hungary. There are significant minorities in Slovenia, Croatia and Serbia, a large group in Slovakia and a very large group in Romania. They have very often in the past been the objects of persecution by the dominant ethnic groups in their states of residence and some of those problems, particularly in Romania and Slovakia, continued after the fall of communism. While only the extreme right wing of the MDF, evolving towards neo-fascism and later to be expelled, entertained serious revanchiste dreams, the issue of sustaining Hungarian culture and Hungarian national identity was a sensitive one for the whole of the MDF. This had implications for a wider range of MTV programming than simply the news and current affairs. Cultural programming, it was argued, also had a major responsibility to re-establish the authentic national Hungarian Christian values that had been eroded by a half-century of foreign atheist communism.

The failure of Hankiss to deliver what the government wanted, either in terms of the political perspective or the cultural content, led to a bitter series of conflicts which became known as the Hungarian 'media wars'. The government put increasing pressure on Hankiss and Gombár to ensure that programming reflected its own political priorities. Hankiss and Gombár reacted by asserting the independence of their organisations.

The struggle moved to overt political methods. The MDF, and in particular its right wing, organised street demonstrations against Hankiss. Some of these used openly anti-Semitic slogans denouncing the policies and personnel of broadcasting and demanding that 'real Hungarians' produced properly national programmes. The supporters of the mainly liberal opposition countered by organising their own, rather larger, demonstrations in support of Hankiss and Gombár.

Unable to exert its influence through either covert or overt political pressure, the government reduced the subsidy from the state treasury to Hungarian broadcasting. Hankiss responded by massively increasing the amount of advertising on MTV in order to make up the shortfall of revenue. The government, for its part, used the money denied to MTV to set up a satellite channel, Duna TV, controlled by a foundation under MDF direction and aimed at providing programming for the Hungarian minorities living in neighbouring countries, although its footprint also covered territory of the Hungarian state itself.

Broadcasting thus became an issue of extreme political sensitivity and it therefore was impossible to secure a sufficient parliamentary majority to allow the passage of the new broadcasting law (Gálik, 1992: 6–11). Since this alone would permit both the licensing of new frequencies and the legal removal of the present heads of radio and television, the government was faced with an impasse. It attempted to resolve this by forcing the resignation of the two leaders. The President, who had formally appointed them, argued that the power to remove them was his and refused to agree to the dismissal. The struggle then moved to the constitutional court, which eventually agreed that the President was in the right.

In the meantime, government supporters in Parliament charged Hankiss and his close supporters with financial mismanagement and forced them to appear before a Committee of Enquiry (Hungarian Embassy, 1993). Hankiss and his aides defended themselves vigorously and the charges collapsed, but in the end the political pressure proved too much. Hankiss, in particular, had not adequately secured his base within MTV. A section of the cultural intelligentsia, while not supporters of the crudities of the MDF, had no serious quarrel with the promotion of Hungarian culture by which they themselves made a living. The journalists were themselves not united in defence of independent journalism: rather, they were divided in their political allegiances and tended to identify independence with support for their own positions. The mass of technical workers were not involved in the debates and were treated simply as auxiliaries in the struggle between the creative and journalistic groups. In addition, they had been constantly informed, by Hankiss and others, that they were underemployed, and that many faced redundancy in the new, slimline organisation (Kováts, 1995: 55–6). As a step towards that, Hankiss had made a number of rather favourable deals with producers who were his close supporters, whereby they were assured contracts and funding if they took their production outside the MTV structure and established themselves as 'independent' producers. Hankiss himself, who retained a teaching commitment in the USA, was also criticised for his lack of direct presence in broadcasting. Lacking the kind of support that would have allowed him to stand up to the government, he stepped down at the end of 1992 (Hankiss, 1995).

The resulting constitutional position was a mess. Hankiss and Gombár, who left radio at the same time, claimed not to have resigned, and that they were still respectively directors of Hungarian Television and Hungarian Radio. On the other hand, the government was unable to appoint successors, since this depended upon the agreement of the President of the Republic, who refused to sanction any replacements. What the government was able to do was to appoint the deputy directors of the organisations, both of whom were their own creatures, to the post of acting director of each organisation, and they set about subordinating news and current affairs output to the MDF line.

The other move by the government was to interpret the legal position freezing the award of new broadcasting franchises to apply only to national franchises. Local franchises were awarded in a number of areas under the Frequency Allocation Act. The decisions as to who got the franchises was taken by a government-dominated committee, and it was widely believed that the committee awarded the franchises to its own political friends.

The subordination of broadcasting to the MDF continued right up to the 1994 elections. During this campaign, radio and television acted as direct propagandists for the governing party. Only a few weeks before the election, 129 journalists were sacked from the national radio system for what was widely believed to be political unreliability (Cunningham, 1994: 18). During this period, it is reasonable to say that broadcasting was even more obviously and openly politicised than it had been under the old regime. The Hungarian 'media wars' thus demonstrate very clearly that the period before the passage of the new media laws was one in which various different factions, representing different political viewpoints and different social groups with interests in television, struggled for positions from which they could hope to exercise long-term influence over the future of broadcasting.

Why no immediate privatisation?

The political views of the first post-communist governments differed quite widely, but most were agreed on the need for a massive amount of privatisation in economies that were essentially state run. There were differences of emphasis as to the extent and speed of this privatisation. The best-known Western advisers tended to stress the virtues of what they termed 'shock therapy', at least as applied to the lives of persons other than themselves, and their views found an echo amongst many influential politicians, particularly in the first post-communist government in Poland (Marer, 1992). Some of the local parties, including the increasingly popular successor parties, claimed at least to want a slower and less stressful transition. There were, however, no substantial voices arguing for any alternative to the market.

In this context, it was apparently surprising that television was not immediately sold off to the highest bidder – of which there were rumoured to be several in the heady months immediately after the fall of communism. After all, that is what happened to a large part of the printed press. One of the more prominent of the foreign investors in the Czech press frankly described the situation as analogous to 'the Wild West [of] America in the last century', and argued that the reason for the great success of his intervention lay in the speed with which his company, Rangier, had acted (Trüb, 1995).

That there was not a similar outcome for broadcasting, even in the Czech Republic, which is the country most clearly and consistently committed to privatised solutions to all economic and social problems, is partly explicable by the clash of the different interests reviewed above, but it also partly reflects a more general set of debates that transcend post-communism in their scope.

The first major difference is in the intellectual framework within which the two kinds of media were approached. In the case of the press, there is today only really one model that is taken at all seriously: the advertising-supported commercial newspaper. Such alternatives as exist, for example the various Nordic subsidy systems, command some international interest amongst academic commentators, but are hardly a force in the world of industry. The political conditions for such state intervention are not present in post-communist countries. Subsidy was one of the means of control of the old government, and subsequently the main use of state subsidy in the printed press has been in those cases where the government wished to sustain a newspaper supporting its own viewpoint that found it difficult to survive in the free market. The idea of a public policy aimed at securing a range of different views in the printed press was, and is, everywhere completely outside the dominant framework of media policy (Kowalski, 1994: 102).

The case is quite different for broadcasting. Although it may plausibly be argued that the future of broadcasting everywhere is set as one of competing commercial channels, it nevertheless remains the case that there are still many different ways in which television systems are actually run. These involve different degrees of commercial dependence, different degrees of political independence, different degrees of competition, different degrees of regulation. There is certainly no clear dominant model. It is rather that there is a spectrum of different actual solutions to the problems of how to run a broadcasting system. The idea that there is a stark alternative between state-run and commercial systems, and, by implication, thus a stark choice between craven government-dependent broadcasting and fearless independent commercial broadcasting is clearly wrong. Reality is much more complex than that. The Western European model of public-service broadcasting, whatever its other limitations, forms an influential alternative to both state and market systems.

Many of the people who discussed broadcasting in the period after the fall of communism were very far from ignorant of the range and variety of Western broadcasting policies. Some of them, indeed, were internationally acknowledged experts in the field. Neither were they lacking in advice from Western experts. Financed by a range of bodies from international organisations through government agencies to private entrepreneurs, a large number of 'experts' (including the current author) on every conceivable subject, but particularly broadcasting, descended on the former communist countries in order to explain how things could be done differently, but better. The main problem was that the experts, both domestic and imported, offered a range of different solutions, and in this they reflected a range of different realities in the West.

There were, and are, ideologues from both East and West who have argued that the only solution to the problems of broadcasting, and in particular the vexed problem of the political independence of broadcasting, lies in the rapid and wholesale privatisation of as much of the spectrum as possible. While there have been relatively few people who have been prepared to argue openly for the continuation of a state-owned and government-controlled broadcasting, there have been plenty of all kinds of ideological hues who have acted to attempt to realise such a system in practice. There have also been a number of determined proponents of the idea of public broadcasting, indeed of public-service broadcasting.

There was, therefore, in the initial stages of post-communism, when a rapid privatisation along the lines adopted in the press might have been possible, a powerful current of opinion opposed to such measures. They had an alternative, and they believed better, view of the way in which the existing state broadcasters could be changed to enhance the democratic life of their countries.

There was also a number of factors quite apart from the international esteem of the public-service broadcasting model that encouraged the legislators to reconsider their general ideological preferences and to think beyond the idea of a market-oriented broadcasting. Some of these problems had to do with the objective constraints under which new systems were being constructed, whilst others were more dependent upon the specific political views of the new governments.

The first of these was the poverty and small size of the majority of the countries emerging from communist rule. Outside the former USSR, the largest single population group is that of Poland, with around 40 million people. Others are smaller and some, like Slovenia with a population of less than 2 million, are very small indeed. The income per head of these populations was low by international standards even in the last years of communist rule, and the collapse of the centrally directed economic system meant a collapse in some sectors of the economy, a fall in the national product and a sharp decline in living standards for much of the population.

Although the advertising market existed in a number of these countries, it was underdeveloped by Western standards, even in Hungary. Elsewhere, it began very small indeed. True, the rate of growth in advertising expenditure in most countries was very fast after 1989, and in many of them there was a distribution towards television that was much greater than the Western European norm. But, nevertheless, the initial figures were so small that even after several years of rapid growth the absolute figures remained tiny by West

European standards. Using figures supplied by the European Audio-Visual Observatory, we can make some rough estimates that illustrate the scale of the income available for commercial television. Spain and Poland have populations of roughly equal size and both have a disproportion towards television advertising relative to the printed press (2:1 in Spain, 3:1 in Poland). In 1993 television advertising expenditure in Spain was US$4,846 million; in Poland, it was US$236 million (European Audio-Visual Observatory, 1995: 276–88).

In such economic circumstances, the prospect of the US model of television broadcasting faces some big problems. The chance of several competing commercial channels financed entirely out of advertising revenues and providing a large proportion of indigenous original programming appear remote. The best that might be expected would be to establish one, or at most two, advertising-funded channels with only limited production commitments, reliant heavily on imported programming for much of their output. This situation of near-monopoly would also increase the possibility of the politicisation of television. The precarious existence of the broadcasters would mean they were constantly tempted to use political methods to advance their interests, and the small number of channels would persuade politicians that it might be possible to strike advantageous deals. While it might therefore be possible to reproduce at least some of the structures of US broadcasting, it is much less likely that these would generate the same kinds of high-quality programming or relative political independence.

The second major problem facing the legislators had to do with the peculiar national and ethnic structures of the region. Since at least the origins of modern nationalism, the patchwork of different ethnic groups has posed problems to politicians. Wilson's experts, descending on Europe after the First World War, with their multi-coloured maps of ethnic distributions, were only the most famous of the various failed attempts to draw borders that commanded general support. The outcomes of the various attempts to align ethnic groups and national boundaries, even ones now sanctified by history, remain highly contentious. It is not only in the countries dominated by the more rabidly militaristic and nationalistic parties that these concerns continue to be live issues. Even though Hungary is one of the least militarised of the former communist states, the Hungarian press still denounces the Treaty of Trianon that set the current boundaries, partly as a punishment for Hungary being on the losing side in the First World War.

As we argued above, a stress upon nationalism has been an important part of the ideological baggage of most of the new governments. Nationalism is a difficult concept even when the boundaries of state and nation happen to coincide, since it is never self-evidently clear how the 'nation' and the 'national culture' are to be defined. In the modern world, it is hardly ever the case that state and nation do coincide, and in Central and Eastern Europe it is not at all the norm. Those governments wedded to ideas of nationalism therefore immediately faced difficulties in carrying their programmes into practice.

Broadcasting, of course, is always one of the central sites in which disputes about nationality are conducted (Schlesinger, 1991). Modern conceptions of ethnic and national identity are so bound up with the nature of the available broadcasting, and in particular television broadcasting, as to make any conflicts in society felt acutely in this field. Most of the new governments, facing a highly contested fit between the boundaries of their states and various national and ethnic divisions, therefore tended to consider television an important instrument in achieving their political goals (Bašić-Hrvatin, 1994).

This drive towards national television cut directly across commitments to the free workings of the market. As is evident from experience elsewhere, an unregulated commercial television system in a small country is particularly prone to penetration by imported programmes. These are often of much higher standard than can be produced internally. They are usually much cheaper to purchase than even their modest indigenous alternatives are to make. They command considerable, if not overwhelming, audience interest and support. Therefore a small broadcaster, particularly if financially pressed, is likely to lean heavily on imports at the expense of local production. To commercialise and deregulate broadcasting is thus to invite it to pursue 'anti-national' programming strategies. The incoming governments were keen to avoid such a situation, and the regulation of television, together with the retention of a large state broadcaster, seemed the obvious solution to these political needs, since in such circumstances broadcasters could be obliged to give priority to whatever definition of 'the national culture' was currently politically dominant.

The third reason why the process of privatisation was not at all simple in the case of television has to do with the relationship between political parties and the emerging class of entrepreneurs. The assumption of a relative distance between political parties and the interests of large corporations is everywhere an unwarranted one. It is very often clearly the case that the owners of capital are aligned with one or another political party. This is a more general phenomenon than the alignment of capital with the 'bourgeois' parties as a bulwark against the 'workers' parties' familiar in Scandinavia. In many countries, different businesses, including broadcasting businesses, are closely related to particular political parties. In Europe, the obvious and well-known case is Italy, but there are numerous other examples from around the world: Brazil and Mexico are particularly famous cases.

In the case of the break-up of the communist regimes, these political links between aspiring capitalists and different political parties were particularly close. They could not be otherwise. The new class of capitalists, foreigners and a few exceptional cases aside, could only come into being through political action. The very process of setting up the conditions in which one particular person would have the opportunity to become an entrepreneur was often a directly political act. The formation of political parties, in terms of their programme and putative social base, had direct implications for the kinds of private ownership that were likely to emerge. In these circumstances, the simple handing over of the franchises for broadcast television to this or that business was thus not a politically neutral, purely business, matter. On the contrary, different parties perceived the award of these franchises as an important element in the political struggle. Those in power were keen to ensure that their friends were rewarded. Those in opposition were keen to prevent more control over the symbolic landscape accruing to the governing party.

One clear example of this was the political struggle between Parliament and the Broadcasting Council set up in the new Czech Republic. This was summarised by one of the casualties, Daniel Korte, with a frankness that is worth quoting at length:

> I'm the ex-Chairman of the Czech Broadcasting Council. It's been exactly one year and one week since my resignation. The Council was elected by Parliament in April 1992 and started working. Very soon there came the elections in June 1992, and the first conflict with the political establishment followed. It concerned the budget, because unfortunately the legislators had forgotten to equip the Council with any funds. And so we worked for five months without absolutely any means, we worked mainly in the underground – or, more precisely, in the underground station museum, because one of the members of the Council worked there. The government does not like the institutions of civil society, and though the first conflict was resolved after five months, the next came at the beginning of autumn when the government, especially the party of Klaus, tried to establish what I call a triple system of broadcasting, composed of public, private and state media organisations, the latter controlled directly by the government. We opposed this tendency with great determination and we won the battle. It was a Pyrrhic victory, however, because just ten months later the fundamental law on the Council was amended and it is now possible to dismiss the Council by rejecting its annual report in Parliament in two separate votes. In fact it means that the Council can be punished for its decisions. Its main crime was that in January 1993 we awarded the national television license to CET 21 [Central European Television for the 21st Century], while rejecting the favourites of the leading party. The punishment came very quickly: our first annual report was rejected under the pretext of some very vague objections as for example, the report is lacking the conception of state broadcasting policy. Two month later came the next vote on the report, and it resulted in a draw 82 to 82 just because two deputies of the leading party were absent from a plenary session of Parliament. At that point I decided to resign my function and leave the Council. My motives were first to attract public attention to the tendency of the party to take control of the media or to manage them in one way or another. Secondly, I hoped that I would blunt the edge of criticism and prolong the life of the Council. (Korte, 1994: 61)

In fact, the charges that the major governing Civic Democratic Party (ODS) laid against the Czech Television Council were directly and unashamedly political. The deputy chairman of the ODS said of the decision to award the contract to CET 21 that: 'it is absolutely unacceptable that so mighty and important a medium like television should be controlled by bankrupt politicians, who have caused so much trouble in the past'. He said he would 'do his best to change this decision' (cited in Šmíd, 1994: n.p.). In fact, as Korte said, the ODS was not quite able to muster the necessary number of parliamentary votes to reject the report, but it was very clear, not only in the Czech case but also in Poland, Hungary and Slovakia, that the running of television would be a political question, and that this would apply at least as much to the award of commercial franchises as it would to that part of broadcasting that remained in state or public hands.

All three of these factors together meant that the new governments were reluctant to follow the advice of the more messianic free market advisers who swarmed over the region. It was the 'European' rather than the 'US' model of broadcasting that found favour in most of the countries. Everywhere, part of the spectrum was privatised, but part of it remained with the successor broadcasting organisation. The open question was whether this would continue to be a pure organ of state and government, or whether it would anywhere develop the kinds of limited autonomy from partisan political pressures that public-service broadcasters claim to enjoy.

The legal position of broadcasters

The laws that were eventually passed all contained very worthy commitments to the freedom and independence of broadcasting, particularly state broadcasting. What is more, they tended to enshrine the notion of public service, defined in terms of representing a range of opinions and views equally and fairly, not discriminating between different sections of the population, and so on. While these public-service commitments were laid particularly clearly upon the state broadcasters, the commercial broadcasters were also subject to varying levels of public obligation as regards the nature and origins of their programming.

A clear example of these conditions comes from Article 21.2 of the Polish Broadcasting Law, which enjoins public television programme services to, among other things:

1 Be guided by a sense of responsibility and the need to protect the good name and reputation of public broadcasting.
2 Provide reliable information about the whole diversity of developments in Poland and abroad.
3 Promote the free formation of citizens' views and of public opinion.
4 Enable citizens and their organisations to take part in public life by expressing diversified views and orientations and exercising the right to supervision and social criticism. (Poland, 1992)

In addition, public television is required to present the political views of organisations 'contesting elections to the Diet, the Senate and local government' (Article 24.1) and to candidates for election to president (Article 24.2). They are also enjoined to undertake various cultural and educational programming tasks.

Similar injunctions to undertaken recognisable public-service goals are to be found in all of the broadcasting Acts. There is a distinction between the public broadcaster, which has quite tightly defined obligations to behave in certain kinds of ways, and commercial broadcasters, which operate under less rigorous conditions. Even these, however, are not freed of programming obligations. The first national commercial broadcaster in the region, TV Nova in the Czech Republic, had appended to its licence a series of conditions as to programme content that enjoined it to operate impartially and to produce original drama and other costly programming, rather than rely purely on imported material and cheap local productions. It was obliged to ensure:

10 That from the beginning of the second year of broadcasting at least forty percent of broadcast time will be dedicated to programs that are domestic productions. By 'domestic productions' are understood productions jointly produced on the territory of the Czech Republic with CET 21 or by its commission with domestic producers. During the first year of broadcasting, domestic production will attain not less than twenty-five percent of broadcasting time. . . .

11 That he [the Licensee] will respect the minimum percentage of programming costs expended on domestic dramatic productions as established by the [Broadcasting] Council . . . the specified percentage will be adjusted in proportion to a reasonable percentage of programming costs. . . . (Czech Broadcasting Council: 1993)

The familiarity of some of this material is the result of the fact that the conditions were drafted with expert advice from the British Independent Television Commission, who have long experience of formulating licenses in such a way as to oblige commercial broadcasters to act in ways other than those that optimise their profits. As we shall see, enforcing these conditions in the conditions of post-communism proved rather difficult.

In the case of the Hungarian law, there is a further distinction introduced. There is a general category of 'Broadcaster', operating under the general provisions of the law and whose ownership and programme obligations are specified in the licence. The existing broadcasting organisations are reorganised as public foundations, and are expected to function as 'Public Service Broadcasters', operating within a legally defined framework, notably a responsibility to ethnic minorities living in Hungary (Hungary, 1995: Section 26). The third category is the 'Public Broadcaster'. This will be a private company, broadcasting under a licence that specifies a certain proportion of public-service programming, which chooses to declare itself a public broadcaster and elaborates a satisfactory plan of activities. Thus the Act specifies that the licence to broadcast on the former MTV2 frequency shall specify that: 'the broadcaster is under obligation to provide public service programme items in not less than twenty-five per cent of daily broadcasting time' (Hungary, 1995: Section 129). Organisations qualifying for 'public' status enjoy the financial advantage of not having to pay a broadcasting fee. In addition, the Act establishes a Broadcasting Fund, which is designed to support 'public service broadcasting, [the] public broadcaster, non-profit oriented broadcasters, public service programmes and programme items, preservation and further development of culture, enuring the diversity of programmes . . .' (Hungary, 1995: Section 77). It is therefore possible, under this latter provision, for a proportion of the programming even of wholly commercially oriented broadcasters to consist of public-service material financed out of the public purse.

In all cases in the Visegrad countries, the legal settlement for the future of broadcasting thus began with a formal recognition of the need for something called 'public-service broadcasting'. This was held to be the main responsibility of the successor broadcasting organisations, although some definite obligations were also laid down upon the award of the new commercial franchises. It was explicitly accepted that certain desirable broadcasting tasks were unlikely to be discharged by the normal workings of a free market, and it was therefore necessary to provide an ownership structure and a regulatory regime that could modify these negative tendencies. In theory, at least, the models that began to emerge from the legal restructuring reflected the advice of the West European public broadcasters and the experts of the Council of Europe rather than that of the free-market ideologues.

In one important respect, however, most of the governments departed from the established norms of West European broadcasting. These usually hold that the discharge of a full public-service remit requires that the broadcaster have two channels, in order to avoid the twin dangers of élitism and populism. The intention in Hungary and the Czech Republic was to restrict public-service broadcasting proper to a single channel, so to this extent it may be said that the commercial principle scored an important victory. Overall, however, the intention was clearly not to allow the unfettered operation of commercial principles. On the contrary, the aim was apparently to create a mixed system of broadcasting that would combine the best of both kinds of organisation, in accordance with the dominant West European pattern.

Defining the tasks of the broadcasters

The law establishing the public broadcasters, and authorising the licensing of their future commercial rivals, contained quite specific provisions about two important aspects of the new services. The first of these concerned the provision of news and current affairs. It was everywhere recognised, in principle, that the provision of balanced and objective reporting and the representation of a diversity of opinion is a desirable objective. The Hungarian law opens with a very clear statement of this intention:

> Parliament, in order to promote the freedom and independence of radio and television broadcasting, and of expressing opinion, to ensure the equilibrium and objectivity of information provided and the freedom of acquiring information, and also to support the assertion of the diversity of opinion and cultural, as well as to prevent the emergence of information monopolies, further, to enforce . . .. the Constitution, has adopted this present Act. (Hungary, 1995: Preamble)

Other countries have similarly written into their laws specific requirements as to covering important public events, both nationally and internationally, and reflecting the range of opinion within society.

We can understand these prescriptions in a number of ways, the most obvious of which is as simple window-dressing designed to present the countries involved in a good light. We shall return to this question in the next chapter, when we examine the actual running of these services in a little more detail. Here, however, we need to note that, however purely formal these provisions might prove in practice, they begin from a recognition that the new political realities are different from the old order, and that broadcasting could not be presented simply as an organ of the state, at the mercy of whoever happened to be in government at a particular time. The new broadcasting institutions were supposed to fulfil the function of fora for public debate.

The second set of concerns has been with what might best be termed 'sustaining the national culture'. The desire to achieve this objective was embodied in two distinct sets of regulations. The first concerned ownership. All of the parliaments were worried about broadcasting following the same route as much of the printed press and falling under the control of foreign owners. Of course, the formal status of the public-service broadcasters prevented this from happening in their case, but the forthcoming commercial services would be much more open to takeover. Left to themselves, purely commercial organisations are vulnerable to acquisition and there is nothing in the laws of the market that demand that the person acquiring a broadcasting right should be of a particular national or ethnic identity. The legislation thus, in Poland and Hungary, introduced quite strict regulations governing the ownership and control of any broadcasting organisation. The details differed between countries, but the intention was in both cases to ensure that the companies that won the broadcasting franchises would have and would retain a strong 'national' component.

The second kind of restriction, this time placed on the broadcasters in all of the countries under review, was the obligation to provide a certain amount of certain kinds of original programming produced in their own country. This condition was applied to both public-service and commercial broadcasters, but more rigorously to the former. The Hungarian law, for example, stated that from 1 January 1997, public-service television must:

> . . . compose at least fifty-one per cent of its annual broadcasting time net of advertising, news, sports coverage, quiz and game shows, of Hungarian produced programme items and, including these, at least seventy per cent of European produced programme items. (Hungary, 1995: Section 28)

In the case of intermediate category of broadcaster, to be granted the former MTV2 frequency, the condition for the award of the franchise is that such programming must constitute 35 per cent of items produced in Hungary (Hungary, 1995: Section 129).

Three factors seem to have influenced the adoption of these kinds of policies. In the first place, there is the obvious political desire to be incorporated into the European Union (EU) and the Council of Europe, and thus to construct legislation that enshrines those organisations' broadcasting policies as much as is possible, and in particular the requirement for a majority of programming originating from within the EU. Second, there is undoubtedly a strongly nationalistic tendency present in the political life of the former communist countries. This is most evident today in Slovakia, but was equally prominent in Hungary during the rule of the MDF government. All the immediate post-communist governments of the region, to a greater or lesser extent, believed it was their duty to repair the damage to the nation consequent on communism and thus to give a relatively high priority to cultural policies designed to achieve that end.

These two factors alone, however, do not entirely explain the policies adopted. They transcend the obvious division between those parties descended from the former opposition and those descended from the former communists. The Hungarian legislation we have reviewed was passed by a Parliament heavily dominated by the communist successor party. A third explanatory factor is that post-communism, in whatever political shade it presented itself, was emphatically not concerned with simple capitulation to the world market. It is certainly true that all the substantial political forces in the region were concerned to break themselves as far as possible from the old, Russian-dominated, patterns of autarkic development embodied in Comecon. All political currents, even an individual such as Slobodan Milosovic, were concerned to integrate their economies into the world market. They did not, however, seek to achieve that by simply auctioning themselves to the highest bidder. On the contrary, they attempted to negotiate terms, in broadcasting as much as in bank loans, with other countries. The new capitalists recognised that they would have to be partners, and very often junior partners, in the emerging economic realities, but they did not wish to become mere employees. The regulations governing broadcasting embody exactly that set of parameters. Foreign programmes and foreign investment are recognised as necessary and inevitable, but the legal framework attempts to set up a situation in which some of the benefits will accrue to the local businessman. If the old ruling élite had been forced to abandon its direct and complete control over the symbolic universe, its immediate inheritors sought to ensure that they retained as much of it as they possibly could.

Conclusions

The legal framework established after 1989 for broadcasting was therefore one that represented a compromise between different tendencies. The option of straightforward privatisation and complete opening to the forces of the market, both local and national, was nowhere adopted. Private broadcasting was now to be permitted everywhere, but under conditions of regulation. The existing broadcasting institutions survived, often reduced in scope and scale, but nevertheless essentially intact. On the other hand, in practice the legislatures recognised the inevitability, and sometimes the desirability, of a closer integration of their broadcasting situations with the world market. They opened both programming and ownership to foreign influence. What they were not prepared to do, however, was to surrender such an important symbolic resource entirely to the possibility of foreign control. They wished to preserve a strong element of the 'national culture' in broadcasting.

In principle, the outcome of the broadcasting legislation was to establish mixed systems in the former communist countries. The main outlines can be seen in Table 6.1.

Table 6.1 *Broadcasting in four countries*

Country	State/public broadcaster	Advertising on state TV	Plurality obligation	Private broadcaster	Ownership restrictions	Foreign capital	Programming obligations
Czech Republic	Yes	Yes	Yes	Yes	No	Yes	In (original) licence
Hungary	Yes	Yes	Yes	Yes	Yes	Yes	In law
Poland	Yes	Yes	Yes	Yes	Yes	Yes	In law
Slovakia	Yes	Yes	Yes	Yes	No	Yes	In law

There was, on the one hand, to be a public-service broadcaster dedicated to providing a range of services and operating independently of the government so far as its news and current affairs were concerned. On the other hand, there was to be commercial broadcasting, free up to a point to run itself as a business, but subject to regulation. The overseeing of both public and commercial broadcasting was to be given to bodies responsible for licensing and general supervision, and sometimes with some powers to control the conduct of public broadcasting. Both public and commercial broadcasters are permitted to raise some of their revenue from advertising, although the public broadcaster is usually more restricted in this than its commercial rivals.

We have already seen how this ideal picture was rather far from the reality that emerged in practice. The membership of the Broadcasting Councils was generally decided by the politicians. The design of broadcasting legislation was a political struggle. Even before the laws were passed, politicians, most notably in Hungary, were keen to establish their power over the broadcasters. The award of private broadcasting licences was itself a matter of intense political debate and struggle. Overall, then, it is obvious that the fine legal provisions about balance, impartiality and so on were under siege, as indeed they have been in Western Europe, although at a rather lower intensity. The chances of the actual practice of broadcasting living up to the proclamations of public-service goals were questionable. Both in its commercial and its public aspects, the initial phase of post-communism suggested that a highly politicised broadcasting landscape would be normal in the region.

That this was the case should not come as a surprise. The process of shifting from a situation in which the state was the sole proprietor of the bulk of productive capital to one in which ownership is dispersed amongst different individuals and firms could only be achieved by political action. If the political revolutions made a start on that possible, they also entailed that the succeeding society would, for the foreseeable future, be one that was saturated with politics. Broadcasting was caught in this field in two ways. On the one hand, the state broadcaster was seen by politicians as one of the spoils of office, and as a necessary means to winning the next election. On the other hand, the award to the potentially profitable private broadcasting franchises represented one of the pieces of patronage available to the government to reward its supporters. Both of these factors meant it was extremely likely that the letter of the law would be placed under considerable strain in the daily practice of broadcasting.

7

The Emerging Media Systems

In the previous chapter, we examined the outlines of the legal conditions under which broadcasting now takes place in the Visegrad countries. There are important differences between different countries, but overall a broadcasting council or similar body is legally charged with important independent powers concerning broadcasting (Hungary, 1995; Robillard, 1995: 39–44, 169–75, 197–200). Legal stipulations, however, are one thing. The concrete conditions under which these objectives are actually carried out are quite another. The differences between a public-service broadcaster, however owned, and, on the one hand a state broadcaster, or, on the other, a purely commercial organisation, depend upon less tangible factors than laws. We have already examined the highly politicised atmosphere surrounding the legislative process. In this chapter, we will examine in more detail how the broadcasting institutions developed in reality. We are particularly interested in seeing how far the potential of both public broadcasting and responsible commercial broadcasting were actually realised.

After a review of the conditions that allow public broadcasters to act independently of government, and commercial broadcasters to adopt non-optimum commercial strategies in their programming, two main questions are considered. The first concerns the extent to which broadcasting in general, and the broadcasting councils in particular, were able to act independently of government. The second considers the impact of the new commercial broadcasters upon the stability of the system as a whole.

The conditions for public-service broadcasting

Public-service broadcasting is usually understood as having two separate aspects. The first of these concerns a measure of political independence from the government of the day, particularly with regard to the news and current affairs output of the broadcaster. The second concerns the pursuit of inclusive and diverse programming strategies aimed at doing something more than reaching the largest possible audience at the lowest feasible cost. These two different aspects raise political and economic questions about the conditions for their existence that are in principle separable, although they tend in practice to be very closely intertwined. It is their interplay that determines the kind of system that actually emerges in any given case (Raboy, n.d.: 5–10).

The political conditions for the existence of public-service broadcasting are something more than a legal situation that proclaims the independence of the broadcasters from political pressures. The legal details are not, of course, themselves unimportant. A system in which the director of the broadcasting institution is appointed and dismissed directly by the office of the Prime Minister is clearly one that invites political intervention. One in which the director is responsible to a body constituted independently of the government and the political élite is clearly one that has more scope to resist political intervention. Neither of these systems is, however, a guarantee. In practice, it is the political conventions within which these powers are exercised that determines the degree of freedom of a broadcaster. A government can be armed with quite Draconian powers over broadcasting and use them only infrequently. The direct powers that the British government has over broadcasting are extremely extensive, and often shock people from former communist countries when they are explained in detail, but they are not often exercised. Conversely, a government may have few formal controls over its disposal, but might in fact have numerous informal mechanisms for influencing broadcasters.

Such a wider definition, however, changes the terms of the debate a little. The rules, written and unwritten, governing the day-to-day exercise of political power can be so constituted that a publicly owned broadcaster is effectively independent. But they can also be constituted so that a privately owned broadcaster is politicised. In this interpretation, the conditions for a broadcaster discharging public-service functions are essentially independent of the mode of ownership. Just as a formally independent broadcaster, owned by a private company, may in fact be very closely linked with a particular political current, as with Berlusconi, Televisa or TV Globo, so a formally independent broadcaster, owned by a private company, may in fact pursue public-service objectives, as with the British ITV companies.

The second set of conditions that govern the practical realisation of broadcasting objectives are those of economics. In order to broadcast according to the public interest, the broadcasters, whether public or private, must be in a position to make programme decisions independent of considerations of audience size, and only secondarily in terms of the relationship between production costs and likely audience. Unless they have this freedom, then it is natural to sacrifice the interests of small sections of the audience in the interests of maximising viewers. Some groups are simply too small, or in commercial systems too poor, to warrant certain kinds of programmes on purely economic grounds. In other words, in order to sustain a genuine public service aimed at providing something of value to all the different groups that make up 'the public', it is essential that the broadcasters operate a system of internal cross-subsidy in programme funding. This, in turn, implies a relatively stable revenue base insulated from the more rigorous kinds of competition.

All commercial companies are subjected to a variety of different disciplines, the most obvious of which is that they need, in the long term, to return a profit on their operations. If they fail in this, of course, they close, unless taken over or specially aided. Another important discipline is the need to return an average level of profitability. Failure to do this need not result in bankruptcy, at least in the short to medium term, but it will expose the company to the threat of takeover by other companies convinced that they can 'work the assets harder' and show a better rate of return on the capital employed.

State companies depending for a large part of their incomes on commercial revenues are, of course, independent of the dangers of takeover. They could, however, in principle go bankrupt. They need at least to raise revenue equal to their programme expenditure and other running costs. The more heavily they are dependent upon commercial revenue for this income, the more their economic behaviour is likely to be similar to that of properly commercial companies.

As we have seen, the starting point for public-service broadcasting is the needs of programming, rather than the needs of profitability. These two may coincide, or they may not coincide. If a commercial company is to be expected to display a consistent commitment to public broadcasting, then it must be in a position to do so in an environment that accords it some form of protection from the natural workings of the market. In return for such privileges, it is possible to ensure that advertising-funded companies, whether public or private in ownership, are in a position to follow public-service obligations. These obligations arise either from the legal instrument establishing the broadcaster or from conditions governing the licence to broadcast issued by a regulatory body.

The condition for the success of public-service broadcasting as a programming model in a multi-channel environment, as opposed to as a political ideal, thus depends upon two conditions, both of which are effectively independent of the type of ownership. The first is that the broadcaster is obliged by either statute or a regulatory body to pursue whatever programming ends are deemed to constitute public service. The second is that the sources of finance are so arranged as to allow the broadcaster to gain sufficient revenue while pursuing what might be termed a 'non-optimum programme strategy'.

Examples of political intervention

In Poland, Hungary, Czechoslovakia and the successor Czech and Slovak Republics the process of direct government intervention has gone far beyond a mere adjustment of the leading personnel of the broadcasters to suit the new political climate. What the regular and frequent interventions of politicians did was to establish the custom and practice that the ability to intervene in broadcasting, and in particular state broadcasting, was part of the prerogative of the government of the day. The direction of broadcasting was thus not only politicised, but party politicised.

We have already seen how this kind of political pressure was used in the 'media wars' in Hungary. As detailed above, similar pressures operated in the

Czech Republic over the award of the initial commercial broadcasting licence. In fact, the struggle between broadcasting council and government did not end with the resignation of the first chair, but continued for the next couple of years, involving matters like the distribution of radio franchises and the conditions for licensing local cable television. Similar attacks were mounted by the government and its supporters on the news coverage by Czech Television (Kettle, 1995: 5–6).

Slovakia provides an even clearer example (Brečka, n.d.; Johnson, 1993; Kalniczky, 1992). In the immediate aftermath of the division of the Federal Republic and the establishment of two new states, Slovakia adopted what was essentially a localised version of the general broadcasting laws. The Parliament, dominated by the nationalist Meciar government, made a number of important changes to the law in the course of this localisation that significantly increased their power over broadcasting. The old law contained the provision for a consulting body for TV made up of 35 people, of whom 16 could be said to be representatives of civil society. The new body was reduced to nine, none of whom were from civil society. Members of this body, and those of the licensing body, could be removed from office by Parliament if it passed a motion on the initiative of 15 MPs. The licensing body itself only had the power to recommend that a national TV licence be granted to a particular company: the final decision lay with Parliament. The director of the national TV station is appointed by Parliament on the initiative of the Council for TV. The general effect of these changes was thus to render all of the intermediary bodies between the broadcasters and Parliament much less independent and much less powerful. In this, they were simply part of the general trend towards disempowering any of the bodies that might be thought to represent civil society rather than the political élite.

The governments of both Meciar and his opponents have been only too ready to use these powers, and to intervene in other ways in the activities of broadcasting. The then head of Slovak Television, Peter Malec, wrote in September 1991 that:

> It would be an illusion to pretend that strong attempts by the current power structure are not made to try to control and influence the content of broadcasting. A great role is played by the persistent thinking of the new politicians and political parties and by the inertia and fear of the broadcasters themselves, and by interchanging the idea of the democratisation of television broadcasting with the absolute control by the politics of the media by politicians, in their concern for democratisation. (Malec, n.d.: 137)

In this sort of political climate, the award of franchises, the running of broadcasting and the composition of the various councils have been determined more or less directly by political advantage. The Meciar-led government replaced nearly all of the members of the Board of Slovak Television in late 1993, but after its fall Parliament appointed six new people of its own choice. Despite this, Slovak Television remained largely pro-Meciar and is credited with an important role in his narrow election victory in October 1994. There followed a particularly dramatic example of political intervention in broadcasting. The Meciar-led coalition purged all of the major state bodies, including the broadcasting council. The Boards of Slovak Television and Slovak Radio were entirely replaced, and the directors of both radio and television were replaced (Fisher, 1995a: 63). The new management of broadcasting is clearly very loyal to the government. In the summer of 1995, there was a conflict between the Prime Minister and the President. The President's statement on the crisis was indeed broadcast by the national television statement, but only after midnight. A content analysis of Slovak TV news from 1 April to 26 May 1995 showed that the government received 272.6 minutes of coverage, against the opposition's 16.4 minutes (Fisher, 1995b). The persistent political interference with the content of journalism in both television and radio remained a prominent feature of the Slovak media scene (Vojtek, 1995: 83).

Poland, too, provides a clear example of these processes. Jakubowicz describes how the National Broadcasting Council was subject to a range of conflicting pressures:

> As in all post-Communist countries, the council came under strong pressure regarding its licensing policy. Because of the spectrum scarcity, it was able, initially, to award only one national commercial television licence, which in the highly charged political situation in Poland naturally became a decision of considerable interest to various political authorities hoping for the licence to go to the company of their choice. It also received political pressure regarding its overseeing of public broadcasters, especially Polish Television, which in 1994 became the object of criticism from the ruling left-wing coalition. The president, displeased by the council's 'excessive' independence and unwillingness to comply with his wishes, acted a number of times to recall the chairman of the council and his other appointees and to replace them with other people. (Jakubowicz, n.d.a: 186)

In the case of President Walesa, there were two grounds for his objections to the Council. He objected to its appointment of Wieslaw Walendziak as head of public television, apparently on the grounds that he was too independent (Vinton, 1995: 44). In the case of the franchise award, Walesa's favoured candidate for the national commercial franchise, Nicolo Grauso, was ruled out of contention by the National Broadcasting Council due to an illegal ownership structure. Walesa's attempts to reverse the ruling were not sustained in the courts, but despite political challenges from Parliament and legal rulings declaring that it was outside his power, he was in fact able to change his nominees to the Council, including twice replacing the chair he had himself appointed (Karpinski, 1995: 13; Netcom, 1994: 2). The former communists who made up the post-1994 government were rather better behaved than the former anti-communists. They perceived the broadcasters, and in particular Walendziak, as acting as a self-appointed 'right opposition' to their policies and complained bitterly about this. They did not resort to using the kinds of pressures that could have achieved the same sort of results as had Walesa, but in the long run their pressure told. Walendziak resigned in February 1996. His replacement, Peasant Party member Ryszard Miazek, moved to establish his own control over television by sacking the head of the First Channel in August 1996 (Reuter, 30/08/96).

These kinds of pressure were and are so prevalent in Central and Eastern Europe that it is tempting to simply regard them as examples of a single uniform process. While it is true that the overall effect has been to produce a highly politicised broadcasting environment, it is valuable in understanding the process to distinguish between the various kinds of political pressure.

We may, broadly, differentiate between three kinds of political intervention, the structural, the routine and the occasional, which are outlined in Table 7.1.

Table 7.1   *Different kinds of political intervention in the media*

Type	Level	Mechanism	Authority	Frequency	Status
Structural	Legal powers	Appointments and legal orders	Government	Intermittent	Highly visible
Occasional	Political pressure	'Telephone calls'	Politicians	Intermittent	Visible and invisible
Routine	Custom and practice	Self-limitation and self-censorship	Editors	Permanent	Invisible

The boundaries between these are perhaps rather blurred, but they point to important differences. By 'structural', I mean those forms of subordination that are written into constitutions, Acts of Parliament, binding legal decisions, and so on. These are instruments that permit politicians to intervene directly and legally in the running of broadcasting. By 'routine', I mean the situation in which both broadcasters and politicians understand very clearly the real relations of power between them, whether legally enshrined or merely the result of custom and practice established by trials of strength. By 'occasional', I mean interventions in which politicians interfere outside of the normal state of affairs, in response to particular issues or as part of a policy of gaining more control over the broadcasters. In formal terms, both occasional and structural subordination are mechanisms by which a particular kind of relationship is established. Routine subordination is the state of relationship that emerges from these processes.

Hungary provides an example of the interrelationship between these different kinds of pressure. The situation during the 'media wars' was, essentially, one of occasional intervention which, after the 1992 resignation of the heads of radio and television, developed towards routine intervention. The first post-communist heads of television and radio had tried to act independently of government and resisted attempts to bring them to heel (Gombár, n.d.: 5–6). Once they had resigned, there were no public protests from the new acting directors and they accepted their subordination, although it should be said that the journalistic staff did still retain some degree of independence and attempted resistance to the subsequent purges.

Despite this complete control over broadcasting, the MDF was very heavily defeated at the elections and the Hungarian Socialist Party, the reformed heirs to the communists, won an overall majority. They immediately formed a coalition government with the liberal Free Democrats. As part of the coalition agreement, the heads of radio and television were replaced. No one suggested that Hankiss or Gombár should return to the posts they always claimed they still legally held, and they displayed no real interest in pressing their claims. The new appointees, particularly Adam Horvath at MTV, were much more neutral figures than their immediate predecessors, but were still thought to be sympathetic to the new government. The extreme intervention of the MDF period ended, but the new appointees dismissed those reporters who they claimed were pawns of the former government (Oltay, 1995a: 35). But although the more dramatic episodes are now in the past, the routine subordination of Hungarian broadcasting remains. The force of custom and practice has established that the relations of power between government and broadcasters are ones of superordinate and subordinate respectively: pressure from Prime Minister Horn was enough to ensure that the editor of a popular news programme was forced to resign his post (Oltay, 1995b: 11). The new legal position, as we have seen, is one that institutionalises a high degree of structural subordination of television to Parliament. The extent to which that represents subordination to the government of the day remains to be seen, but we should note that the law does in fact provide for a plurality of voices from the major parties to be heard in the running of broadcasting.

It is routine subordination that is the most common and most pernicious form of political control over broadcasting. It exists, in one form or another, in every country. Obviously, in some cases it is much more harsh and direct than in others. Romania is perhaps an extreme case, but a survey of 362 journalists in June 1994 found that 74.8 per cent thought that political considerations were the most important influence on news writing in the written press, and 74.6 per cent were of the same view for Romanian Television. Only Radio Bucharest, in which only 29 per cent held that view, and 60.8 per cent believed professional considerations were paramount, formed an exception (Dragan, 1995: 63–4). It is nevertheless naïve to imagine that any large social organisation like broadcasting could anywhere be entirely independent of the influence of the strongest centre of power in a society. What is important in discussions about public-service broadcasting, and it implications for theories of the relationship between broadcasting and democracy, is the nature and extent of this subordination. In all of the cases that we have been studying, routine subordination was established through a very sharp trial of strength that resulted in the effective reduction of broadcasting to a political instrument. The current government in this or that country may not choose to use that instrument in quite such a blunt manner as its predecessor, but it retains the power to do so.

It might in general be said that the routine outcomes of subordination are the result of a combination of the structural subordination present in the legal situation and the occasional interventions of government. Legal instruments usually specify a certain range of powers, whose exercise by the political authorities is a matter of discretion. Thus the Draconian powers that the British government has over broadcasting have seldom been employed in reality. It is the practice of intervention, either through the legal channels or through more informal methods of pressure, that establishes the actual limits of subordination and establishes what, for a given political conjuncture, constitutes the routine of subordination.

The political conditions for the realisation of the public-service intentions expressed in the various broadcasting laws were thus nowhere present. The routine subordination of broadcasters to the political élite was clearly established quite early on in the former communist countries and it was of a sufficiently developed kind as to render broadcasting a party-politicised question. This was, however, politicisation of a different kind to that which had prevailed under communism, The best, or worst, that the post-1989 governments could, in most cases, achieve was influence rather than control. In the old order, with a single dominant party subordinated to its own central leadership, there were no serious institutional counter-pressures to the desires of the government. In the new system, with a variety of parties, the governments were only one, albeit often the strongest, of the different forces attempting to ensure that broadcasting developed in the desired direction. The two examples where the award of a commercial franchise was contested on political grounds demonstrate this very clearly. While both Walesa in Poland and Klaus in the Czech Republic objected to the award of the franchises to the particular candidates chosen by the broadcasting councils in their respective countries, in neither case were they able to have the decisions reversed. Although they could put pressure on the councils, and force through changes in their personnel, in neither case was it possible for them to exert sufficient pressure to make the council act differently on the franchise allocations.

Developments in journalism

This politicisation of broadcasting was the result neither of the inexperience of particular groups of politicians nor of the malign intent of particular parties. There were parallel developments in the newspaper press, which was largely outside government control. Everywhere, the press made substantial efforts to demonstrate its new political independence. In part at least this was a wholly legitimate result of journalists wishing to exercise a degree of autonomy and freedom, which they fondly imagined to be the norm of journalism in capitalist countries, after decades of overt political subordination. In this, it was a process similar to the one that we have noted amongst broadcast journalists. On the other hand, there was also a sense in which opposition to the government of the day was a necessary condition for the newspapers to transform themselves from mouthpieces of the state into organs that were purchased by readers in the perception that they were genuinely politically independent. The clearest and easiest way to demonstrate that a newspaper was now a different sort of institution from a newspaper published under the old regime, even if it was the same newspaper edited by substantially the same journalists, was to attack the government on each and every front.

In part, however, this process also raised a question about the nature and role of the kinds of journalism practised in these societies. Many writers have observed that the journalists in both press and broadcasting were reluctant to abandon what was seen as the 'old-style' journalism, based upon political criteria, for a 'newer' model based upon objective reporting (Plenkovic and Kucis, 1995: 26–7; Vihalemm, 1995: 39). At the same time as he was engaged in a fight for institutional autonomy from the government, the president of Hungarian Radio argued that his own staff displayed considerable short-comings from the point of view of democracy:

> The never ending daily question is: is it against or for the government? But this question is not a good one. The better and more basic question is: are our news and current affairs balanced, unprejudiced and objective, that is impartial? My answer is that we have many faults but impartiality is our main aim; a growing number of us agree on this and work accordingly. In a pluralistic society, in a multiparty system, we – as public service broadcasters – have to be impartial. But, here comes the 'but': the prevalent attitude, stemming from the living tradition, is a critical one nurtured in a less democratic system. And it means that the journalists feel on many occasions that giving the news in itself is not enough. They are inclined to be on guard. They feel that the nation, public interest, public morale, and many other important elements may get into some danger: they feel they have to act, they have to speak out, they have to unveil the bad guys. And independently of a journalist's political leanings, the result is to damage impartiality. (Gombár, n.d.: 5–6)

This partisan journalism, believed to be an inheritance from the old order, was pervasive in both the newspaper press and broadcast journalism throughout the region.

It would be wrong to see this as a political hostility on the part of journalists to governments that were bent on introducing as much of a market economy as possible in as short a time as possible. For one thing, the newspapers themselves were often the most visible representatives of the new marketisation. For another, although some newspapers had obvious editorial affiliations with one political party or another, they were hardly ever hostile to the establishment of private capitalism. Even the larger of the allegedly 'leftist' parties descended directly from the old communist parties were concerned only to haggle over the terms of the transition: they had abandoned any hostility to private capitalism and effectively transformed themselves into modern social democrats. The hostility that was often expressed towards politicians in the newspapers arose partly from cultural differences between different groups of the intelligentsia and partly from disputes over the best ways in which to establish a market economy. The corruption and incompetence that was everywhere consequent upon the attempt to shift away from the centrally directed economies provided plenty of examples of both of these shortcomings for the newspapers to concentrate on.

Despite this mixture of motives, the new governments perceived that all, or at least a majority, of the newspaper press were consistently hostile to their political views, and keen to impute disreputable motives to them. For this reason, the apparently international desire of politicians to exert as much control as possible over the presentation of their ideas in the media received an additional impetus in that part of the media that the politicians could directly control: broadcasting.

Overall, then, the kind of media systems emerging in the former communist countries were ones characterised by a high degree of overt politicisation. This may well have been inevitable, given the sorts of stresses that the social and economic transitions following on the end of communism were bound to produce. They did, however, depart very radically from the aims that had been dreamed of by oppositionists. Not only was their ownership and control very distant from the dreams of empowering the ordinary citizen that had inspired the more democratically inclined of the opposition, but their journalistic content bore little apparent relation to the output of the *New York Times* or the BBC.

The contradictions of advertising finance

Apart from political instability, the other major problem concerning the possibility of public-service broadcasting is the question of financial stability. The state broadcasters in the region have all enjoyed some income from taxation, either directly in the case of a government subsidy, or indirectly through a licence fee, and sometimes through a combination of both. The new commercial broadcasters, of course, expect to depend very largely on the sale of advertising space for their income, although we have seen how in Hungary there is provision for some of their programming to receive a subsidy. If this were the simple division of revenue streams, then there would be considerable grounds for optimism regarding the possibilities of public-service broadcasting. At the very least, the fact that there were protected revenue streams for the public broadcaster would ensure that it was financially possible for it to attempt to discharge some of its more inclusive programming functions.

In fact, in all cases the situation is in reality rather different from this. The broadcasting laws in all the Visegrad countries permit the public broadcasters to raise at least some of their revenues from the sale of advertising space. The public broadcasters are thus encouraged, indeed enjoined, to try to make up for any shortcomings in their direct income through commercial activities. Potentially, at least, they are thus in direct competition with the nascent commercial broadcasters.

An additional problem is that everywhere there are restrictions on the kind and amount of advertising that can be carried. Many of these are uniform across all broadcasters, and refer to generally accepted European norms concerning, for example, the advertising of tobacco products. There are, however, specific regulations that restrict the public broadcasters rather more tightly in terms of the amount of advertising time they may sell than they do the commercial broadcasters. The amended Czech Broadcasting Law, for example, while it lifted many of the constraints on the kinds of advertisements that could be carried, allowed public broadcasters to carry advertisements for up to 1 per cent of their total daily transmission time, but permitted commercial broadcasters to carry up to 10 per cent (Czech Republic, 1995: Article 7.1).

The licensing of commercial broadcasters could thus be expected to precipitate some sort of programming and financial crisis in the public broadcasters. Such crises have been familiar features of the Western European broadcasting scene for some decades now. In the case of the UK, for example, the introduction of commercial broadcasting in the 1950s produced an audience and programming crisis for the BBC. This was not converted into a financial crisis, due to the complete separation of sources of income. It was, however, only with the imposition of strict regulation on the activities of the commercial broadcasters that the relatively stable public-service system across all channels that characterised the UK up to the early 1990s was actually established. More recently, other European public broadcasters have faced similar crises, exacerbated by the fact that in many cases they themselves depended upon advertising for much, or in the case of Spain all, of their income. The expectation of any reasonably informed observer would be that similar crises would emerge in the former communist states.

In the short term, things appeared very differently. The ability to sell advertising revenue appeared to all broadcasters as an immense and unalloyed boon. One reason for this was that everywhere the state budgets were under severe strain, and the sums available to pay for broadcasting were kept under tight control. Even to maintain the same level of services, the broadcasters needed, if anything, more money after 1989. This was partly to improve their plant and facilities to international standards after decades of decline, and partly to help integrate themselves more fully into the world programme market. For example, the collapse of the Organisation Internationale de Radiodiffusion et Télévision (OIRT), the 'Eastern' equivalent of the European Broadcasting Union (EBU), meant that the broadcasters now had to pay the standard international rates for important sporting fixtures. Advertising, which grew very rapidly throughout the region, for obvious reasons, in the aftermath of the collapse of communism, seemed to provide the goose that could lay such desperately needed golden eggs. Enjoying, at least in the short term, a monopoly on the sale of television advertising time, the broadcasters found that they had the proverbial licence to print money. Thus, in the year 1994, advertising accounted for 32.7 per cent of Slovak Television's income (Slovak Television, 1995: 16). In the case of Poland, the 1.48 trillion old zlotys profit made by Polish Television in 1994 was partly achieved as a result of the fact that the biggest source of revenue, at 48.5 per cent, was from the sale of advertising space (Reuter, 31/05/95). Czech television, while it enjoyed its advertising monopoly, raised more than 30 per cent of its revenue from these sales (Czech Television, 1995: 37). At the same time, it bent the legal restrictions on the amount of advertising that it was permitted to carry in any one hour of prime time television, which then stood at six minutes, so that 'the audience had to endure during the period of 72 minutes up to 18 minutes of commercials, i.e. 25 per cent' (Šmíd, n.d.: 1).

The second major reason was that advertising revenues constituted a source of funding that went directly to the broadcaster and was quite independent of the political struggles of the day. It thus seemed to provide revenue that the politicians could not easily touch, and thus to constitute a material base for editorial independence. This factor led many of the policy advisers in the region to support advertising funding even though they were in principle in favour of a 'pure' type of public broadcasting along British lines.

This was particularly clearly illustrated in the case of the Hungarian 'media wars'. When, during these struggles, the government tried to force Hankiss out of MTV by withholding the licence fee payments, and by using them to establish the more directly controlled Duna TV, Hankiss's response was to dramatically increase the amount of income from advertising. Apparently, both radio and TV were so successful in this strategy as to become 'almost totally self-reliant financially' (Kenedi and Mihancsik, 1994: 13). This enabled the broadcasting organisations to weather the initial political shocks.

It is important to recognise that, while this ability to raise money outside government control did indeed allow the broadcasters some degree of freedom from direct political intervention, it was not in the long run sufficient to win the battles. It was, ironically perhaps, economic charges arising from the circumstances surrounding the sale of advertising that contributed to the climate that finally forced Hankiss out. What is more, acceptance of a subordinate role was very far from preventing the broadcasters from continuing with their commercial activities on a large scale. Advertising in 1995 still accounted for just over 50 per cent of the budget of MTV, even though it was then much less than totally independent.

The Nova experience

Based on this experience, an observer could predict that a number of things would happen. First, the introduction of a commercial channel would lead to the collapse of the audience for the existing state channel. The newcomer would programme aggressively and innovatively across the range of its output and would expose the limitations, political and cultural, of the existing channel. As a result of this, the existing state channel would lose a considerable amount of its advertising revenue. It would therefore enter a financial crisis that would lead to a reconsideration of its programming objectives. It would need to decide whether, on the one hand, to continue to pursue what may be termed a public-service remit or whether to meet the new challenger head on and to programme commercially. If it followed the former course, it would be certain to become more than ever financially dependent upon the state and to continue in its role as political subordinate. If it followed the latter course, it would be forced to abandon, or at least dilute, its public-service remit.

For its part, the commercial service would be likely to chafe against both the fact that the state channel was permitted to have any of the very limited available advertising and against the programming obligations that prevented it optimising its expenditure strategy. It is likely that a campaign would develop against the state channel's continued subsidised commercial activities, which would be represented as unfair competition, and against the obligation to carry certain kinds of local programming.

It requires no particular brilliance to outline this scenario: it is simply a compilation of the Western European experience since the introduction of commercial television in the UK in the mid-1950s. It is also exactly the scenario that has developed in the Czech Republic over the last few years as TV Nova has developed its programming and begun to exercise its muscles as an established, rather than an aspirant, broadcaster.

Nova began full-time broadcasting on 4 February 1994, technically a little later than its licence specified but still only just over 12 months after it was awarded. By May 1994, it was already the leading broadcaster in the Czech market and by the first quarter of 1995, it had achieved a 70 per cent share of the audience. It has, more or less, held on to this dominance ever since. The first channel of Czech Television was reduced to around 23 per cent of the audience, and the second Czech channel to around 3 per cent. The main commercial competitor, the cable-based Premiéra, struggled to win 2 per cent (Nova, 1995: 2–6).

Nova's rapid growth in audience was achieved as a result of aggressive tactics both in programming and in attitude towards the regulatory body. In its first 11 months of operation, Nova broadcast 53 per cent of acquired foreign programmes, as opposed to 28 per cent on the first Czech Television channel and 35 per cent on the second (Czech Television, 1995: 20; Nova, 1995: 2). The series it chose to highlight in its publicity were those up-to-date and authentically Central European dramas, 'Dallas' and 'M.A.S.H.' (Nova, 1995: 23). One supporter of privatised media characterised its programming as a 'diet of imported soap operas, game shows, films, and sports' (Kettle, 1995: 4). The general director of Nova TV, Dr Vladimir Zelezny, a former leading dissident, summed up the programming policy in the following terms:

> We never overestimate our viewer. We accept the fact the our viewer is a well-educated normal European, he's not over-educated with very sophisticated or unique cultural needs. Our programming reflects this . . . we have not only created TV programming. With marketing merchandising, a logo and a mascot, we have created an institution called TV Nova . . . and we have regular programming. (Madden, 1996b: n.p.)

Zelezny saw no need to do anything other than 'fine tune' this strategy. In other words, the continuing strategy is to broadcast the kind of programming characteristic of a low-budget, unregulated commercial television station.

This combination of programming policies and audience ratings proved very attractive to advertisers and very profitable to the broadcasters. In the financial year ending in April 1995, TV Nova made a profit of US$7,000,000 (Kc181 million) after taxes. The overall position of the operating company, Central European Media Enterprises Group (CME) was less impressive. Heavy losses in the much more mature and competitive German market meant that overall there was a loss of US$20,000,000 (Reuter, 4/04/95).

At the same time, the management of Nova have carried out a continuous campaign against regulatory restraint. The issue of what kind of advertising could be carried and when it could be broadcast quickly became an issue of dispute. Czech law, in line with European norms, forbids the television advertising of some commodities, most notably alcoholic drinks. Both Nova and its small commercial rival Premiéra, were asked on 26 May 1994 by the Broadcasting Council to desist from carrying advertisements for these products. Nova seems to have ignored this request. On 11 October the Broadcasting Council imposed a penalty on Nova 'for repeated violations of Act Nr. 468/91 Coll. and Act Nr. 37/89 Coll. (advertising alcoholic beverages)' (Czech Council, 1995: n.p.). Under the original law of 1991, advertisements were to be broadcast between programmes, rather than inserted into them as is usual in Britain and the USA. The exceptions were programmes that fall naturally into parts, like some sports that have half-time and so on, and works like concerts that have a natural interval. From very early on, Nova was in breach of this provision and was censured by the Council (Czech Council, 1995: n.p.). Zelezny mounted a very aggressive public campaign against the Council, and extended it to include an attack on the demand for certain kinds of expensive local programming that had been written into the licence. Subsequent amendment (Act No. 40/1995 Coll.) moved in a much more commercial direction and allowed the broadcasting of advertisements during other works of more than 30 minutes in length, although insisting on an interval of at least 20 minutes between commercial breaks (Czech Republic, 1995: Article 6).

There continued to be outstanding items of dispute between the Council and the newly successful commercial operator. The first of these concerned the takeover by Nova of Radio Alfa, a national FM licence-holder. The new management altered the programming in such a way as to break the terms of the licence, and there was a struggle between Nova and the Council, which the Council effectively lost (Czech Council, 1996: n.p.). Its own political position, and its legal resources, were so insecure that it was not prepared to enter into a direct trial of strength with such a well-funded opponent.

The political weakness of the Council might be thought surprising, since it had already been firmly subordinated to Parliament by the rejection of its 1994 Report and the replacement of some of its members, and that it was the Klaus party that objected most strongly to the award of a licence to Nova in the first place. To the extent that it attempted to implement the existing law, however, it came up against political pressures, particularly from those factions in Parliament that wanted a much more deregulated broadcasting market (Šmíd, 1994: n.p.). For its own part, Nova proved as astute about political advantage as have Berlusconi and Murdoch, and patched up relations with the Klaus government. In June 1994, it withdrew an interview with Klaus that he objected to. In September 1995 it went further by offering the Prime Minister a weekly television slot, in the nine months before the election, to put his own views to the nation. Klaus, of course, accepted this kind offer (Kaplan and Šmíd, 1995: 43). In those circumstances, the Council was rendered effectively powerless. According to Jiri Pehe, director of research for the Open Media Research Institute (a successor to RFE):

> The broadcasting council has threatened to revoke TV Nova's operating licence on a number of occasions, but TV Nova has become such a factor in Czech politics and culture that to do so would be a scandal of such proportion that I really can't imagine that the councils would take such a step. (Kenety, 1997: A5)

Nova has used this political influence to achieve changes in the media law to bring it into line with its own commercial requirements. Zelezny spelt out his objections to the current situation in a speech to an American Chamber of Commerce in February 1996. He claimed that the original licence conditions were 'so strict it converted us before we even launched into a purely public interest and educational venture' (Madden, 1996a). He identified the source of the 'over-regulation' as being the result of pressure on the Broadcasting Council from the rest of Europe, and in particular the EU, and argued that it was necessary to abolish the restrictions on broadcasting activities. As a result of this political pressure, the Czech media law was amended during the course of 1996 to remove all the conditions that Zelezny objected to.

The final objectionable condition concerned the transfer of the licence, which was specifically prohibited without prior notification to the Broadcasting Council and its express agreement to the change, by Clause 17 of the conditions of the original licence. This became an issue when documents filed with the US Security Exchange Commission by the publicly traded CME, which backs Nova, were discovered by Czech journalists. These revealed that there were well-developed plans to change the ownership of the broadcasting licence. The original licence was awarded to a group of prominent intellectuals with dissident backgrounds calling themselves Central European Television for the 21st Century (CET 21). Two organisations, CME and the Czech bank Ceska sporitelna, have very small shares in this company. Nova's operator is a separate company, the Czech Independent Television Company (CNTS), with a different ownership structure. Ceska sporitelna owned 22 per cent of CNTS. CME, technically titled Central European Development Corporation–Central European Media Enterprises, a Bahamas-registered company controlled by the Lauder perfume family, owned 66 per cent of CNTS. The remainder of the shares are owned by CET 21. There are, apparently, struggles between the various elements for increased control of the various companies (PSMLP, 31 March 1996: 8–9). These complex relations provided a small group of former dissidents, working together with a major successor institution, with access to considerable US capital and expertise.

The new developments involved CME providing a loan to Zelezny to allow him to buy out his fellow dissidents, and in return for this to agree to exercise his voting rights on the direction of CME, until such time as the loan was discharged. This arguably constitutes a de facto change of ownership. When it was agreed, in July 1996, this procedure was in breach of the licence agreement, not least because it was secret. In the event, despite a very considerable public debate, the Broadcasting Council has not proved strong enough to take any effective actions against Nova.

These complex negotiations and political struggles have commanded an audience far wider than simply the Czech Republic, since CME is expanding rapidly into a number of other markets. It has an established television presence in Slovakia and Slovenia, as well as less developed interests elsewhere, and was one of the unsuccessful bidders for a terrestrial licence in Hungary. At the same time, it is expanding into print publishing in the Czech Republic. It looks very much as though Lauder wishes to become the Murdoch of the formerly communist countries.

The effect on public broadcasting

The effect of this sudden competition upon the existing broadcaster was immediate. Faced with a loss of their advertising monopoly, the public broadcasters proved equally willing to ignore the law, broadcasting more than their permitted share of advertising during prime time and earning a censure from the Broadcasting Council (Czech Council, 1995: n.p.). At the same time, a political struggle developed between Czech Television and Nova, who wanted the public broadcaster to be prevented from advertising in prime time (Rohwedder, 1995: 6).

Even in 1994, when it faced the first year of competition from a fledgling broadcaster, Czech Television faced a 25.7 per cent drop in its advertising revenue, and its declared operating surplus was down to US$609,050 (Czech Television, 1995: 36–7). Despite the intensified competition, there were grounds for thinking that the financial position of Czech Television might improve in the near future. The first of these is that the total advertising market in the Czech Republic is growing very quickly, and thus to hold on to a reduced share would still mean an increase in income. The second was that the original law contained the provision that the second channel of public television should be privatised in late 1996. This would reduce Czech Television operating costs considerably, while not reducing its total audience very much. By the end of 1995, however, few people wanted the privatisation to go through. Certainly, Nova did not want any new competitors. Zelezny argued that countries like the Czech Republic are too small and poor to sustain more than one commercial station in the short term, and that the public broadcaster was competition enough for Nova (Madden, 1996b: n.p.). A second factor is that there has been a shift in mood amongst the intellectual élite in the Czech Republic. While they were initially very enthusiastic for privatisation and all its works, particularly in broadcasting, the experience of the real thing has changed their minds. The mass audience may well still be interested in Nova's programming, but 'the enlightened and socially engaged part of the public has realised the potential of commercial TV and started to push the pendulum into the more balanced position' (Kaplan and Šmíd, 1995: 42). Bluntly, just as in Britain, the middle classes want a special channel that caters to their minority interests. Finally, although Czech television has not yet followed Nova downmarket, it has begun to modify its programming strategies to give itself a more competitive edge, apparently with some very modest success.

The worst predictions based on the experience of Western Europe have thus not been wholly fulfilled. The commercial broadcaster has operated in an utterly predictable manner, and managed to avoid any public-service obligations. There has not as yet, however, been a complete collapse in the advertising revenues of the public broadcaster. Thus, even while there are signs that it may be beginning to alter its own programming strategy to meet competition head on, it has not as yet been obliged to duplicate its rival's offerings. Its news, for example, is not as 'tabloid' as that of Nova, but it has been very careful to follow a safe and responsible agenda in order to avoid provoking the government into completely removing its right to carry advertising (Kaplan and Šmíd, 1995: 43).

It is, however, clear from the constant amendments to the broadcasting laws, the frequent breaches of the law, the massive public squabbles between different public figures involved in broadcasting, and the general financial uncertainty that surrounds the whole field, that there is no stable base for the development of a public-service broadcasting policy on the part of Czech Television. Politically cowed, the broadcaster will also find it hard to continue with its job of subsidising uncommercial local production in the name of diversity.

Conclusion

We can draw a number of important conclusions from the overall experience of the former communist countries, and from the Czech and Slovak cases in particular. In the first place, we can conclude that, whatever the laws might say, the political and economic conditions for the flourishing of a recognisable 'public-service broadcasting' do not really exist in Central and Eastern Europe. The idea that if one established 'the rule of law', with a freely elected Parliament and an independent judiciary, one had reached a state when the collective will could be formulated democratically and administered impartially, was clearly naïve. Irrespective of legal frameworks, political realities have been such as to ensure that the control of broadcasting remains a highly politicised question throughout the region. In pursuit of political advantage (Walesa) or economic profit (Zelezny), the former protagonists of the rule of law have been only too willing themselves to flout the law.

In the case of the public broadcasters, the first post-communist governments moved very quickly to try to exert control over their output. They made a number of very definite interventions in staffing and programming that aimed to curb the freedoms that the journalists had abrogated to themselves in the collapse of the old system. By the time the broadcasting laws came to be finalised, the reality of subordination was already established as part of the routine of broadcasting. To the extent that the intensity of the attacks by government and Parliament was reduced, this was in large measure because the public broadcasters were already cowed.

The case of the new private broadcasters was slightly different. The inability to construct genuinely independent public broadcasters had led some of the intellectuals who were part of the initial coalition aiming to prevent the wholesale privatisation of broadcasting to change their minds. They became convinced that it was only by establishing commercial broadcasters that independence could be guaranteed. Despite the strong international evidence against such a claim, particularly from Italy, they came to believe that the demands of the market would prevent political partisanship. This proved mistaken for two reasons. In the first place, the award of the franchises was itself a highly politicised process, with different bidders having links with different political forces. Second, once the licenses were awarded, and the logic of commercial broadcasting began to operate, the new broadcasters themselves became important political actors. They did not regard the circumstances in which they found themselves as fixed and rigid, and chafed against the restrictions placed on their commercial operations. In order to improve their own position, to weaken their rivals, or to allow themselves to expand, they were forced to enter into political battles. In all of this, the political involvement of the commercial broadcasters was enhanced, and their desire to protect their positions intensified, by the fact that the small size of the advertising market meant that the first franchisees have a very good chance of becoming entrenched monopolists. Although none of the new commercial operators has yet emerged as a Berlusconi, Zelezny has been less than firm in his denials of renewed political ambitions.

This link between political power and commercial broadcasting will only surprise those who have an oversimplified view of the distinction between economics and politics in a capitalist society. It is true, as we have consistently argued, that a private capitalist society, and in particular one in which bourgeois democratic norms prevail, is characterised by much weaker links between politics and economics than are totalitarian societies. Even in the USA, however, the prevalence of lobbying groups is a testimony to the continued link between economic and political power. In societies attempting to manage the transition between a state-owned economy and a privately owned one, such links are inevitable. The very process of converting institutions into private concerns involves political action, and the only way in which control can be gained is by being the beneficiary of such decisions. Very far from being an aberration, then, the highly politicised nature of commercial broadcasting in the formerly communist countries is a function of the nature of the transition within those countries.

Finally, the structure of the deal whereby the region's first commercial television station is run provides a microcosm of the relationships between the new ruling class in the former communist countries and the world market. The general strategy of CME, practised in the Czech Republic, Slovakia and Slovenia, and under development in Hungary and Poland, is to seek to build an alliance with powerful local figures. In the Czech case, these consist of two different social groups. On the one hand, there are the prominent former dissidents of CET 21, politically credible in the new order and without too many compromising links with the old regime. On the other hand, there is a bank that traces its structure directly from the communist epoch. Blended together in the CNTS share-structure are the survivors of the old order, an infusion of new blood from the former opposition, and international capital bent on constructing a media empire in the region. The attempt at autarkic development has failed and been finally buried. The new Republic is open to foreign capital and to trade. The representatives of the old order have found internal allies that help them survive in the new conditions, and struck a deal with the world market. The new order is a seamless blend of former oppositionists and their former enemies.

8

Conclusions:
Understanding the Transition

The main contours of the post-communist media systems in the Visegrad countries are becoming visible. The process of restructuring has been a slow one, certainly much slower than many of the enthusiasts of 1989 predicted. It is still far from complete. It has, however, now reached a point when we can begin usefully to draw some conclusions as to its nature and dynamics. The new media are embedded in legal forms and social practices, and are no longer a matter of hope, fear or speculation. On the basis of what we have seen of these systems, we can also begin to draw some conclusions about the more general intellectual issues with which we began this book.

The shape of the new systems

So far as television is concerned, there are today, either actually or potentially, two kinds of broadcaster. The old state broadcasters of the communist epoch have survived as institutions, and many of their staff remain the same. Their legal position has been transformed. They are today officially 'public broadcasters'. In reality, however, they are everywhere subordinated to the government of the day, and this is reflected in their programming, in particular their news and current affairs. The interventions today are more public, more contested and more likely be unsuccessful than those of the communist epoch, but it remains the case that nowhere can it be said that they correspond to a model of robust political independence.

These public broadcasters all face, either now or in the near future, competition from new commercial stations. The award of the franchises for these stations has everywhere been highly contested politically. Where they have been established, the commercial stations have introduced aggressively competitive programming policies, using large amounts of imported entertainment material and scheduling it for audience maximisation. They have won a large share of the audience. They have not, however, established themselves as politically independent, although their degree of identification with political parties is rather lower than that experienced in, notably, Italy.

Broadcasting is everywhere the responsibility of broadcasting councils. These are, in their majority, appointed by the different political forces in the Parliament and the other arms of the legislature. The members of these councils are therefore widely perceived as political appointees. Their tenure depends upon the good offices of politicians, and in most cases these latter have been quite willing to use their powers to suborn the councils.

Although we have not looked in any detail at radio in this book, the story there is structurally similar to that of television. Private stations were set up much more quickly there, and the extent of specialised commercialisation familiar in the West is much greater. The ownership, control and political direction of radio stations, however, remains as much a matter of contention as does that of television.

At first sight, the press provides a contrast. There have been many new foundations, both of newspapers and magazines. The old party- and state-owned newspapers have everywhere passed into private hands. The titles, and indeed many of the journalists, display a remarkable continuity from the communist epoch. In the first instance, these papers were often seized by their journalists. In many cases today, these private hands are those of the same international media companies that are familiar players on the world stage, sometimes with local partners, sometimes alone. The press market remains highly competitive, although there is a high casualty rate amongst the new foundations of 1989. The press, too, remains highly politicised and partisan.

There has thus been a definite shift towards a much more commercial media system, integrated into the world market, although a surprising amount of the old order survives. One strongly marked feature of these new systems is that they are highly politicised throughout.

In considering these new systems, we have first to answer the obvious question of how they fit into a typology of world media systems. We can then begin to answer the specific questions about media theory and the more general ones concerning social theory that have provided the motive for our detailed investigations.

Models of media systems

There is a widespread tendency to measure the media systems of the post-communist countries, and in particular their journalism, against what is often termed the 'Anglo-Saxon' model. This is said to be characterised by fearlessly independent media employing brave investigative journalists who, whatever their personal feelings, are dedicated to the separation of fact and opinion in their reporting, who are even-handed and impartial between contending viewpoints, and whose main task is to inform their readers and viewers without fear or favour about all that is most important in the world today. Measured against this yardstick, the media of the post-communist world are manifestly inadequate and must be encouraged, bullied or persuaded to become better. To this end, missionary expeditions, often from US schools of journalism, pass through the region with great frequency.

The trouble with this view is that all and any media, measured against this yardstick, are manifestly inadequate. The 'Anglo-Saxon' model of the media is a largely imaginary construction. Like some mythological beast, it is an impossible amalgam of selected features of two incompatible systems, joined together without regard to its possibility of existence. In this case, the two parts might be characterised as the *New York Times* and the BBC – although with both presented in an idealised form.

The fact that this 'Anglo-Saxon' model does not and cannot exist does not mean that we should dismiss it out of hand. On the contrary, it is very illuminating to ask just what it is that makes each part, and the impossible whole, so attractive to the observer. In doing that, we will beg two important questions. First, how far and in what ways the reality of these institutions differs from their ideal image. These are much studied and are of great importance in themselves, but they are not our concern here. Second, whether the kinds of media content they embody – objective, impartial and serious – are preferable to alternatives that stress interpretation, advocacy and entertainment. This is also an important debate, and one that is too often dismissed without serious attention, but let us here assume, since such an assumption makes the issues at stake very much clearer, that the former are indeed better.

The material conditions for the existence of the *New York Times*, or more generally the US press, are that it does not exist in a free market. Since such a statement would no doubt cause apoplexy if uttered in Freedom House, the Freedom Forum and other such neutrally named bodies, it is important to be clear exactly why that is the case. The US press is certainly commercial, but it generally operates in a monopoly situation. Monopoly is the negation of the free market, and its economic effects are well known, much deplored and generally legislated against. Unfortunately, legislation in the USA has proved inadequate to arrest the normal processes of capitalism. The journalistic consequences of monopoly are also well known. The characteristic impartiality of journalism in this situation is a function of the need to serve a diverse audience, and the desire not to offend any significant section through the adoption of a partisan stance. The 'seriousness' of the press, embodied in the amount of journalistic resources and editorial space that it is prepared to devote to public enlightenment matters, is a function of its need to superserve the élite audience that is particularly attractive to advertisers. We can see how peculiar that situation is by comparing the US situation with another developed 'Anglo-Saxon' press market: that of the UK. National newspapers in the UK exist in a free market and are highly competitive – there are currently 10 major daily morning titles. As a result of this, newspapers are partisan and their readership is class-stratified. These papers are not impartial. On the contrary, they regularly adopt highly party-political positions. The vast majority of the copies sold are not of the 'serious' papers. Newspapers have definite, clear and well-known political profiles, since these form part of their ability to secure a section of their target audience. The majority of newspapers are built around entertainment, because that is the route to a mass audience. There is a sharp gap between those few readers who get serious information and the vast majority who do not. These factors do not constitute an aberration, but a rational business response to generating profit in a competitive market.

If we consider the case of the BBC, or more generally British broadcasting of recent memory, when the whole system, including the commercial part, was essentially public service, we see that similar conditions prevailed: there was an effective absence of capitalist competition. The broadcasters who made up this duopoly, state-owned and privately owned, were serious because they could afford to be, as they did not compete for revenue. They were impartial because they were obliged to be by regulation. They were able to be impartial because they existed in a political environment in which government intervention in broadcasting was a relative rarity. Again, we can see how peculiar this situation was by comparing it with the USA. While the political environment was similarly hostile to direct intervention in broadcasting, even limited competition led the broadcasters towards a much more entertainment-oriented notion of their functions.

Manifestly, neither of these sets of conditions exists in the former communist countries. The press finds itself in a highly competitive situation, at both the national and the regional level. There are a plethora of titles competing with each other. In these circumstances, political alignment is a fact of marketing every bit as much as it is the result of the personal attributes of journalists. Although the legal situation of broadcasting speaks of the duties of public service, we have seen that neither the economic nor the political conditions for such an activity exist. The commercial broadcasters find themselves struggling in a small and poor market. The would-be public broadcasters confront a political world in which their subordination to the government is a normal and accepted part of the routines of daily life.

Given these circumstances, it is naïve in the extreme to imagine that the media systems of post-communist countries can be assimilated to those of some Anglo-Saxon model. The social and political realities of the change from a centrally directed to a market economy necessitate that all aspects of society will be saturated with politics, and the mass media do not form an exception.

It does not follow, however, that we need to abandon any attempt to place these media systems within an international typology. One possibility is that the systems are something *sui generis*, examples of a unique historical formation, the post-communist media system. This is the position that would, logically, follow from arguments like that of Schöpflin about the condition of post-communism. There are strong grounds for rejecting this claim. The structure of the system – dual broadcasting system, competitive press, highly politicised media – is hardly unique. On the contrary, they can be seen as close to the common features of western European media systems, as Table 8.1 shows.

Certainly, the peculiar features of the historical experience of communism mean that these systems are not identical with other European examples. They are not so different, however, as to be examples of a distinct type.

Table 8.1   *Comparison of main features of media systems*

Type	Press monopoly	Press impartiality	Press stratification	Private broadcaster	Major state broadcaster
USA	Yes	Yes	No	Yes	No
Western European	No	No	Yes	Yes	Yes
Former Communist	No	No	Yes	Yes	Yes

In this context, it is tempting to follow Splichal and identify the emerging systems as 'Italian'. Certainly, the Italian, or more generally the southern European, media type does have some features in common with that of post-communism. The parallel can only be accepted, however, with three important reservations. In the first place, the underlying structure of the Italian model of media, which persisted through a number of different manifestations, was a rather stable one. It was designed to cope with a society that was paralysed at the political level by a fundamental division between the PCI on the one hand and the DC on the other. In essence, this fundamental fault lasted 40 years from the moment the US Sixth Fleet anchored in Naples Bay to the *Tangentopoli* crisis. The various shifts within the media, which were very substantial indeed in television, can nevertheless be mapped more or less accurately on to the underlying social rift. The complete control by the Christian Democrats of television, the 'DC in your living room', which persisted up until the 1970s, was a complement of the single party domination of the state. The pluralism that ensued, with the main RAI channels clearly aligned with the major political forces, constituted a political compromise resulting from the entry of the PSI into government and the failed attempt at a historical compromise. The 'Italianness' of the Italian media was thus an enduring historical formation. There is no evidence that these sorts of enduring and relatively stable divisions exist in the former communist countries. In particular, and for understandable historical reasons, there is no mass party that presents itself as the natural champion of the working class, fundamentally opposed to the state and the system that it defends. Conversely, there is no single obvious political force that the rich see as their natural bulwark against the poor. Legal, political and social arrangements for the mass media in post-communist countries are likely to prove much less long-lasting than was the case in Italy.

Second, and partly because of its stability, the Italian model was at a later date able to build government and opposition into the very structure of the system. The press was always more or less plural and the PCI was able to sustain a powerful presence there. In broadcasting, the eventual division of RAI into three competing channels exactly embodied both the deep political division of the society and the way in which the DC benefited from the manner in which institutions were divided up. There is no sign whatsoever that this kind of institutionalised political pluralism is likely to be enshrined in the broadcasting systems of the post-communist societies. Although broadcasting is the site of struggles, the evidence so far is that the aim of all of the participants is to seize the institutions rather than to negotiate some kind of 'equitable' sharing of influence between the major political forces.

The third reason applies more directly to the press. The Italian daily press has, by north European standards, a relatively restricted circulation. It is not, in many ways, a mass press. There is not that sharp division between serious and popular, tabloid and broadsheet, quality and gutter, intellectual and yellow, that is so clearly present in Britain or Germany. The evidence in a number of former communist countries, notably Slovenia, but also Hungary and the Czech Republic, strongly suggests that the sharp decline in overall newspaper readership that has been such a marked consequence of falling living standards and rising prices has been accompanied by a recomposition along lines that broadly suggest a repeat of the 'northern' press model (Erjavec, 1996).

It seems best, then, to try to understand the media systems of post-communism as variants of a more general European model rather than specific examples of a definite Italian type. Such a perspective allows us better to understand both the common features of the different national instances and their different historical dynamics. There is no evidence that there is operating a secret teleology that will result in 'Anglo-Saxon' media, and against which the current progress, or lack of progress, of the existing media may be measured.

Consequences for media theory

The most important consequence of our investigations for media theory follows directly from the above discussion. *Four Theories of the Press* provides no insights whatsoever into the past, present or future of the media systems of post-communism. Whatever other qualities it may have, it is completely useless as a reference point for understanding what is, on any account, a major development in the world media. At the most obvious level, its counter-position of the world's media systems into two opposing camps provides no space for a recognition of the specific features of the European systems that we have just examined, and certainly no purchase on why the formerly communist systems should change to approximate to them rather than some other model. If we accept that the first test of any social theory is its ability to illuminate the real world, then that book has failed spectacularly. It cannot be brought up to date. It cannot be improved. It cannot be modified to take account of subsequent developments. It cannot be replaced by a new edition more in tune with the times. It was plain wrong and it is plain useless as a starting point for media analysis. It should be relegated forthwith to the gloomiest recesses of the Museum of the Cold War and visited only by sensible graduate students of a historical persuasion.

We can also observe that, in failing so comprehensively the test of historical relevance, the internal weaknesses of the book were exposed. Even if one were to accept the notion that it is value systems that determine social institutions, the fact that the methodological basis of *Four Theories of the Press* is that there is a single, dominant value system that determines all of the significant features of a society and a media system is clearly inadequate to deal with a historical change of the kind that we have examined. It may, arguably, be the case that the USA is the kind of monolithic and unified society that this approach assumes, but it is clearly not true of the bitterly contested social terrain of the countries we have been examining. It is precisely the clash of value systems that is the most striking immediate feature of their media landscapes.

In fact, when we look at the actual evidence of the ways in which the media have changed and developed over the last few years, it is very difficult to make the claim that media systems can best be understood with reference to value systems, whether dominant or contested. On the contrary, the evolution of broadcasting, for example, seems to be much better explained with reference to the conflicting logics of economic and political forces rather than clearly defined values. We might take the intention to establish independent public-service broadcasters precisely as one such attempt to impose a value system upon reality. As we have seen, this proved quite impossible in practice, since neither the political nor the economic conditions for such a system existed anywhere in the region. Indeed, even some of those who had initially held strongly to the idea of public service themselves were forced to change their views by their experiences, and came to be advocates of the commercialisation of broadcasting. They did so on the grounds that only commercial organisations were capable of breaking the politicisation of television news. The experts, many of them very sophisticated by world standards, held this view, mistakenly as it turned out, not on the grounds that such broadcasters would be more likely to cherish the values of independence as matters of principle, but because they believed that commercial considerations would force commercial operators to act in this way.

The evolution of the press provides a similar illustration. This rapidly evolved into a fiercely competitive, market-based system. But, as we have seen, to the extent that it is possible to claim that a dominant value system in these countries is revealed by examining the results of social surveys, it is clear that only in the Czech Republic does the market ideal command majority support, and there only very narrowly indeed. Unless 'core social values' mean something quite impenetrable to empirical analysis, there is a strong case for saying that, at least in three out of the four countries we have looked at closely, the societies have had forced upon them press systems modelled after social values that they do not themselves adhere to. A much better explanation, surely, is one that starts from a recognition of the material nature of media structures and practices, and which accepts that all developed societies are characterised by conflicting sets of values.

The search for general models of the mass media, or for theories that allow us to classify the vast range of existing media systems into recognisable types, remains an essential one. The utter failure of the framework that permeated this effort for nearly half a century, and which continues to shape contemporary discussion to an unconscionable degree, makes the project more urgent, rather than discrediting the entire enterprise. We have seen how the evidence of media change in Central and Eastern Europe strongly indicates that an approach to this task based on the material determinants of media systems, along the lines suggested by Raymond Williams, is more likely to generate a robust theory. The ideas and values that human agents bring to situations are important elements in determining historical outcomes. They are not negligible after-effects of other, more important, factors. On the other hand, people act in circumstances that they themselves do not define or construct. It is those circumstances not of their own choosing, to coin a phrase, to which this branch of media theory needs to pay much more attention.

The conditions for public-service broadcasting

The other consequence for media theory is minor and local, although it does have methodological implications that are exactly opposite to those considered above. It concerns the continued discussion of the concept of public-service broadcasting. Despite its well-known international crisis, this way of organising broadcasting continues to be influential in debates both in the industry and amongst scholars. The experience of post-communism provides two small, and essentially confirmatory, notes to those debates. In the first place, the evidence we have reviewed demonstrates that the legal status of a broadcaster is not a sufficient condition for establishing it as a public-service institution. If the history of British commercially owned broadcasting demonstrates the positive case that, in the right conditions, private broadcasters could behave in more or less the same way as public broadcasters, Central and Eastern Europe provides two pieces of negative evidence. It restated the well-known fact that state, or public, ownership is not a sufficient condition for the kinds of independence essential to public-service broadcasting. It also confirmed that the negative consequences of dependence upon advertising revenue in a competitive system are at least as great as the positive advantages of relative financial independence.

The second implication of our study is that there needs to be something of a shift in emphasis in discussions as to the continued viability, or otherwise, of public-service broadcasting. Much of the discussion in the last decade or so has been, it might be argued, about issues internal to the broadcasters. Under this heading, we might identify the threats to public broadcasting posed by shifts in the funding situation, the impact of globalisation as mediated through technological changes, the impact of the end of spectrum shortage, and so on. What the experience of Central and Eastern Europe throws into sharp relief is the importance of organisations outside the direct ambit of broadcasting, and in particular of political parties and governments, to the viability of the public service remit. The reasons why it has proved impossible to translate the legal provisions into functioning and healthy public broadcasters anywhere in the region has nothing to do with cable and

satellite delivery systems. It has nothing to do with the organisational structure of the broadcasters. It even has nothing to do with the fragmentation of
the audience as a result of the proliferation of channels. The primary reasons
are located in the political conditions of the different states. It is what politicians have done that has made the project unviable.

The rules governing the relations between powerful social institutions, and
in particular the government and state institutions, a complex I would be
tempted to call the 'political culture' of a society if that term did not have
such an unfortunate history, is much more important in the existence or
otherwise of a public-service broadcaster than are the well-known internal
factors. This has been obscured by the fact that much of the international
debate has taken for granted the fact that it was centred on institutions in relatively stable bourgeois democracies. Given that the degree of political
conflict in such societies is, more or less by definition, limited and constrained
within mutually agreed limits by the major political forces, it is sometimes
assumed that states, governments and politicians have no direct influence on
public broadcasters.

This is, of course, an untenably naïve assumption. One of the prime examples in the debate, the BBC, in fact provides considerable evidence of the
ways in which changes in political culture had immediate consequences for
the degree of independence of broadcasters, but these consequences were
admittedly fairly limited in their scope. Those societies experiencing post-
communism are much more intensely, and necessarily, saturated with politics
than are stable bourgeois democracies. In stable societies, much of the way in
which the political situation shapes the mass media is normal and accepted.
It is what we have here called 'routine' intervention by politicians in the mass
media. In transition societies, intervention is much more dramatic, overt and
contested. It is therefore much more visible to the analyst and much easier to
understand. It is impossible to understand any of the main features of broadcasting in Central and Eastern Europe without considering the prevailing
political conditions. What these experiences demonstrate is that major institutions like parties, governments, states and major economic actors act to set
the terms and terrain upon which broadcasting takes place. It is reasonable to
assume that the structures that are so visible in these cases are ones that are
present, albeit in a more disguised form, in all contemporary societies.

This point, of course, applies particularly strongly to discussions about
public-service broadcasting, but it is clearly of relevance not only to all of
broadcasting but also to the mass media as a whole. One of the major faults
of what is usually called 'political economy' with reference to the mass media
has been that, in practice, it has tended towards the purely, one might almost
say vulgarly, economic. In stressing the extent to which the contemporary
mass media have to be considered primarily as economic institutions, and
demonstrating the pertinence both of general economic laws and the peculiar
economic features of the culture industries, there has been a tendency to
ignore the consequences of political action. Politics may well be concentrated
economics, but political power is not a pure expression of economic power,

any more than brandy is just wine with a higher alcohol content. Examining and understanding the operation of political power on the media, and the extent to which particular outcomes are the consequence of the relationship between political and economic power, remains an important task.

Overall, we may say that the consequences of the study of post-communism for media theory proper are first to reaffirm the importance of beginning from the real relations existing in societies in any attempt to theorise why media are the way they are. But the second consequence is that an adequate account of the mass media needs also to take into account factors other than simple materialism understood as economic determination. There remain other levels of analysis that are necessary to any convincing account. If the approach to the mass media must be materialist, it has to be a materialism that recognises the importance of, at least, political activities in deciding outcomes.

Issues in political theory

The politicisation of public television highlights the two main problems for political theory revealed by this study. Neither the concept of 'civil society' nor that of 'a state of laws' can really survive a close examination in the light of what has actually occurred.

The concept of civil society was a unifying theme to the opposition in communist countries, and indeed to other oppositions fighting repressive regimes around the world. To the extent that it embodied a vague aspiration to a better society in which the atrocities of the existing regime were impossible, it was of course an extremely valuable, even admirable, idea. Its fundamental incoherence could be ignored in the press of the struggle. The construction of some space, however small, in which a life different from that dictated by the regime could even be imagined was an immense victory. Subsequent to the victory of the former opposition, however, the situation changed. The concrete meaning of the term was subjected to the harsh criticism of reality.

Of the three different major interpretations of the meaning of civil society, only the most crudely 'materialist' gives any purchase on what has happened. Neither what we termed the 'poetic' nor the 'idealist' versions are adequate to account for the ways in which the mass media developed. If either of the latter were even remotely accurate guides as to how people behave in post-communist societies, then we would expect to find evidence for them in the ways in which the mass media were structured. The fact is that in the press there seem to have been few if any attempts to empower civil society. On the contrary, the press has become private property and is at the mercy either of the market or of political patronage. In broadcasting, it is true that there were some attempts to find ways in which civil society might be represented in the governing bodies. However, even in those cases like Slovenia and Hungary, where this attempt has continued, the reality has been that it is political parties that are the decisive forces in the appointment of the broadcasting councils and other powerful institutions and individuals. In other countries, the appointment and tenure of the members of the governing bodies is openly and obviously the result of political decisions taken by the Parliament and the President. Nowhere, in no part of the media, has the ambition to construct a civil society along the lines envisaged been realised.

What has been constructed is a media system that fits quite well into the materialist interpretation of civil society. This version of the idea essentially used the term to refer to the construction of a market economy. In the press this is what, overwhelmingly, has happened. In broadcasting, it has begun to happen in terms of ownership, and in terms of the economic dynamics, even of the state broadcasters, it has made considerable advances. Compared with the situation prevailing in the last years of the communist epoch, the media landscapes of Eastern and Central Europe are today a fair approximation of what would be predicted by the 'materialist' version of civil society.

The inadequacy of 'poetic' and 'idealist' ideas that claimed that civil society was some sphere independent of both politics and economics, and that it could be populated by men and women of goodwill, is thus manifest. There is no room for such ideas in serious discussion of the mass media. The 'materialist' version is much more robust. It does indeed go part of the way towards explaining what has happened. There are, however, two very good reasons for rejecting the utility even of this version in debates on communication.

The first of these concerns that substantial part of the predictions about civil society that have not been borne out by developments in the region. All of the proponents of civil society were arguing not only against communism but for a version of society that they believed would be better. It would be better materially, because it would be more efficient than the planned economy. It would be better spiritually, because the individual would be able to develop free of the chains of dogma. It would be better politically, because it would be much more democratic.

In the case of economic advance, it is much too soon to make any final judgement. It is true that in the short term most of the economies suffered severe shocks, and the living standards of the mass of the population, as opposed to the fortunate proto-capitalists, fell very substantially. People struggled for West German or Swedish capitalism but, with the exception of the people of East Germany, what they got was much more like Turkey. On the other hand, six years is a relatively short time in terms of economic development – unless one still believes in five-year plans as the solution, that is. In the longer term, it may well be that the pressures of the global economy will have the effect of equalising living standards for the mass of the population throughout Europe, although of course we in the richer countries may find that is not wholly a process of levelling-up.

In terms of personal freedom, there is no doubt that the end of communism meant an enormous advance. This is despite the appeal of the most atavistic forms of nationalism. It is despite the renewed strengths of various kinds of crude racial prejudice. It is despite the vigorous assertion of various kinds of very crude masculinity. All of these are severe limitations to the promises of 1989, but none of them amounts to its negation.

In the case of political life, the record is ambivalent. There was, immediately, a vast extension of the range of political opinions that can find expression. There are, in all of the Visegrad countries, elections which, while not perhaps models of democratic procedures, are at least good enough to be recognised as some sort of expression of popular will. The promise of the theory of civil society, however, was that the sphere of politics would be greatly reduced, not that it would simply become pluralised. As we have seen, in the case of the mass media, this was only marginally true, if at all. The politicisation of the mass media, and in particular of broadcasting, would seem to suggest that the theory of civil society as market capitalism linked necessarily to Western democratic norms is a little wide of the mark. The norms that do exist are different from, and, from the point of view of bourgeois democratic theory, weaker than, those prevailing in Western Europe and the USA. What is more, it is very far from certain that the strengthening of the market economy is necessarily linked with an extension and improvement of democracy. There is little in the record of the former communist countries to suggest that they are any different from any other political system: abrupt changes in material circumstances can lead to sharp changes in political forms. While it thus correctly identified the economic dynamic of market capitalism, the materialist version of civil society was rather too optimistic about its political potential.

The second objection to accepting this term at face value is that, to the extent that it does accurately describe the real historical process, it is in fact a euphemism. If what is meant by 'civil society' is in fact 'private capitalism', why not just call it that? It is true that, sometimes, the term is used by critics of capitalism in order to find an unobjectionable point of rhetorical departure from which to mount a critique of the democratic inadequacies of existing social institutions in general and media in particular. It is also true that the term is used by enthusiastic advocates of capitalism, who wish in turn to find an unobjectionable rhetorical point of departure for arguing to extend the market. Neither of these groups has any convincing intellectual case for retaining the term in scholarly, or indeed political, discourse. The issues are much clearer if one confronts them without obfuscation.

One of the issues that becomes dramatically clearer if one employs the term 'private capitalism' instead of 'civil society' is the actual structure of existing social relations and their inscription in the mass media. As a matter of systemic logic, private capitalism requires capitalists and proletarians, entrepreneurs and wage workers. It cannot exist without imbalances of economic power. In the days of Hegel these were relatively undeveloped, although already a few years later the point of Marx's critique was precisely that the term 'civil society' obscured this issue. Today, obviously, these imbalances of power are very much greater. To speak today, in Britain, of the 'press of civil society' is simply to conceal the salient fact of a very highly concentrated ownership structure in the newspaper industry. So, too, with other areas of debate: our view of social reality will be very much clearer, and our chances of understanding that reality very much greater, if we stop using terms that obscure essential features of contemporary reality. It would be much better for serious enquiry if everyone stopped using the term 'civil society' forthwith.

The second term that needs questioning as a result of our investigation is the notion of the 'state of laws'. Like civil society, this term has a descriptive and a normative dimension. We can readily agree that most contemporary developed societies have codified systems of laws, and that it is a good idea that these are enacted constitutionally, or better still democratically, that they are administered fairly and impartially, and that they are only changed as a result of agreed procedures. What is much more questionable is whether any society actually is 'a state of laws', in the sense that the legal framework actually constrains the actions of powerful interests in all and every case. The evidence presented here is that the societies emerging from communism are marked by highly contested laws. Governments, powerful politicians, media owners and others seem to act in pursuit of their interest without undue regard for the precise detail of the law. In those circumstances when their actions are found to be illegal, the judgments do not appear either to alter the situation or modify the behaviour of the law-breakers. One might venture to suggest that in this respect, as in so many others, the countries of Central and Eastern Europe are examples, albeit extreme examples, of more general features of capitalist societies.

It is therefore questionable whether the concept of a state of laws adds anything to our understanding of the specific nature of those societies emerging from communism. To the extent that the concept is banally about the fact that all developed societies require an elaborate code of regulations called laws, it is obviously true. To the extent that it purports to be a description of any actually existing society, it is, at the very least, highly questionable. To the extent that it is a normative statement about the desirable society it is open to debate, but the outcome of such a debate would not impinge on its utility for analysis. What is not at all evident is the extent to which the concept of a state of laws adds to our understanding, and therefore, on the principle of parsimony in theoretical matters, it is probably better to do without it.

Theories of transition

If the idea that the changes in Eastern and Central Europe can be adequately explained in terms of the rebirth of civil society, or the emergence of a state laws, has to be rejected, there remains the problem of explaining what actually has occurred. In Chapter 4 we identified four substantive theories about the nature of the transformation, which could in turn be grouped broadly into two general camps.

On the one hand, there are those theories that stress the radical and fundamental nature of the transformation. There are those, like Francis

Fukuyama, for whom 1989 represented a total and complete break with the past, ushering in a society completely different at every level from the spiritual to the material. Less grandiose claims are made by those, like the late Ralph Miliband, who saw the old communist regimes as ruthless tyrannies running what were essentially socialist economies. For them, the main change of 1989 was the restoration of capitalism in the economy. The main economic and social institutions were completely recast by the fall of the communist system.

On the other hand, there are those who argue that the main changes consequent on the fall of communism are relatively small, if not non-existent. For those, like Alex Callinicos, for whom the previous regimes were tyrannous forms of class exploitation best understood as state capitalism, the main changes have been at the political level. Many of the major institutions have survived more or less unscathed, and the fundamentally exploitative productive relations have continued. The shift to private capitalism, however, is most easily handled through the political framework of democracy, and the fragmentation of the old ruling class means that competitive divisions will become ever more apparent in the societies as a whole. The final group of theories question the extent to which there has been any significant change as a result of the fall of communism. The mass of the population remains dominated by a narrow, and substantially unchanged, élite group that monopolises social and political power.

The evidence that we have reviewed above must lead us decisively to reject the first group of theories. The broadcasting institutions of the former regime were generally not seriously disturbed by the events of 1989. There were some changes at the top, but the basic structures remained intact. In those few cases where there was some upheaval, and the prospect of radically different, and much more democratic, ways of organising the media were present, the interlude was brief, and the bureaucratic order was reimposed without serious conflict. Large, state-owned broadcasting institutions with essentially the same personnel continued to exist in the period after the transition. The transition in the press seems on the surface to have been swifter and more complete but, analysed more closely, demonstrates that many of the leading titles of the earlier period continued in production, with many of their former staff in place. The degree of continuity is much too great to support any theory of total transformation.

The continuity theories of the second group thus find much more support from the evidence. To the extent that there have been changes in these countries, it has been change that has left in place substantial legacies of the old order and which has been very far from a total transformation. Although some of the more notorious of the old regime's leaders may have vanished from view, the political, social and media life of the former communist countries remains heavily peopled with representatives of the former regimes. Social continuity in the élite groups is one of the strongest and most striking features of the transition. The institutional continuity of large-scale social organisations is another.

Given these continuities, there remains the question of whether there has been any substantial change, or if the essence of the old order remains in place. The latter argument has a great deal to recommend it, but must ultimately be rejected. There have indeed been systemic changes, at the level of politics. Whereas in the past the societies can be understood as having a totalitarian political structure, today there is everywhere a fragmentation. This has immediate consequences for the mass media, which are no longer under quite such direct and complete control as in the past. Broadcasting, in particular, has become the site of political contestation in a way that would have been impossible even in the dying days of the old regimes. The press, no matter how subject to the imperatives of the market, is able to report and advocate a wide range of different views. Thus, while the substantive changes might not have been so far reaching at the immediate level, they nevertheless constitute a change in the ways in which the mass media relate to the wider society, and to the political élite in particular.

This political shift should be understood as more than a simple transition from a dictatorial to a parliamentary way of running society. Indeed, it is by no means certain that the latter will be the final outcome of the process everywhere in the region. The transformation is political in a much deeper sense. The old order achieved its economic and social dominance, and was able to exercise its overall social power, only as a result of its unity. This was often achieved, against the centrifugal pressures of interests in the real world, through the forced unity of the purge. Once that political unity was removed, then the fragmentation of the economic and social life of the ruling group was inevitable. While it is true that the great mass of the population today finds itself confronting exactly the same exploitative conditions and social exclusions as it did in the past, often administered by exactly the same individuals, for the ruling group the transformation is much deeper. They have splintered into different factions, absorbed some new, formerly dissident, elements, and begun to integrate themselves into the world market. It may well be that the same people rule. It is certainly true that people of the same gender rule. It is also true, however, that they rule in a fundamentally different way.

It therefore seems that the view advanced by Callinicos is the one that best passes the test of practical experience. There was indeed a change in 1989, and it was of a sufficiently fundamental nature to warrant being considered a real revolution. It was, however, primarily a political revolution, which left relatively untouched many of the key structures of economic and social dominance, including in particular the mass media. The oppressive and exploitative social relations that were characteristic of the old order have not been altered fundamentally.

In some ways, perhaps, the changes in the mass media were the clearest expression of the essentially political nature of the transformation. Throughout all of the changes, the vast mass of the population remains the object of the techniques that are commonly termed mass communication. At no point did the people succeed in transforming the fundamental terms upon which the media are organised. At the same time, the media themselves did change. They ceased simply to be the property of a single, unified ruling group. They no longer spoke with one single voice determined by the Central Committee. Now they responded to the pulls of different competing groups of rulers. They were part of the stakes in, and indeed one of the sites of, the political struggle.

The future of the critical project

The final area of interest concerns the continuing viability of what we called in the first chapter the 'critical project'. We saw how the collapse of communism represented a fundamental challenge to this critical project, since it is necessarily based on the notion that there could be an alternative, and better, society than that of capitalism. For most advocates of the project, social democrats as well as communists, that different society was embodied, however imperfectly, in the Soviet Union and similarly structured societies. For most of the adherents of the critical project, the state machine was the great antidote to the evident barbarities of the market: societies in which the state had apparently negated the market were, whatever their limitations in terms of democracy and human rights, some sort of model of an alternative. For decades, it had been possible to point to these countries as examples of greater, or at least equal, economic vigour than private capitalism. For many, it had also been true that these societies seemed to embody greater distributive equality, social justice, and even substantive democracy, compared to their competitors.

All that ended in 1989, at least for the vast majority of commentators. So deeply were the critical project and the fate of communist societies intertwined that no honest observer could fail to recognise a crisis. Time might make it seem less pressing, and some of the horrors of succession might tint the view of the past a little more favourably, but it was impossible not to acknowledge that, unless the critical project could offer a convincing account of the origins, dynamics and collapse of communism, it was doomed to irrelevance.

This book has only considered a tiny fragment of that gigantic problem. Our conclusions, however, do make some contribution to resolving it. If the structures of the mass media altered so little in the transition from communism to its supposed mortal enemy, capitalism, then it suggests that there was little to choose between them. It is difficult to accept that, when the evidence points so strongly to the social continuity between communism and post-communism, these constitute fundamentally different social systems. It is much more credible to see this as evidence of structural similarities between the two orders. Both operated to exclude the vast mass of the population from any voice or any control. Neither allowed for any substantial degree of democratic participation in the running of broadcasting or the press. Both were concerned with what are sometimes termed system-maintaining functions.

The implication of our evidence, and of the theoretical explanation offered for it, is that the communist societies were not alternatives to capitalism but one especially horrible variant of it. They have been replaced by another, currently rather less horrible, variant of the same system. It therefore follows that there was and is no organic link between these societies and the critical project, which after all has been concerned in almost all of its forms not only to advance a critique of the shortcomings of capitalism but to suggest an alternative and better way of organising human society. There appears to be no logical reason for linking the critical project to communist societies.

That is not to say that there have not been historical links between the critical project and communism, both as an oppositional movement and as a ruling ideology. On the contrary, there have indeed been very powerful links. The rulers of these countries certainly claimed to embody the critical project. They said they spoke for the working class even when they were ordering tanks to drive over the bodies of real workers. For many sincere opponents of capitalism, communism was thought to embody the living form of a better society. Those who admitted the limits, indeed the crimes, of the real communist societies could yet defend their position with the belief that, given time, things would get better and the superior nature of socialism would manifest itself. The collapse of communism terminated that line of defence. Historical developments have clearly demonstrated that people who held such views, however brave and sincere, were fundamentally mistaken.

The collapse of those links has certainly had profoundly demoralising effects on the people who believed in them. Some, like Eric Hobsbawm, have fallen into a deep epochal pessimism that is often almost tragic. Other responses have been frankly risible. Martin Jacques, another very well-known member of the British Communist Party, claimed, unbelievably, to be shocked to discover that there had been financial links between his party and Moscow, and scuttled off to a new career in mainstream journalism. These demoralisations and defections undoubtedly all depleted the slender human resources of the critical project. In the short term, it got harder to oppose capitalism.

In the long term, however, the collapse of the links with communism is a condition for health. No convincing programme for human liberation can be built on the denial of some of the most evident truths about the contemporary world. No serious analysis can be based on wilful blindness to such obvious facts. No trust can be placed in an ideology that demanded silence about the most horrible of crimes. It is only by reasserting the fundamental difference between the critical project and what passed for communism that there is any hope for its renewal. Freed of the need to contort itself to explain the world, to think that a state that murdered workers was a workers' state, to claim that a society in which the most privileged élite in the world ruled over impoverished masses had abolished class antagonisms, to believe that an economy that made raising output its primary goal had ended exploitation, to imagine that a country armed to the teeth with weapons of mass destruction was a force for world peace, freed from all of this, the critical project is a much more convincing proposition.

To the extent that it is possible, within the terms of the critical project, to explain not only what occurred in capitalism but also within communism, it is possible to continue with it. This study of the collapse of the old order and the birth of the new in Central and Eastern Europe, as embodied in the restructuring of the mass media, attempts to do precisely that.

State, market and self-emancipation

If the critical project can survive 1989 only by recognising that the infatuation with what was called communism was a near-fatal mistake, then in most variants it will need considerable rethinking. In general, what the collapse of communism demonstrated was that the state was not the alternative to the market. That opposition will have to be abandoned. The first thing that the critical project needs to do is stop thinking of the state as a kindly, if regrettably bureaucratic, agency of social regulation and recapture the old truth that it is essentially a special body of armed men with prisons etc. at their disposal, and that its primary role is to carry through social repression. In its place, the critical project needs to place much more emphasis on the extent to which it is only realisable through self-activity and self-emancipation.

The debate between state and market has been central to many versions of the critical project in the study of the mass media. As an example of such debates, one thinks immediately about debates over cultural imperialism, both in terms of developing countries and, increasingly, in advanced countries faced with globalised media conglomerates. The question of salvaging whatever is valuable about local cultures, like the British, from the workings of the global market through state action is not only a matter of debates about practical possibilities. It is also, for any renewed critical project, a theoretical issue. To put it crudely, it is no longer possible to imagine that state institutions are constituted as mechanisms for sustaining a culture. They are not, naturally and inevitably, the enemies of the market. They are not, naturally and inevitably, the expression of popular will. The media that can embody a living culture cannot be built straight out of the existing models.

We can see that it is to the divisions within state organisations, rather than to the organisations themselves, that the critical project should address itself if we re-examine the history of the collapse of communism. Looked at from the perspective of a critical project that has learned the lessons of recent history, the end of communism displays remarkable similarities with the class struggle in normal capitalist countries. In particular, the issue of the fate of the mass media is subject to forms of contestation that are instantly recognisable. In Prague and Berlin, every bit as much as in Paris or Lisbon a generation before, those moments that catch our attention most immediately are the ones where the hierarchical order of established authority was challenged from below. They are the points when we can gain brief glimpses of what a world that was organised to try to do away with class oppression and exploitation would be like.

In this account, pride of place, of course, goes to the Polish workers during the high period of Solidarity. Not only did the union put forward radical plans for bringing the existing mass media more directly under the control of the mass of the population, but it explored ways in which groups who had previously been denied any public voice could set up and run their own organs. At the same time, the workers in the media industries, including those self-same journalists who had spent their entire professional lives fitting their stories as neatly as possible to the latest party line, found themselves in conflict with the men who ran the system. It is one of the characteristics of great revolutionary moments that people whom one would have thought lost entirely to social progress find a new consciousness and a new voice. The Polish journalists were part of that huge self-transformation.

It was this potential that was dribbled away in the redefinition of civil society, that evaporated in the 'round table' discussions, that was squandered by the leaders of the opposition in deals with the reformist-minded communists. For the communists, of course, it was precisely the function of the moderate leaders of Solidarity that they provided a bulwark against the threat of a serious social upheaval, should the masses get out of hand. Like the German Social Democrat Scheidemann, addressing the armed masses from the Reichstag balcony in 1918, Walesa and the rest were the people who saved the social essence of the system only by destroying its political forms.

In the revolutions of 1989, the masses were a stage army at best. Without the energy of that great social force behind it, it is not surprising that even the best-intentioned schemes for fundamental change faltered. No doubt many people wanted new and more democratic media institutions. No doubt memories of the early 1980s continued to inspire people. But without the kind of living, struggling mass movement that was Solidarity in its prime, the ideas of radical change remained mere ideas.

The second set of things that strike the critical eye are the brief exceptions to the negotiated deals that dominated the end of communism. The short rule of 'The Garage' in Czech television, and much more substantially the debate and questioning around the media in the GDR, form the obverse of the official story of 1989. They are a glimpse of the sort of change that was possible. They pointed clearly to an ending for communism that would amount to a great deal more than the replacement of one indifferent system of exploitation by another.

Perhaps, neither in the case of Solidarity nor in Prague or Berlin in 1989, were the ideas of those who started to go beyond mere regime-swapping sufficiently clear as to provide a programme for successful change. That, surely, is something we have all shared and can sympathise with. Certainly, one of the limits of the study of 1989 is that these ideas were never developed and never seriously tested. We cannot point to any wonderful blossoming of a different order as a positive affirmation of the critical project. But, whatever their shortcomings, those ideas were ones that we can recognise as addressing the same problems as we face. The oppositionists were worried about the massive and unaccountable concentrations of power in media organisations. They were worried about the marginalisation or exclusion of dissenting voices. They were worried about the ways in which hierarchical organisations find ways of taming even the rare maverick journalist. They were, in fact, worried about exactly the same things as we are worried about.

Finally, the revolutions of 1989 produced their times of joy and celebration, but they have also had their moments of misery and suffering. The collapse of employment and the fall in living standards are the two most obvious examples of misery and suffering. They have not been unknown amongst media workers, either. The talk, from the new rulers in the East and their expert advisors from the West, is all of making the broadcasters more efficient, of reducing overmanning, of becoming more competitive. Talk, in other words, of destroying peoples' lives. It is also talk we have heard in the West, certainly in the BBC.

If one lesson from the study of the collapse of communism is that only a narrow line divided our rulers from theirs, and that line was easily obliterated in the marriage of convenience that followed 1989, then another lesson is that it is almost impossible to notice the line between media workers here and media workers there, either before or after the fall of communism. They wanted, and want, the same things as media workers here want.

An academic study of the recent past can illuminate certain things quite well. I hope that this one has illuminated the possibility of continuing with the critical project. But what such a study cannot do is to realise the critical project. The other story of the fall of communism should give us at least hope that the agency of that social transformation is still a historical potential.

References

Ahmad, A. (1992) *In Theory: Classes, Nations, Literatures*. London: Verso.

Andorra, R. (1993) 'Regime transitions in Hungary in the 20th century: The role of national counter elites', *Governance*, 6 (3): 358–71.

Androunas, E. (1993) *Soviet Media in Transition*. Westport, CT: Praeger.

Arato, A. (1981) 'Civil society and the state: Poland 1980–81', *Telos*, 47: 23–47.

Arato, A. (1993) 'Interpreting 1989', *Social Research*, 60 (3): 609–46.

Arato, A. (1994) 'The rise, decline and reconstruction of the concept of civil society, and directions for future research', *Javnost/The Public*, 1 (1–2): 45–54.

Arendt, H. (1958) *The Origins of Totalitarianism*. Second edition. London: George Allen and Unwin.

Aron, R. (1950) 'Social structure and the ruling class', quoted in T. Bottomore (1966), *Élites and Society*. London: Penguin.

Ash, T.G. (1990) *We the People: The Revolution of '89*. London: Granta.

Banac, I. (1992) (ed.) *Eastern Europe in Revolution*. Ithaca, NY: Cornell University Press.

Bašić-Hrvatin, S. (1994) 'Television and national public memory'. Paper presented to the European Film and Television Studies Conference, London, 3–6 July.

Bauman, Z. (1981) 'On the maturation of socialism', *Telos*, 47: 48–54.

Bauman, Z. (1992a) *Intimations of Postmodernity*. London: Routledge.

Bauman, Z. (1992b) 'The Polish predicament: A model in search of class interests', *Telos*, 92: 113–80.

Bayard, C. (1993) 'The changing character of the Prague intelligentsia', *Telos*, 94: 131–44.

Bayliss, T. (1994) 'Transformation and continuity among East European élites', *Communist and Post-Communist Studies*, 27 (3): 315–28.

Benda, V., Šimečka, M., Jirous, I., Dienstbier, J., Havel, V., Hejdánek, L. and Šimsa, J. (1988) 'Parallel polis, or an independent society in Central and Eastern Europe: An enquiry', *Social Research*, 55 (1–2): 211–46.

Berglund, S. and Dellenbrant, J. (1994) 'The failure of popular demoncracy', in S. Berglund and J. Dellenbrant (eds), *The New Democracies in Eastern Europe*. London: Edward Elgar. pp. 14–35.

Berglund, S., Grzybowski, M., Dellenbrant, J. and Bankowicz, M. (1988) *East European Multi-Party Systems*. Helsinki: Societas Scientarium Fennica. Commentationes Scientarium Socialum, No. 37.

Bertsch, G., Vogel, H. and Zielonka, J. (eds) (1991) *After the Revolutions: East–West Trade and Technology Transfer in the 1990's*. Boulder, CO: Westview.

Bihari, P. (1991) 'From where to where? Reflections on Hungary's social revolution', in R. Miliband and L. Panitch (eds), *Communist Regimes: The Aftemath. Socialist Register 1991*. London: Merlin. pp. 279–301.

Blackburn, R. (ed.) (1991) *After the Fall: The Failure of Communism and the Future of Socialism*. London: Verso.

Bobbio, N. (1988) 'Gramsci and the concept of civil society', in J. Keane, (ed.), *Civil Society and the State: New European Perspectives*. London: Verso. pp. 73–99.

Boyle, M. (1992) 'The revolt of the Communist journalist: East Germany', *Media, Culture and Society*, 14 (3): 133–9.

Boyle, M. (1994) 'Building a communicative democracy: The birth and death of citizen politcs in East Germany', *Media, Culture and Society*, 16 (2): 183–215.

Bozóki, A. (1992) 'Political transition and constitutional change', in A. Bozóki, A. Körösényi and G. Schöpflin (eds), *Post-Communist Transition: Emerging Pluralism in Hungary*. London: Pinter. pp. 60–71.

Brar, H. (1992) *Perestroika: The Complete Collapse of Revisionism*. London: Harpal Brar.

Brečka, S. (n.d.) 'The transformation of Slovak Television'. Unpublished paper. (Probably 1993.)

Bruszt, L. (1988) '"Without us but for us": Political orientation in Hungary in the period of late paternalism', *Social Research*, 55 (1–2): 43–76.

Bruszt, L. (1989) '1989: The negotiated revolution in Hungary', *Social Research*, 57 (2): 365–87.

Bruszt, L. (1992) '1989: The negotiated revolution in Hungary', in A. Bozóki, A. Körösényi and G. Schöpflin (eds), *Post-Communist Transition: Emerging Pluralism in Hungary*. London: Pinter. pp. 45–59.

Brzezinski, Z. (1956) *The Permanent Purge*. Cambridge, MA: Harvard University Press.

Brzezinski, Z. (1967) *Ideology and Power in Soviet Politics*. Second edition. New York: Praeger.

Brzezinski, Z. (1989) *The Grand Failure: The Birth and Death of Communism*. New York: Charles Scribner's Sons.

Brzezinski, Z. (1993) 'The Cold War and its aftermath', *Foreign Affairs*, 71 (3): 31–49.

Bunce, V. (1995) 'Should transitologists be grounded?', *Slavic Review*, 54 (1): 111–27.

Callinicos, A. (1991) *The Revenge of History*. Cambridge: Polity.

Calvert, P. (1990) *Revolution and Counter-Revolution*. Milton Keynes: Open Unviersity Press.

Cerutti, G. (1994) 'The military against the publc sphere: The case of Argentina', *Javnost/The Public*, 1 (4): 59–71.

Clarke, N. (1987) 'The Hapsburg footprint', *Airwaves*, Summer: 21–4.

Cliff, T. (1974) *State Capitalism in Russia*. London: Pluto Press.

Cliff, T. (1975) *Lenin, Volume 1: Building the Party*. London: Pluto.

Cohen, J. (1993) 'The public sphere, the media and civil society'. Paper presented to the conference on The Development of Rights of Access to the Media, Budapest, 19–21 June.

Cohen, J. and Arato, A. (1992) *Civil Society and Political Theory*. Cambridge, MA: MIT Press.

Coppieters, B. and Waller, M. (1994) 'Conclusions: Social democracy in Eastern Europe', in M. Waller, B. Coppieters and L. Deschower (eds), *Social Democracy in Post-Communist Europe*. London: Frank Cass. pp. 188–97.

CST (1980) *Čzeskoslovenska Televizia Ročenka CST 1980 (za Slovensku Televiziu)*. Prague: Czechoslovak TV.

CST (1985) *Čzeskoslovenska Televizia V SSR, Ročenka 1985*. Prague: Czechoslovak TV.

Cunningham, J. (1994) 'The "media war" in Hungary'. Paper presented at the European Film and Television Studies Conference, London, 3–6 July.

Czech Council (1995) *Report on the Situation in Broadcasting and Activities of the Council for Radio and TV Broadcasting of the Czech Republic (July 9, 1994 to January 31, 1995)*. Prague: Council for Radio and TV Broadcasting of the Czech Republic. (Unpaginated.)

Czech Council (1996) *Report on the Situation in Broadcasting and Activities of the Council for Radio and TV Broadcasting of the Czech Republic (February 1, 1995 to January 31, 1996)*. Prague: Council for Radio and TV Broadcasting of the Czech Republic. (Unpaginated.)

Czech Television (1995) *Facts and Figures 1994/1995*. Prague: Czech Televison.

Dahl, R. (1991) 'Transitions to democracy', in G. Szobojzlai, (ed.), *Democracy and Political Transformation*. Budapest: Hungarian Political Science Association. pp. 9–20.

Dahrendorf, R. (1990) *Reflections on the Revolution in Europe*. London: Chatto and Windus.

Delano, A. and Henningham, J. (1995) *The News Breed: British Journalists in the 1990s*. London: The London Institute.

Dennis, E. and Vanden Heuvel, J. (1990) *Emerging Voices: East European Media in Transition: A Gannett Foundation Report*. New York: Gannett Foundation Media Centre. (The publishing organisation renamed itself the 'Freedom Forum' on 4 July 1991.)

Dougan, D.L. (1990) *Eastern Europe: Please Stand By. Report of the Task Force on Telecommunications and Broadcasting in Eastern Europe*. Washington, DC: US Department of State.

Downing, J. (1995) 'Media, dictatorship and the reemergence of "civil society"', in J. Downing, A. Mohammadi and A. Sreberny-Mohammadi (eds), *Questioning the Media: A Critical*

Introduction. Second edition. London: Sage Publications. pp. 184–204.

Downing, J. (1996) *Internationalizing Media Theory: Transition, Power, Culture*. London: Sage Publications.

Dragan, I. (1995) 'Les médias roumains: la crise de crédibilité', *The Global Network/Le Reseau Global*, 2: 61–6.

Erjavec, K. (1996) 'The impact of commercialisation on journalism in the daily newspapers of Slovenia'. Paper presented to the 10th Colloquium on Communication and Culture, Piran, Slovenia, 11–15 September.

European Audio-Visual Obervatory (1995) *Statistical Yearbook*. Strasbourg: Council of Europe.

Fedorowicz, H. (1990) 'Civil society as a communication project: The Polish laboratory for democratisation in East Central Europe', in S. Splichal, J. Hochheimer and K. Jakubowicz (eds), *Democratization and the Media: An East–West Dialogue*. Ljubljana: Communication and Culture Colloquia. pp. 73–87.

Fisher, S. (1995a) 'Slovakia: Turning back?', in *Transition: 1994 in Review, Part One*. Prague: Open Media Research Institute. pp. 60–3.

Fisher, S. (1995b) 'Slovak media under pressure', *Transition*, 1 (18): 7–9.

Folger, A. (1994) 'Changes in Polish cinema'. Paper presented to the European Film and Television Conference, London, 3–6 July.

Friedrich, C. and Brzezinski, Z. (1956) *Totalitarian Dictatorship and Autocracy*. Cambridge, MA: Harvard University Press.

Fukuyama, F. (1992) *The End of History and the Last Man*. London: Penguin.

Gagarkin, A. and Kushnereva, O. (1988) 'TV and public opinion: Problems of interaction', in P. Hemanus (ed.), *Mass Media and Public Opinion: Report of the Fifth Soviet–Finnish Seminar*. Tampere: University of Tampere. Publications, Series B, No. 24. pp. 51–9.

Gálik, M. (1992) 'The media scene in Hungary'. Paper presented to the Fourth European Conference on Public Service Local/Regional Radio, Budapest, 7–9 October.

Gálik, M. and Dénes, F. (1992) *From Command Media to Media Market: The Role of Foreign Capital in the Transition of the Hungarian Media*. Budapest: Budapest University of Economics, Department of Business Economics.

Galtung, J. (1974) *A Structural Theory of Revolutions*. Rotterdam: Universitaire Pers Rotterdam.

Garfinkle, A. and Pipes, D. (eds) (1991) *Friendly Tyrants, An American Dilemma*. London: Macmillan.

Gellner, E. (1993) 'The price of velvet: On Thomas Masaryk and Vaclav Havel', *Telos*, 94: 183–92.

Giorgi, L. (1995) *The Post-Socialist Media: What Power the West?*. Aldershot: Avebury.

Giorgi, L. and Pohoryles, R. (1994) *Media in Transition: The Cases of Hungary, Poland and Czechia*. Vienna: Interdisciplinary Centre for Comparative Research.

Gluckstein, Y. (1952) *Stalin's Satellites in Europe*. London: George Allen and Unwin.

Gluckstein, Y. (1957) *Mao's China: Economic and Political Survey*. London: George Allen and Unwin.

Goban-Klas, T. (1990) 'Making media policy in Poland', *Journal of Communication*, 40 (4): 50–5.

Goban-Klas, T. (1994) *The Orchestration of the Media: The Politics of Mass Communication in Communist Poland and the Aftermath*. Boulder, CO: Westview.

Gombár, C. (n.d.) 'Introductory address', in A. Pragnell and I. Gergely (eds), *The Political Content of Broadcasting*. Manchester: European Institute for the Media. European Institute for the Media Monograph No. 15. pp. 4–6. (Probably 1992.)

Gross, P. (1990) 'The Soviet Communist press theory – Romanian style', in S. Splichal, J. Hochheimer and K. Jakubowicz (eds), *Democratization and the Media: An East–West Dialogue*. Ljubljana: Culture and Communication Colloquia. pp. 94–107.

Gross, P. (1996) *Mass Media in Revolution and National Development: The Romanian Laboratory*. Ames: Iowa State University Press.

Hale, O.J. (1973) *The Captive Press in the Third Reich*. Princeton, NJ: Princeton University Press.

Hall, A. (1977) *Scandal, Sensation and Social Democracy: The SPD Press and Wilhelmine Germany 1890–1914*. Cambridge: Cambridge University Press.

Hanke, H. (1990) 'Media culture in the GDR: Characteristics, processes and problems', *Media, Culture and Society*, 12 (2): 175–94.

Hankiss, E. (1988) 'The "Second Society": Is there an alternative social model emerging in contemporary Hungary?', *Social Research*, 55 (1–2): 13–42.

Hankiss, E. (1990) *East European Alternatives*. Oxford: Clarendon Press.

Hankiss, E. (1995) 'The Hungarian media's war of independence: A Stevenson Lecture, 1992', *Media, Culture and Society*, 16 (2): 293–312.

Hardy, J. and Rainnie, A. (1996) *Restructuring Krakow: Desperately Seeking Capitalism*. London: Cassell.

Harman, C. (1983) *Class Struggles in Eastern Europe, 1945–83*. Second edition. London: Pluto.

Havel, V. (1988) 'Anti-political politics', in J. Keane (ed.), *Civil Society and the State: New European Perspectives*. London: Verso. pp. 381–98.

Haye, J. and Shi, Z. (1993) 'Alternative strategies for the reconstruction of the state during economic reform', *Governance*, 6 (4): 463–91.

Haynes, M. (1996) 'Eastern European transition: Some practical and theoretical problems', *Economic and Political Weekly*, 31 (8): 467–82.

Hegel, G. (1967) *Hegel's Philosophy of Right*, translated with notes by T.M. Knox. Oxford: Oxford University Press.

Held, D. (1992) 'Liberalism, Marxism and democracy', in S. Hall, D. Held and T. McgGrew (eds), *Modernity and its Futures*. Cambridge: Polity. pp. 13–47.

Hobsbawm, E. (1968) *Industry and Empire*. London: Weidenfeld and Nicolson.

Hobsbawm, E. (1994) *The Age of Extremes: The Short Twentieth Century, 1914–1991*. London: Michael Joseph.

Hopkins, M. (1970) *Mass Media in the Soviet Union*. New York: Pegasus.

Horkheimer, M. and Adorno, T. (1973) *Dialectic of Enlightenment*. London: Allen Lane.

Horváth, A. and Szakolczai, Á. (1990) 'The dual power of the state–party and its grounds', *Social Research*, 57 (2): 275–301.

Hungarian Embassy (1993) 'Looking behind the news: The Hungarian media saga', press release, 5 February.

Innes, A. (1993) 'Political developments in the new Czech Republic', *Policy Studies*, 14 (4): 22–30.

Iordanova, D. (1995) 'Bulgaria: Provisional rules and directorial changes: Restructuring of national TV', *Javnost/The Public*, 2 (3): 19–32.

Jakab, Z. and Gálik, M. (1991) *Survival, Efficiency and Independence: The Presence of Foreign Capital in the Hungarian Media Market*. Manchester: European Institute for the Media.

Jakubowicz, K. (1987) 'Advertising in Poland – a time of transition', *Media Development*, 1987/3: 16–18.

Jakubowicz, K. (1989) 'The media: Political and economic dimensions of television programme exchange between Poland and Western Europe', in J. Becker, and T. Szecskö (eds), *Europe Speaks to Europe*. Oxford: Pergamon. pp. 148–64.

Jakubowicz, K. (1991) 'Musical chairs? The three public spheres in Poland', in P. Dahlgren and C. Sparks (eds), *Communication and Citizenship*. London: Routledge. pp. 155–75.

Jakubowicz, K. (1992) 'The restructuring of television in East-Central Europe: Polish television'. Paper presented to the symposium Restructuring Television in East-Central Europe. University of Westminster, London, 14 July.

Jakubowicz, K. (1993) 'Stuck in a groove: Why the 1960s approach to communication democratization will no longer do', in S. Splichal and J. Wasko (eds), *Communication and Democracy*. Norwood, NJ: Ablex. pp. 33–54.

Jakubowicz, K. (1995) 'Poland: Television: What mix of continuity and change?', *Javnost/The Public*, 2 (3): 61–80.

Jakubowicz, K. (1996) 'Civil society and public service broadcasting in Central and Eastern Europe', *Javnost/The Public*, 3 (2): 51–69.

Jakubowicz, K. (n.d.a) 'Poland: Prospects for public and civic broadcasting', in M. Raboy (ed.), *Public Broadcasting for the 21st Century*. Luton: John Libbery Media. (Undated but probably 1996.)

Jakubowicz, K. (n.d.b) 'The new communication and information technologies in Poland – stopgap policy making by default'. Unpublished paper.

Johnson, O. (1993) 'Defining interests: Slovak broadcasting and its Czechoslovak inheritance'. Paper presented at the conference on East-Central European Broadcasting, University of Westminster, London, 20–23 October.

Kalniczky, A. (1992) 'Slovak television: Back to state control', *RFE/RL Research Report*, 8 November: 64–8.

Kaplan, F. and Šmíd, M. (1995) 'Czech Republic: Broadcasting after 1989: Overhauling the system and its structures', *Javnost/The Public*, 2 (3): 33–45.

Kaplan, F., Jirák, J. and Šmíd, M. (1993) 'The Broadcasting Law: First steps in defining a media policy for the Czech Republic'. Unpublished paper.

Karch, J. (1983) 'News and its uses in the communist world', in J. Martin and A. Chaudhary (eds), *Comparative Mass Media Systems*. White Plains, NY: Longman. pp. 111–31.

Karpinski, J. (1995) 'Information and entertainment in Poland', *Transition*, 1 (18): 13–18.

Keever, B. (1991) 'Wilbur Schramm', *Mass Comm Review*, 18 (1–2): 3–26.

Kenedi, J. and Mihancsik, Z. (1994) 'The mass media war in Hungary'. Unpublished paper presented at the conference on The Present of Public Broadcasting and the Direction of its Expectable Development until 2000, organised by Budapesti Kommunikációs RT., Budapest, 24–25 February.

Kenety, B. (1997) 'Nova TV: New democracy or old-fashioned greed?', *Prague Post*, 12–18 February: A1–A7.

Kennedy, M. (1992) 'The intellegentsia in the constitution of civil societies and post-communist regimes in Hungary and Poland', *Theory and Society*, 21 (1): 29–76.

Kettle, M. (1995) 'The Czech Republic struggles to define an independent press', *Transition*, 1 (18): 4–6.

Kilborn, R. (1994) 'All change! The new face of East German broadcasting'. Paper presented to the European Film and Television Studies Conference, London, 3–6 July.

Kirkpatrick, J. (1982) *Dictatorship and Double Standards*. New York: Simon and Schuster and The American Enterprise Institute Press.

Kirkpatrick, J. (1990) *The Withering Away of the Totalitarian State . . . And Other Surprises*. Washington, DC: American Enterprise Institute Press.

Kiss, Y. (1992) 'Privatization in Hungary – two years later', *Soviet Studies*, 44 (6): 1015–38.

Klaus, V. (1991) 'Creating a capitalist Czechoslovakia', in T. Whipple (ed.), *After the Revolution*. New York: Freedom House. pp. 149–56.

Kloc, K. (1992) 'Polish labour in transition', *Telos*, 92: 139–48.

Kolarska-Bobinska, L. (1988) 'Social interests, egalitarian attitudes, and the change of economic order', *Social Research*, 55 (1–2): 111–38.

Kolarska-Bobinska, L. and Rychard, A. (1990) 'Economy and polity: Dynamics of change', *Social Research*, 57 (2): 303–20.

Kolodko, G. (1993) 'From recession to growth in post-communist economies: Expectations versus reality', *Communist and Post-Communist Studies*, 26 (2): 123–43.

König, K. (1993) 'Bureaucratic integration by elite transfer: The case of the former GDR', *Governance*, 6 (3): 386–96.

Kornai, J. (1990) *The Road to a Free Economy*. New York: Norton.

Korobeinikov, V. (1988) 'Press and public opinion: Relationship in the process of restructuring', in P. Hemanus (ed.), *Mass Media and Public Opinion: Report of the Fifth Soviet–Finnish Seminar*. Tampere: University of Tampere. Publications, Series B, No. 24. pp. 51–9.

Körösényi, A. (1992a) 'The decay of communist rule in Hungary', in A. Bozóki, A. Körösényi and G. Schöpflin (eds), *Post-Communist Transition: Emerging Pluralism in Hungary*. London: Pinter. pp. 1–12.

Körösényi, A. (1992b) 'The Hungarian parliamentary elections of 1990', in A. Bozóki, A. Körösényi and G. Schöpflin (eds), *Post-Communist Transition: Emerging Pluralism in Hungary*. London: Pinter. pp. 72–87.

Korte, D. (1994) 'Speech', in Polish National Broadcasting Council (eds), *The Mass Media in Central and Eastern Europe: Democratization and European Integration*. Proceedings of a conference held in Jadswin, Poland, 3–5 June. pp. 61–2.

Kosik, K. (1993) 'The third Munich', *Telos*, 94: 143–54.

Koss, S. (1990) *The Rise and Fall of the Political Press in Britain*. London: Fontana.

Kováts, I. (1995) 'Hungary: The causes of the stalemate situation in television', *Javnost/The Public*, 2 (3): 47–59.

Kováts, I. and Tölgyesi, J. (1990) 'The media – A change of model or continuity?'. Paper presented to the August 1990 Conference of the International Association for Mass Communication Research, Bled, Yugoslavia (Slovenia).

Kováts, I. and Tölgyesi, J. (1993) 'On the background of the Hungarian media changes', in S. Splichal and I. Kováts (eds), *Media in Transition: An East–West Dialogue*. Budapest–Ljubljana: Communication and Culture Colloquia. pp. 35–47.

Kováts, I. and Whiting, G. (1992) 'Evolution and revolution in the Hungarian mass media'. Unpublished paper.

Kowalik, T. (1991) 'Marketization and privatization: The Polish case', in R. Miliband and L. Panitch (eds), *Communist Regimes: The Aftermath. Socialist Register 1991*. London: Merlin. pp. 259–78.

Kowalski, T. (1994) 'The economic aspects of media transformation: Case of Poland', in Polish National Broadcasting Council (eds), *The Mass Media in Central and Eastern Europe: Democratization and European Integration*. Proceedings of a conference held in Jadswin, Poland, 3–5 June. pp. 99–103.

Kuczyńska, T. (1992) 'The capitalists among us', *Telos*, 92: 159–63.

Kuhn, R. (1995) *The Media in France*. London: Routledge.

Kumar, K. (1971) *Revolution: The Theory and Practice of a European Idea*. London: Wiedenfeld and Nicolson.

Kumar, K. (1992) 'The revolutions of 1989: Socialism, capitalism and democracy', *Theory and Society*, 21 (3): 309–56.

Kurant, T. (1991) 'Now out of never: The element of surprise in the East European revolutions', *World Politics*, 44 (1): 7–48.

Kux, E. (1991) 'Revolution in Eastern Europe – revolution in the West?', *Problems of Communism*, Vol. xl, May–June: 1–13.

Laba, R. (1991) *The Roots of Solidarity: A Political Sociology of Working Class Democratization*. Princeton, NJ: Princeton University Press.

Lendavi, P. (1981) *The Bureaucracy of Truth: How Communist Governments Manage the News*. London: Burnett Books.

Lenin, V.I. (1961) *Collected Works*, volumes as numbered. Moscow: Progress.

Lipset, S. and Bence, G. (1994) 'Anticipations of the failure of communism', *Theory and Society*, 23 (2): 169–201.

Lomax, B. (1993) 'From death to resurrection: The metamorphosis of power in Eastern Europe', *Critique*, 25: 47–84.

Luxemburg, R. (1970) 'Reform or revolution?', in M.A. Waters (ed.), *Rosa Luxemburg Speaks*. New York: Pathfinder. pp. 33–90.

McIntosh, I., MacIver, M., Abele, D. and Smeltz, D. (1994) 'Publics meet market democracy in Central and Eastern Europe, 1991–1993', *Slavic Review*, 53 (2): 483–512.

McIntyre, I. (1989) 'Economic change in Eastern Europe: Other paths to socialist planning', *Science and Society*, 53 (1): 5–28.

McQuail, D. (1987) *Mass Communication Theory*. Second edition. London: Sage Publications.

McQuail, D. (1994) *Mass Communication Theory*. Third edition. London: Sage Publications.

Macek, V. (1994) 'Looking for the Slovak film industry'. Paper presented to the European Film and Television Studies Conference, London, 3–6 July.

Madden, N. (1996a) 'Text of speech by Vladimir Zelezny', distibuted electronically by eemedia@mcfeeley.cc.utexas.edu. February.

Madden, N. (1996b) 'Interview with Dr. Vladimir Zelezny, TV Nova', *Prague Business Journal*, 9 September. (Unpaginated electronic redistribution form eemedia@mcfeeley.cc.utexas.edu.)

Mahr, A. and Nagle, J. (1995) 'Resurrection of the successor parties and democratization in East Central Europe', *Communist and Post-Communist Studies*, 28 (4): 393–409.

Malec, P. (n.d.) 'Concluding remarks', in A. Pragnell and I. Gergely (eds), *The Political Content of Broadcasting*. Manchester: European Institute for the Media. European Institute for the Media Monograph No. 15. pp. 136–9. (Probably 1992).

Manaev, O. (1993) 'Mass media in the political and economic system of transition society', in O. Manaev and Y. Pryliuk (eds), *Media in Transition: From Totalitarianism to Democracy*. Kiev: Abris. pp. 119–48.

Manaev, O. (1995) 'Rethinking the social role of the media in a society in transition', *Canadian Journal of Communication*, 20 (1): 45–66.

Mandel, E. (1991) 'The roots of the present crisis in the Soviet economy', in R. Miliband and L. Panitch (eds), *Communist Regimes: The Aftemath. Socialist Register 1991*. London: Merlin: pp. 194–210.

Marer, P. (1992) 'Roadblocks to changing economic systems in Eastern Europe', in W. Kern (ed.), *From Socialism to Market Economy: The Transition Problem*. Kalamazoo, MI: W.E. Upjohn Institute for Employment Research. pp. 9–33.

Marinsecu, V. (1995) 'Romania: private versus state television', *Javnost/The Public*, 2 (3): 81–95.

Marody, M. (1988) 'Antimonies of collective subconsciousness', *Social Research*, 55 (1–2): 97–110.

Marody, M. (1990) 'Perceptions of politics in Polish society', *Social Research*, 57 (2): 257–74.

Mason, D. (1995) 'Attitudes toward the market and political participation in the post-communist states', *Slavic Review*, 54 (2): 385–406.

Mazowiecki, T. (1989) Speech to Parliament on 12 October 1989, cited in J. Oledzky (1991) (ed.), *Polskie Media w Okresie Przemian*. Warsaw: Osrodek Badan Spolecznych. p. 163.

Meillassoux, C. (1993) 'Towards a theory of the "social corps"', in H. De Soto and D. Anderson (eds), *The Curtain Rises: Rethinking Culture, Ideology and the State in Eastern Europe*. Atlantic Highlands, NJ: Humanities Press. pp. 2–42.

Meiskens Wood, E. (1990) 'The uses and abuses of "civil society"', in R. Miliband and L. Panitch (eds), *The Retreat of the Intellectuals: Socialist Register 1990*. London: Merlin. pp. 60–84.

Michnik, A. (1985) *Letters from Prison and Other Essays*. Berkeley, CA: University of California Press.

Miliband, R. (1973) *The State in Capitalist Society*. London: Quartet.

Miliband, R. (1991) 'What comes after communist regimes?', in R. Miliband and L. Panitch (eds), *Communist Regimes: The Aftermath. Socialist Register 1991*. London: Merlin. pp. 375–89.

Millard, E. (1994) 'The Polish parliamentary elections of September 1993', *Communist and Post-Communist Studies*, 27 (3): 295–313.

Misztal, B. (1993) 'Understanding political change in Eastern Europe: A sociological perspective', *Sociology*, 27 (3): 451–70.

Mrozowski, M. and Pomorski, J. (1989) *Partners in Production: The Polish Film and TV Industries*. London: International Institute of Communications.

MTV (1991) *Hungarian Television 1991: Facts and Figures*. Budapest: MTV.

Myant, M. and Waller, M. (1994) 'Parties and trade unions in Eastern Europe', in M. Waller and M. Myant (eds), *Parties, Trade Unions and Society in East-Central Europe*. London: Frank Cass. pp. 161–81.

Nelson, J. (1993) 'The politics of economic transformation: Is the Third World experience relevant to Eastern Europe?', *World Politics*, 45 (3): 433–63.

Netcom (1994) 'Poland: Sacking of broadcasting council members', *Leipzig Letter*, 1 (3): 2.

Nova (1995) *Nova and its Audience*. Prague: TV Nova.

Novak, M. (1996) 'The transition from a socialist to a market-led media system in Slovenia'. Unpublished PhD dissertation, University of Westminster, London.

Offe, C. (1991) 'Capitalism by democratic design? Democratic theory facing the triple transition in East Central Europe', *Social Research*, 58 (4): 865–92.

Oltay, E. (1995a) 'The return of the former communists', *Transition: 1994 in Review Part One*. Prague: Open Media Research Institute.

Oltay, E. (1995b) 'Controversy and crisis deluge Hungary's broadcast media', *Transition*, 1 (18): 10–12.

Ost, D. (1989) 'The transformation of Solidarity and the future of Central Europe', *Telos*, 79: 69–94.

Ost, D. (1990) *Solidarity and the Politics of Anti-Politics*. Philadelphia, PA: Temple University Press.

Ost, D. (1993) 'The politics of interest in post-communist Eastern Europe', *Theory and Society*, 22 (4): 453–85.

Papácsy, E. (1992) 'The new Hungarian media bill – a legal presentation'. Paper presented to the Konrad Adenauer Foundation Conference on Media Rights, Bonn, November 1992.

Pateman, C. (1988) 'The fraternal social contract', in J. Keane (ed.), *Civil Society and the State: New European Perspectives*. London: Verso. pp. 101–27.

Pelczynski, Z. (1988) 'Solidarity and "The Rebirth of Civil Society" in Poland, 1976–81', in J. Keane (ed.), *Civil Society and the State: New European Perspectives*. London: Verso. pp. 361–80.

Petras, N. (1993) 'Eastern Europe: Restoration and crisis', in *Critique*, 25: 13–45.

Piccone, P. (1988) '20 Years of *Telos*', *Telos*, 75: 3–25.

Pickel, A. (1993) 'Authoritarianism or democracy? Marketization as a political problem', *Policy Sciences*, 26 (3): 139–63.

Plenkovic, M. and Kucis, V. (1995) 'Structuring media elite in Croatia', *The Global Network/Le Reseau Global*, 2: 25–8.

Pogany, C. (1988) 'Hungary', in M. Alvarado (ed.), *Video World-Wide*. Paris, UNESCO. pp. 223–34.

Pomorski, J. (1988) 'Poland', in M. Alvarado (ed.), *Video World-Wide*. Paris, UNESCO. pp. 181–96.

Pospelov, P.N. (1971) 'Leninism and the building of communism in the USSR', in D. Skvirsky (trans.), *The Development of Revolutionary Theory by the CPSU*. Moscow: Progress. pp. 9–53.

Poszgay, I. (1989) 'Interview', cited in T. Szecko, 'Games people play: Changes in the mass communication system in Hungary'. Unpublished paper (1991).

Poznanski, K. (1992) 'Privatization of the Polish economy: Problems of transition', *Soviet Studies*, 44 (4): 641–64.

Poznanski, K. (1993) 'An interpretation of communist decay: The role of evolutionary mechanisms', *Communist and Post-Communist Studies*, 26 (1): 3–24.

Prevrátil, R. (1993) *Communication in the Transition to Democracy: East Europe*. London: World Association for Christian Communication.

PRTV (1989) *PRiTV: Information*. Warsaw: PRTV Foreign Relations Department.

PSMLP (31 March 1996) 'Nova's success spurs attacks by potential competitors', *Post-Soviet Media Law and Policy Newsletter*, Issue 27/28: 8–9.

Raboy, M. (n.d.) 'Introduction: Public service broadcasting in the context of Globalization', in M. Raboy (ed.), *Public Broadcasting for the 21st Century*. Luton: University of Luton Press. (Probably 1996.)

Raycheva, L. (1994) 'Film and television industry in Bulgaria during the transition period'. Paper presented to the European Film and Television Studies Conference, London, 3–6 July.

Reading, A. (1994) 'The people v the King – Polish broadcasting legislation', *Media Law and Practice*, 15 (1): 7–12.

Reading, A. (1996) 'Socially inherited memory, gender and the public sphere in Poland'. Unpublished PhD thesis, University of Westminster, London.

Reiman, M. (1989) 'Prague Spring and Perestroika', *Telos*, 79: 155–62.

Reuter (4/04/95) 'Czech Republic: TV Nova has $7m profit in 1994, owner expanding to Radio Alfa', *Reuter's Business Briefing*.

Reuter (31/05/95) 'Poland: State television makes 1.48 trillion old zlotys net profit in 1994', *Reuter's Business Briefing*.

Reuter (30/08/96) 'New row erupts in Polish public television', *Reuter's Newswire*.

Reykowski, J. (1994) 'Why did the collectivist state fail?', *Theory and Society*, 23 (2): 233–52.

Robillard, S. (1995) *Television in Europe: Regulatory Bodies. Status, Functions and Powers in 35 European Countries*. London: John Libbey.

Rohwedder, C. (1995) 'Central Europe's broadcasters square off', *Wall Street Journal Europe*, 15 May: 6.

Rose, R. (1992) 'Towards a civil economy', *Journal of Democracy*, 3 (2): 13–26.

Rutland, P. (1993) 'Thatcherism, Czech-style: Transition to capitalism in the Czech Republic', *Telos*, 94. 103–29.

Sanford, G. (1991) 'The Polish road to democratisation: From political impasse to the "controlled abdication" of communist power', in G. Sanford (ed.), *Democratization in Poland, 1988–90. Polish Voices*. London: Macmillan. pp. 1–34.

Schapiro, L. (1972) *Totalitarianism*. London: Pall Mall Press.

Schlesinger, P. (1991) *Media, State and Nation: Political Violence and Collective Identities*. London: Sage Publications.

Schmitter, P. and Karl, T. (1994) 'The conceptual travels of transitologists and consolidologists: How far to the East should they attempt to go?', *Slavic Review*, 53 (1): 173–85.

Schöpflin, G. (1993) *Politics in Eastern Europe*. Oxford: Basil Blackwell.

Schöpflin, G. (1995) 'Post-communism: A profile' in *Javnost/The Public*, 2 (1): 63–72.

Selucky, R. (1989) 'The irrelevance of Perestroika in Czechoslovakia', *Telos*, 79: 149–54.

Shore, E. (1988) *Talkin' Socialism: J.A. Wayland and the Role of the Press in American Radicalism, 1890–1912*. Lawrence: Univeristy of Kansas Press.

Siebert, F., Peterson, T. and Schramm, W. (1963) *Four Theories of the Press*. Urbana: University of Illinois Press.

Šiklová, J. (1990) 'The "gray zone" and the future of dissent in Czechoslovakia', *Social Research*, 57 (2): 347–63.

Šiklová, J. (1991) 'The solidarity of the culpable', *Social Research*, 58 (4): 765–73.

Simon, J. (1993) 'Post-paternalist political culture in Hungary: Relationships between citizens and politics during and after the "Melancholic Revolution" (1989–1991)', *Communist and Post-Communist Societies*, 26 (2): 226–38.

Slovak Television (1995) STV *Slovenská Televízia/Slovak Television*. Bratislava: Slovak Television.

Šmíd, M. (1992) 'Television after the velvet revolution'. Paper presented to the symposium on Restructuring Television in East-Central Europe, University of Westminster, London, 14 July.

Šmíd, M. (1994) 'Broadcasting law in the Czech Republic'. Unpublished paper, December. Unpaginated.

Šmíd, M. (n.d.) 'Public media and public interest in East and Central Europe'. Unpublished paper.

Sparks, C. (1993) 'Raymond Williams and the theory of democratic communication', in S. Splichal and J. Wasko (eds), *Communication and Democracy*. Norwood, NJ: Ablex. pp. 69–86.

Sparks, C. (1994) 'Civil society and information society as guarantors of progress', in S. Splichal, A. Calabrese and C. Sparks (eds), *Information Society and Civil Society: Contemporary Perspectives on the Changing World Order*. West Lafayette, IA: Purdue University Press. pp. 21–49.

Sparks, C. and Reading, A. (1995) 'Re-regulating television after communism: A comparative analysis of Poland, Hungary and the Czech Republic', in F. Corcoran and P. Preston (eds), *Democracy and Communication in the New Europe: Change and Continuity in East and West*. Creskill, NJ: Hampton Press. pp. 31–50.

Splichal, S. (1994) *Media Beyond Socialism*. Boulder, CO: Westview.

Splichal, S. (1995) 'Slovenia: The period of "Capitalist Enlightenment"', *Javnost/The Public*, 2 (3): 97–114.

Staniszkis, J. (1989) 'The obsolescence of Solidarity', *Telos*, 80: 37–50.

Staniszkis, J. (1991) *The Dynamics of Breakthrough in Eastern Europe: The Polish Case*, translated by C. Kisiel. Berkeley: University of California Press.

Szablowski, G. (1993) 'Governing and competing élites in Poland', *Governance*, 6 (3): 341–57.

Szecskö, T. (1986) 'Encounters with the new media: Perspectives from a socialist country', *Nordicom Review*, 1: 15–18.

Szecskö, T. and Fodor, G. (1974) *Communication Policies in Hungary*. Paris: Unesco Press.

Szekfü, A. (1989) 'Intruders welcome? The beginnings of satellite television in Hungary', *European Journal of Communication*, 4 (2): 161–71.

Szelenyi, I. and Szelenyi, B. (1994) 'Why socialism failed: Towards a theory of system breakdown – causes of disintergration of East European state socialism', *Theory and Society*, 23 (2): 211–31.

Tankard, J. (1988) 'Wilbur Schramm: Definer of a field', *Journalism Educator*, 43 (3): 11–16.

Telos Staff (1991) 'Populism versus the new class', *Telos*, 88: 2–36.

Terry, S. (1993) 'Thinging [*sic*] about post-communist transitions: How different are they?', *Slavic Review*, 52 (2): 333–7.

Tesar, I.(1989) 'Television exchange of programmes and television co-operation between Czechoslovakia and Western Europe: Experience, problems, proposals', in J. Becker and T. Szecskö (eds), *Europe Speaks to Europe*. Oxford: Pergamon.

Thomas, R. (1976) *Broadcasting and Democracy in France*. London: Bradford University Press.

Trüb, T. (1995) 'Speech of Mr Thomas Trüb, Ringier AG Switzerland. Central and East Europe: Obstacle-ridden awakening', in Adam Smith Institute (eds), *Media in Central and Eastern Europe: Television and Radio Broadcasting, Publishing and Advertising*. Documentation of the First International Conference and Exhibition, Vienna, 11–12 May.

Tsagrousianou, R. (1995) '"God, Patria and Home": "Reproductive Politics" and nationalist (re)definitions of women in East/Central Europe', *Social Identities*, 1 (2): 283–95.

TVP (n.d.) *40 Lat TVP*. Warsaw: Przewodinczacy Komitetu d/s Radia i Telewizji.

Urban, L. (1989) 'Hungary in transition', *Telos*, 79: 108–18.

Varis, T. (1985) *International Flow of TV Programmes*, Unesco Studies in Mass Communication, No: 100 (Paris: UNESCO, 1985). pp. 35–6.

Vaughan James, C. (1973) *Soviet Socialist Realism: Origins and Theory*. London: Macmillan.

Vihalemm, P. (1995) 'Media élite in Estonia', *The Global Network/Le Reseau Global*, 2: 37–42.

Vinton, L. (1995) 'Velvet restoration', *Transition: 1994 in Review Part One*. Prague: Open Media Research Institute. pp. 42–8.

Vojtek, J. (1995) 'The media in Slovakia since 1989', *The Global Network/Le Reseau Global*, 3: 81–4.

von Beyme, (1993) 'Regime transition and recruitment of élites in Eastern Europe', *Governance*, 6(3): 409–25.

Voslensky, M. (1984) *Nomenklatura: Anatomy of the Soviet Ruling Class.* London: The Bodley Head.

Walker, M. (1993) *The End of the Communist Power Monopoly*. Manchester: Manchester University Press.

Wasilewski, J. (1990) 'The patterns of bureaucratic élite recruitment in Poland in the 1970s and 1980s', *Soviet Studies*, 42 (4): 743–57.

Wesołowski, W. (1990) 'Transition from authoritarianism to democracy', *Social Research*, 57 (2): 435–61.

Westoby, A. (1981) *Communism Since World War II*. Brighton: Harvester.

Wiatr, J. (1995) 'The dilemmas of re-organising the bureaucracy in Poland during the democratic transition', *Communist and Post-Communist Studies*, 28 (1): 153–60.

Williams, R. (1962) *Communications*. London: Penguin.

Witkowska, A. (1990) 'The changing face of Polish television'. London: BFI. Unpublished report.

Wolchik, S.L. (1991) *Czechoslovakia in Transition: Politics, Economics and Society*. London: Pinter.

Ziółkowski, M. (1988) 'Individuals and the social system: Values, perceptions and behavioural strategies', *Social Research*, 55 (1–2): 139–77.

Zubek, V. (1992) 'The rise and fall of rule by Poland's best and brightest', *Soviet Studies*, 44 (4): 579–608.

Laws, bills and licence documents

Czech Broadcasting Council (1993) *Conditions to Licence #001/93*. Prague: Czech Broadcasting Council.

Czech National Assembly (1991) *Czech Broadcasting Act*. November 1991.

Czech Republic (1995) *Act on Radio and Television Broadcasting, As Amended.* (Act No. 468/1991, as amended up to Act No. 301/1995.)
Czechoslovak Federal Republic (1991) *Federal Broadcasting Act.* October 1991.
Hungary (1991) *Draft Broadcasting Bill.* October 1991.
Hungary (1992) *Draft Broadcasting Bill.* November 1992.
Hungary (1995) *Radio and Television Services Act.* December 1995.
Poland (1990a) *Draft Broadcasting Bill.* December 1990.
Poland (1990b) *Post and Telecommunications Act* (No. 504): November 1990.
Poland (1991) *Draft Broadcasting Bill as developed by a Parliamentary Sub-committee on the Basis of Two Members.* March 1991
Poland (1992) *Broadcasting Law.* December 1992.
Slovakia (1992) *Amendment to Slovak TV Law* (294/1992). 29 September 1992.

Personal communications

Goban-Klas, T., interviewed by A. Reading, Krakow, 28 September 1992.
Hankiss, E., interviewed by A. Reading, Budapest, 20 November 1992.
Jakobec, M., interviewed by A. Reading, Prague, 16 October 1992.
Jakubowicz, K., interviewed by A. Reading, Warsaw, 1 November 1992.
Kostal, J., interviewed by A. Reading, Prague, 15 October 1992.
Malec, P., interviewed by A. Reading, Bratislava, 26 October 1992.
Vajdova, K., interviewed by A. Reading, Bratislava, 26 October 1992.
Varga, F., interviewed by A. Reading, Budapest, 15 November 1992.
Wasiuta, L., interviewed by A. Reading, Warsaw, 28 September 1992.

Index